Staying Human

Katharina Stegelmann

Staying Human
The Story of a Quiet WWII Hero

Translated by Rachel Hildebrandt

Skyhorse Publishing

To my husband, Henning

Foreword

I met Heinz Drossel on a hot August day in 2003. He had already agreed to give me an interview that would serve as the basis for a biographical article about him as a "quiet hero" for the *Spiegel* publication, *Die Gegenwart der Vergangenheit* (*The Presence of the Past*). Soon afterward, I decided that I wanted to tell the story of this man and his family in more detail than I had been able to at that time. Heinz Drossel immediately agreed when I asked him if he would allow me to write the history of his family. We met numerous times, telephoned regularly, and exchanged countless emails. We traveled together so that he could introduce me to his daughters, grandchildren, and acquaintances. We became friends.

I wrote the history of Heinz Drossel and his wife Marianne after many conversations with him, readings of his memoirs *Die Zeit der Füchse* (*The Time of the Foxes*), analysis of the legal records related to the reparations proceedings connected with Marianne Drossel, and conversations with the family members and friends who are still alive today. I also pursued research in various institutions and archives. I have pulled the facts together in order to present a truthful depiction of the events. However, "the truth" cannot be found in this book. At least, not "the full truth."

The memories of those still alive and the statements of family members about the now deceased protagonists did not produce a unified picture. There were contradictory, illogical pieces of information. Holes remained, and some things could not be clarified through research. I had to stay silent on some things because those involved wished this. I have made some deductions, choosing the most likely variation and occasionally risking enhancement, in order to create a picture of how it could have been.

"Do It Better!"

Osterholz-Scharmbeck, near Bremen, May 24, 2004
It is pretty close quarters in the high school music room. Almost 150 teenagers, students from all five tenth-grade classes, are present. The guest sits behind a desk with a glass of water to his right, a microphone to his left, and a few pieces of paper in front of him. He is slight and gray-haired. He wears no glasses. He is old. As he stands up from his chair, his movements are hesitatingly uncertain, as if he has balance problems. Then he pulls himself together and suddenly seems somewhat younger. He crosses to the edge of the little stage. The general noise is disrupted by "shh" and "quiet." The small, old man looks quietly out across his audience. He pulls his shoulders back a little and says: "Good morning." It is now quiet.

"I was born in the old German empire," relates Heinz Drossel. For the students, this is fascinating. It is as if all 150 teenagers are briefly holding their breath. In the empire! The man up there on the podium is truly ancient.

"I was born in the old German empire. I experienced the collapse after World War I, and I very consciously experienced the Weimar Republic. With effort, I survived Adolf Hitler's thousand-year Reich and his horrendous war. And since that time, I have lived in the Federal Republic of Germany."

The teenagers who do not have their regular lessons on this sunny May day are about 16 years old.

Heinz Drossel, 2005 in Jerusalem

They are here to listen to a "contemporary witness." On the teaching plan for today, the words "National Socialism" are written. Drossel might well be the first person that these young people have ever met in person who experienced this dark period in Germany's history as an adult. Certainly, some of them might have grandparents who were adults in the so-called Third Reich, perhaps even a grandfather who lost his life as a child soldier. However, these young people are now hearing a firsthand account of what it was like to live under the Hitler dictatorship, what it meant to live through this, what it was like for the parents of an acquaintance to suddenly disappear, or what one felt as a 16-year-old when a friend was no longer permitted in a café because he was Jewish.

Heinz Drossel lifts up several worn-out notebooks. As he explains, these were his war diaries. They are over 60 years old and were with him in France and in Russia. At the conclusion of his talk, the students, whom he formally calls "dear friends," are welcome to come up and look at the little books.

Walking back and forth across the small stage and imitating a Gestapo officer, Drossel tells the story of how he went to this officer as an 18-year-old to ask about one of his father's business partners who was missing. He reports how he wanted to have a farewell cup of coffee with his friend Salomon, and how a Nazi loudly demanded, "The Jew must get out!" Drossel's voice becomes quiet, as he looks sadly across the audience: "I was ashamed to be a German then."

Drossel talks about his role models, his father and his grandfather, and how both of them encouraged him to explore and analyze the world. He returns to the confusion of the Weimar period. As a schoolboy, he was sent out to buy bread in the morning for his family; this minor purchase was acquired with million-mark bills. And he talks about how he saw the Orthodox Jews from the East, who lived in the Scheunen Quarter in Berlin.

Drossel only spends a little time describing his experiences as a soldier and an officer on the front. Soldier stories are not emphasized. Even in this phase of his life, he had his own ideas, and he tried to remain true to his convictions. It is obvious that, above all, humanity is of the greatest value to him. And that he did not seek to avoid any discomfort or risk when he recognized that this value was in danger. How else could he have decided in a second's time to organize a hiding place for four Jews in January 1945 in order to enable them to escape from the Gestapo? One of the rescued Jews, Ernest Frontheim, became his best friend. According to Drossel, a meeting with his grown daughter years later revealed to him the true significance of what he had done: "As I held her in my arms, I was suddenly aware that this woman probably never would have existed, if I had done things differently."

There are many moving moments during this two-hour talk, which resembles a story more than a lesson. Drossel always stays objective in his word choices, even during the description of dramatic situations. Succinctly he describes how in 1942 he prevented a young Jewish woman from taking her own life. Later, this woman became his wife. It is completely still in the room.

However, after an hour and a half a little commotion does develop and a break is called. The students are divided about this, however the teachers present at the talk make this decision. Reinhold Egge, former army officer, member of the association

For Democracy-Against Forgetting, and planner for this event gets upset at a student who had eaten something during Drossel's talk. Drossel stays quiet. "I know that I cannot reach all of them, but I cannot change that," he comments. After the short interruption, Drossel is asked to take the microphone. Over the course of the talk, his voice has become somewhat raw and more subdued. The 87-year-old man feels compelled to sit down to use the microphone. He is not pleased by this, but surrenders because the microphone is on the table and not portable.

In conclusion, Drossel again directly addresses his listeners: "Dear friends, that was my life under the most brutal dictatorship and during the bloodiest war of the 20th century. You could survive that period, but you had to pay a high price. A national socialist dictatorship requires that you sell yourself completely. Your conscience and perhaps most importantly, your personal freedom. And the meaning of personal freedom can only be gauged if you have lived a period of your life without freedom. As you know, many people at that time sold their souls. I do not condemn these individuals. In such a situation, the decision is a matter of conscience, one that everyone must make for him- or herself. However, it was a decision that shaped Germany's future. Do it better!"

A short silence, then loud applause. Slowly, the assembly dissipates. At the front, a cluster of girls assembles around Drossel's desk. They look through his diaries and thank him. One of them trots forward, climbs up on the small stage, and hugs the perplexed man. She kisses him sweetly on the cheek. And then she quickly runs away.

I. A Fateful Meeting

An Attempt at Reconstruction

Jungfern Bridge, Berlin, November 1942

With a rumbling in her stomach, the woman stands on the bridge. Beneath her, the Spree River splashes quietly. Black and cold. So cold that it should not last long. Marianne Hirschfeld is afraid of what will happen after she jumps. Not of death, but perhaps she is stronger than she thinks and she will fight. Perhaps she will be pulled from the water half-dead, taken to a hospital, identified, and then be taken to a concentration camp. In the camp, there would perhaps be no more opportunities to end her suffering on her own.

She had learned only a few hours before that her landlords, the Fleischers, a Jewish couple, want to leave Berlin earlier than planned. Actually, they were supposed to leave the city together, all three of them. That was the last hope to which Marianne had clung. It is completely impossible to continue to exist in Berlin. Every day brings with it the threat of deportation to certain death, every day the bombs fall, and the finding of food had become a catastrophe long before. Now she has to stay behind, since she does not have enough money saved up.

She has already found a place for her six-year-old son. He is protected by his "Aryan" father and his Lutheran baptism certificate, as was often the case in such instances. He is a tough, clever boy, and he would make it, surely. And the baby, did it have a chance? It is hardly possible to think about the tiny girl. Marianne had no choice when she gave birth to her daughter Judis in August 1942 in the Jewish hospital. There were serious complications during the birth, ones that almost cost Marianne her life. In order to protect her and the man she loved, she had to lie. She claimed that the father, too, was a Jew; she gave a false name for the father.

The little girl is still there. Born prematurely, she needed special care, and the day-to-day life of a persecuted woman is no place for a baby. Marianne did not dare visit her daughter, out of fear that the Gestapo would arrest her. In the interim, they had begun to continuously monitor the hospital and to use it as a collecting station for the deportation of Jewish people.

Marianne had planned not to think about her children. However, she was not successful. She does not know which is more frightening: to desert them—either by fleeing or by suicide—or the conviction that she could not protect them anyway. Again she wishes that she had died at Judis's birth or that she had never been born. Upset, she walks up and down the walkway. Do it! Now! She tries to spurn herself on and bends far over the guard rail.

She does not hear the steps approaching her through the darkness. Boot steps. Her arms are grabbed from behind. She looks over her shoulder and sees an army uniform. She sees nothing but the uniform and tries to tear herself free in order to jump over the rail. However, the man holds her tightly. Marianne almost faints, the blood rushes in her ears. She is now frozen and doesn't hear clearly what he is saying.

Marianne Hirschfeld with her son William (Billy) Albinus, Berlin 1941–1942

The subordinate officer Heinz Drossel, who is on leave in his native city, does not believe his eyes. He immediately recognizes that this is the young, pretty woman from 1938, before the war. They had crossed paths in Tempelhof, and her young son was with her. He was the reason why they even spoke in the first place, and they exchanged a couple of friendly sentences. Now she stands before him here, completely unable to move. He holds her arm. However, in the same moment that he asks it, he realizes what a dumb question he is posing: "Are you not doing well?" The person in front of him is terrified and numb. And then he asks: "Are you a Jew?"

Marianne collapses, and her eyes fill with tears. She nods. He puts his arm around her, holds her, and says: "Do not be afraid. I will take you somewhere safe." Safety. For Marianne Hirschfeld, this word had lost all meaning over the previous years. Nothing was safe anymore. Everything was in flux, uncertain, and threatening. Could she trust this army officer? There is nothing else she can do. She follows him.

Heinz Drossel does not pause to think on the Jungfern Bridge. He simply pushes the woman gently away from the rail. Everything would be figured out. It had to be. The very next thing was to take this woman home with him.

Disjointed thoughts, mainly images, pass through Heinz Drossel's mind as he walks to the tram station, side by side with this delicate, unduly exhausted figure.

He sees her boy before them. And then he sees the boy from Dagda, who would forever remain nameless to him. He was one of the countless victims of the mass murder of Jews to which Drossel had secretly been a witness in 1941. The boy was about six years old. He stood there, naked and shaking, with his parents and other relatives and acquaintances, at the edge of a ditch in which corpses already lay. He stretched his hand out to one of the adults at his side. In that moment, an SS man shot him in the head. His small body pitched onto the bodies in the ditch, and then he was covered by other murder victims.

For added protection against the bombers, the street lamps are kept dim. Even in the tram station, only a few emergency lights are burning. Both of them stand on the platform, nestled close to each other. The conductor discreetly ignores the officer and the woman. They seem to be a couple. They do not suspect that this pose, which is assumed to protect them from curious glances, foretells the future. They will actually become a couple, establish a family, and spend their lives together. Until then, though, much time must still pass, time during which they must fight to survive and will have no word of each other. It will be almost three years exactly before they see each other again.

II. Before the War (1916–1939)

One against the Other

Berliner Strasse 79, Berlin-Tempelhof, April 1, 1933

Heinz had never seen his father so irate. Paul Drossel screamed in rage. During the early morning hours of this April 1, 1933, members of the SA (Sturmabteilung, or Storm Division/Brownshirts) had smeared the word *Jude* ("Jew") and a Star of David, in white, on the display window of his linens business. Sixteen-year-old Heinz hovered in the hall and watched as his father raced for the telephone. He was visibly shaking as he grabbed the telephone receiver. After calling the NSDAP (Nationalsozialistische Deutsche Arbeiterpartei, or Nazi Party) administrative office, he demanded that "this mess" be removed. And of course, this cleaning should not just take place at his business but at that of the Levy business across the street. The perpetrators should be sent over, and "lickety split" too!

Drossel's wish was fulfilled, but only in part: two young SA men trotted over and cleaned his window. However, they left the window of the Jewish neighbor untouched. Father Drossel's calm did not last long. He loathed the boycott of Jewish businesses. As the graffiti indicated, the members of the new ruling party knew that Paul Drossel took no stock in their new regime. He had never made a secret of this, and he had refused to "ornament" his business with the already obligatory swastika flag. The house chairman had already warned him several times about this. This period of resistance was now over. Drossel had followed the rise of the Nazis with suspicion and was one of the few in his circle of acquaintances who did not trivialize the "brown mob."

Now, he finally special-ordered a swastika flag measuring 15 inches by 20 inches, which he hung on his door.

It was very hard for Paul Drossel to make this concession to the new regime. However, in light of his responsibility to his family and also to his customers, many of whom had repeatedly urged him to not be so stubborn, he was moved to back down. Some of his customers were afraid to be seen coming and going at a business owned by an overt opponent of the Nazi Party. Drossel prophesied to his son Heinz that the Party would not forget his outburst of fury and that the family would eventually feel the ramifications of this. He was right.

The Gestapo summons arrived as unsealed letters, clearly marked with a swastika stamp and naming the Gestapo as the sender. Thus, the mailman knew what was happening and could tell tales to the neighbors, who began to gossip secretly among themselves. This method was often calculated to result in the marginalization of the individuals who received these notorious letters. People usually chose to avoid any connection with those the Gestapo was watching. Paul Drossel was repeatedly called to the Gestapo headquarters. However, nothing is known about the interrogations of the businessman. The Gestapo liquidated his linens business in May 1943.

Paul Martin Drossel was born on December 15, 1880, the oldest son of a tailor. After the conclusion of his business apprenticeship period and several years of employment as a bookkeeper for Meder & Thiele, a laundry company in Berlin, he married Elfriede Labové in 1911. She had been born in Berlin in 1892, the daughter of a locksmith, and worked as a seamstress for Meder & Thiele. Soon, Paul and Elfriede were prospering financially. In 1916, when their only son, Heinz, was born, they were living in a large, lovely six-room apartment in the middle-class neighborhood of Berlin-Tempelhof. Paul could not be present for the birth of his son on September 21. Since August 1914, he had been fighting at the front as a soldier for "Emperor and Fatherland" in Infantry Regiment Nr. 18.

Drossel was involved in World War I as an active soldier from start to finish. He spent most of this time on the eastern front. He never wrote home about his war experiences, only that the Russians were

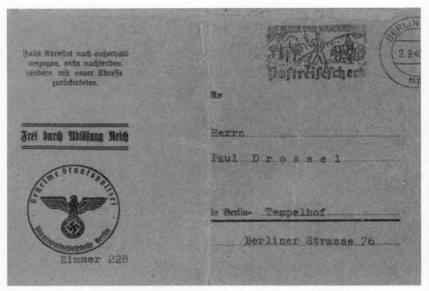

Gestapo summons for Paul Drossel

quite wonderful people. This he told his son at a very young age. After Private Drossel's release from military service on January 9, 1919, he had a difficult time providing for the financial well-being of his family. Like millions of others in the German Reich, he could find no work.

On November 9, 1919, Philipp Scheidemann announced the establishment of the Weimar Republic in Berlin. After the Kaiser abdicated and Friedrich Ebert took over the government as Chancellor, a period of chaos and violence began in Germany. Supported by the military and industrial complexes, the conservative powers did not wish to accept the shift in power which benefited the Social Democrats, a group that the conservatives demonized as traitors of the Fatherland. Street fights were the order of the day in Berlin; the murders of Rosa Luxemburg, Karl Liebknecht, and Kurt Eisner in 1919 were only the start of the multitude of bloody actions that shook the Weimar Republic.

Already by the first parliamentary elections on June 6, 1920, only two months after the Kapp Putsch which sought to overthrow Ebert's government, the young republic's coalition parties lost their absolute majority. The conservative, nationalist-oriented DVP

Paul and Elfriede Drossel, wedding photograph

(German People's Party) and DNVP (German National People's Party) won numerous seats. Organized by the trade unions in reaction to the Kapp Putsch, the general strike only briefly fired up the democratic powers; the unity between the bourgeois and leftist voters and parties that opposed the militaristic, nationalist conservative putschists was short-lived.

For the Drossels, the rent for their relatively large apartment became unaffordable. In 1920, the head of the family found a shop with adjacent rooms and a small kitchen in Tempelhof. The bathroom was in the courtyard. The situation was a personal nightmare for Elfriede. With childhood nonchalance, Heinz adapted to his new surroundings. For the first two years, his bed was an ironing board laid between two chairs and wrapped in blankets. Paul Drossel grit his teeth; with his final savings and a loan, he wanted to build a new existence for himself and his family. He opened a shop for custom-made shirts, and table and bed linens.

The first years were ones of privation for the Drossel family. Even little Heinz had to do his part in the new business; as an elementary school student, he ran errands to the sewing shop at the Hackescher Market. The so-called *Scheunenviertel* (Barn Quarter) lay in this area. This was the part of Berlin in which numerous Eastern European Orthodox Jews lived. The Grenedier and Kanonier streets teemed with traditionally garbed men, replete with yarmulkes and sidelocks. The exotic residents of these streets did not irritate the child. He had already had good experiences with one of these people's fellow believers.

Directly adjacent to his father's shop, a Jewish used clothing merchant ran his business. Day after day, the first-grader Heinz Drossel walked past this old man, who regularly sat on a stool in front of his door. The boy's curiosity about the foreigner grew, and after a short time, the two of them became friends. The Jewish man told the boy stories from the Old Testament, which the little boy found fascinating. The old man's manner made a lasting impression on the boy.

Almost 80 years later, Drossel recalled that "the clothing merchant Jud Flieg was the first foreigner I ever got to know. And I have never forgotten his sad eyes."

The early school years passed by without any notable events. Heinz's contact with other children was fairly rare. He spent most of his free time lending his parents a hand. Besides running errands for the business, he took care of some shopping at a young age. As the lower multiplication tables were being taught in school, he traded in million- and billion-valued currency. 1923 witnessed the progression from economic depression to hyperinflation. The German economy collapsed.

In September, the first billion-mark bills appeared on the market, soon followed by trillion and even hundred-trillion notes. In October, a kilogram of rye bread cost up to 78 billion marks. Unemployment benefits peaked at 21 billion marks a week. Noisy protests and fights

Heinz with an acquaintance in front of the linen shop in
Berlin-Tempelhof, ca. 1922

became fixtures to the street scene. Sometimes the altercations became
quite violent, even in front of the Drossel linen shop. Streetcars
were tipped over, noses were bloodied. Communists fought against
infamous SA squads, Nazis against Social Democrats.

In November, over half a million Berliners received unemployment
payments. No one could exist on this, and the wages could not keep
up with the rapidly escalating devaluation of the currency. Food
became increasingly hard to find, as the farmers held back their
stock. Eventually, there was even a shortage of paper. The currency
presses could not keep up with the printing of money. Emergency
currency, gold bonds, and "stable value city treasury notes" were
introduced, based on pre-war pricing standards. New prices were

calculated every day based on the old German Gold Mark. The result was total confusion.

The *Rentenmark* was introduced on November 15, 1923, and slowly the state of affairs calmed down. The economic situation in Germany began to stabilize. The living conditions again became bearable, and people rediscovered hope. This was also the case with the Drossel family. The low point seemed to have passed, and the financial situation even allowed Elfriede to take Heinz on a vacation. Between 1924 and 1932, mother and son together took a short trip every year. In the meantime, the father took care of the running of the business, which was prospering. Soon he was even able to hire several employees.

The first mother-son trip was to the Thuringian Forest. It was meant to help Heinz recuperate fully from his serious bout of pleurisy and a lung infection. His parents had feared for their only child's life for seven long weeks.

A nun was hired to help care for him. The experience of watching someone pray for him, which he observed between his serious fever attacks, touched the boy deeply. As Drossel described later, this was his first "inner experience of religion."

In 1925, Paul Drossel rented an extra room for his son on the first floor at the front of the house. Until now, the back room of the shop had been all that the family had had as living space. In 1928, Heinz received another room on the third floor. From his new kingdom, he could easily see the apartments across the street. On Friday evenings, the view into the Levy family's living room in particular fascinated him, fixing him to his observation post. One year before, Mr. Levy had opened his large, modern linen shop, and he was Paul Drossel's only direct competition in Tempelhof. Both businessmen had quickly arranged that if either of them could not fulfill the wishes of a customer, he would send him or her across the way to the other shop.

On every Friday, the Levy Family celebrated the traditional Sabbath. The solemnity and earnestness of the ceremony deeply impressed the school-age Heinz. This was the period in which he

Drossel Family, ca. 1931

seriously explored world religions. He would soon be confirmed. Heinz's observations of what happened in the neighboring apartment motivated him to explore Judaism, and his maternal grandfather encouraged the boy to read various texts related to Buddhism, Christianity, and Judaism, as well as the Gilgamesh Epic.

Grandfather Hermann Labové was a formative figure in Heinz Drossel's life. The locksmith came from Western Pomerania, and he worked for the national railroad system (*Reichsbahn*). He had never received much formal education, however he was quite well read. As he grew older, Hermann Labové became increasingly interested in philosophical and religious writings. Already at a young age, he involved Heinz in his studies, explaining to him about Kant and the firmament. He conveyed to the boy his first impression of what it was like to have a personal worldview.

As Catholics, the Drossel Family celebrated Heinz's first communion with great festivity. Relatives were invited to dine with the family at Veith's *Gesellschaftshaus*. With his son's move into the adult world, Father Paul offered a toast to him. Heinz Drossel never forgot his closing words, which became his life's motto: "Always stay human, my boy, and decent, even in hard times and even when a sacrifice is demanded of you."[1]

The one and only time that Heinz took a trip with both of his parents was around New Year's 1932. Father Paul believed that this might be the last opportunity for a long time. He possessed a keen political awareness, and the outcome of the previous election had made him very concerned. The Nazi Party had been forced to accept a small decrease in numbers, but with 33.1 percent of the vote, it was still the strongest party.[2]

At the weekly meetings of business acquaintances from Tempelhof at the Drossel home, much was discussed. Often the men, most of whom were inclined toward the center party, listened to the radio together to learn about the political and economic situation in Germany and around the world. Starting in 1931, they gathered regularly in Heinz's room and used the radio that he had received as a gift for his 12th birthday in 1928. (Prior to this point, Paul had rented a four-room apartment including a water closet in the rear house.) The boy was allowed to sit in on these meetings, and he listened as heated debates were waged, often fueled by a chocolate factory owner and a master butcher.

Early on, father Drossel vehemently argued against the Nazi Party at these meetings, while most of the others were of the opinion that this new party should not be taken seriously. Even when Hitler came to prominence in the government, it was not so bad, and the Browns would, sooner or later, vanish. This was a position that many Germans held at this time. Drossel Senior had a very different opinion. His son remembered that he prophesied: "Once they are in, we will not get rid of them so quickly."

Shortly before the election in November 1932, the high schooler asked his father which party was the best and for which he would

Hermann Labové Family, Heinz Drossel's mother is seated to the left at the front.

vote. Instead of answering him, Drossel told his son to inform himself on this subject by reading the newspaper, studying party platforms, and visiting the rallies. As soon as Heinz had formed his own impressions, they could talk again. He only gave him the following terse advice: "If you go to the radicals and there should be a shooting, leave quickly."

Drossel Junior followed his father's advice. He observed the Communists' parades, listened to the speeches of the Social Democrats, and even visited the gatherings of the Nazis. And he did what few other Germans did: he read Hitler's *Mein Kampf*. The 16-year-old found the book to be confusing and poorly written, but the message was clear. Hitler wanted war, and he wanted to persecute and annihilate the Jews.

For the Nazi Party, the election on November 6 was not especially favorable. They lost 34 parliamentary seats but remained the strongest party. On the other hand, the Communists could chalk up an increase in 11 seats. The dissatisfaction of the working class was reflected in the election results. However, the support of numerous influential members of the upper industrial complex, including bankers and large landowners, helped propel Hitler into power. They demanded that *Reichspräsident* von Hindenburg make Hitler the head of the government.

Hitler successfully undermined the position of Kurt von Schleicher, who had been named Chancellor on December 3. Hitler conspired with Franz von Papen, who had lost his position to Schleicher, and they came to a mutual agreement on January 4, 1933, on a joint Hitler/von Papen government with von Papen as Vice Chancellor. The new government would have full presidential authority and would have two main goals: "the removal of all Social Democrats, Communists, and Jews from leadership positions in Germany" and "the reestablishment of order in public life." According to the new allies, another key issue would be "the dissolving of the Versailles Treaty . . . and the reestablishment of a strong Germany, both militarily and economically."[3]

Two days after Schleicher was forced to resign, an aged President von Hindenburg named the leader of the Nazi Party, Adolf Hitler, Chancellor on January 30, 1933. The Drossel family heard the news on the radio and was outraged.

In his memoirs, Heinz Drossel recounted what happened that day: "Already that afternoon, columns of SA men marched through the streets. The radio incessantly blared calls to join a great celebratory gathering in front of the chancellery: 'for the Führer.' Around 7:00 p.m., I decided to go into the city.

"Masses of people in plain clothes stormed from all sides. Singing their fight songs, the SA columns marched by. Everything was moving in the direction of the inner city. 'Today Germany belongs to us—tomorrow the entire world.' . . . I reached the chancellery. Illuminated from all sides by spotlights, a man with a stone face stood above at a window. . . . I returned home on foot and climbed up the now-dark Kreuzberg Hill. I looked back at the city that had been consumed by madness. Far away now, I heard the muted throbbing of the uproar. The flickering light of thousands of torches lit everything. The sky above the inner city glowed with fire. Was this the writing on the wall?"[4]

Only one month later, on February 27, the *Reichstag* (Parliament Building) burned. Immediately Hitler blamed the Communists and justified the "Emergency Regulation for the Protection of the People and the State," which went into effect the following day. With its passage, the most important basic rights set forth in the Weimar Constitution were abolished. Personal freedom, freedom of the press, freedom of thought, the right to gather and form societies, protection of the private sphere and private property, the protection of keeping your mail private—all of these democratic rights were now subordinated to "restrictions," which were also "applicable outside of the otherwise stipulated legal boundaries."[5]

The Enabling Act of 1933 went into effect on March 21. On the basis of this mandate "for the alleviation of the suffering of the people and the Reich," the government could create laws, claiming that they were emergency decrees, over the next four-year period. The Parliament no longer held any power; the terror began. The Communist Party was banned, elected officials were arrested, and numerous officials were suspended and replaced by Nazi Party members. Already in late February, Berlin's police chief, Hermann Göring, had appointed 40,000 SA and SS (*Schutzstaffel,* a major paramilitary organization) men as assistant policemen, and he demanded the indiscriminate use of guns.

On Monday, March 27, 1933, the headlines of one Berlin newspaper read, "Mass Action Prescribed."[6]

Starting on April 1, all Jewish business, as well as Jewish attorneys and doctors, were to be boycotted. SA patrols and guards would control and guarantee the observance of this action. The official justification of these measures was just as flimsy as it was absurd: in other countries, the Jews were spreading lies about and defaming the "New Germany," thus the boycott was intended to be a kind of defensive and retaliatory action.

Even those who had, until now, chosen to ignore or deny the deeply rooted antisemitism in the Nazi movement, could no longer turn their heads away. *The* Jews—often lumped together with *the* Social Democrats or *the* Communists—were guilty of everything: of the humiliating peace drafted at Versailles, of the unemployment rates, of the bad economic situation of the individual.

The list of boycott measures was long. No German was to buy anything from a Jew. All "Aryan" businesses were to fire their Jewish employees. All Jewish business proprietors were to appoint "Aryan" managers, fire their Jewish employees, and only utilize and pay their Aryan workers. The basis for the complete and systematic destruction of the Jewish Germans' means to live was established for years to come.

On the first day of the Jewish boycott, Heinz Drossel skipped school and walked around the city. He noticed other defaced show windows and barricaded businesses. He watched as SA men, armed with cardboard signs, tried to block the entrances to Jewish businesses: "Do not buy from Jews!" However, in front of a woolens shop in New Tempelhof that was operated by a Jewish merchant, he witnessed a scene that encouraged him or, at least, quieted him somewhat. Here, two resolute female Berliners shoved the SA men aside, calling them "dumb boys," and made their way into the shop where they took care of their shopping.

Such public instances of defiance of the "ordered mass action" and the more covert, yet clear, disapproval of the measures caused the Nazis to view this first pogrom as a failure. The propaganda machine only occupied itself briefly with this "uprising of the Germans." As planned, the "Law for the Reestablishment of the Official Offices" went into effect on April 7. The mass firings of Jewish university professors, doctors in public hospitals, teachers, and court employees were rigorously pursued. The authorities were showing their "Aryan" people what was expected of them: the complete exclusion of Jews from the public arena.

Jews were forbidden from going for walks or sitting in public parks. They could no longer frequent cafes and restaurants, cinemas, theaters, or sporting events. Signs hung everywhere: "Jews not desired" or "Not permitted for Jews." Starting on April 25, 1933, it was considerably harder for Jewish children to gain access to public schools.[7] After November 1938, Jews were totally banned from public schools, and they were only permitted to attend Jewish institutions. Even before the passing of this law, many parents had decided to send their daughters and sons to Jewish schools to spare them the constant teasing and cruelties of the "Aryan" school children and the teachers.

In 1936, six of the sixteen students in Heinz Drossel's class were not members of the Hitlerjugend (HJ, Hitler Youth) or other Nazi youth organizations. The Nazi *Gleichschaltung* (enforced conformity) was so far advanced at this point that the previously independent *Jugendbunde* (youth societies), whether church-oriented or secular in nature, had been completely absorbed—or banned—by the Nazis. After an HJ leader from his school asked Heinz why he was not participating in the organization, the high schooler spoke with his father. For tactical reasons, Paul advised his son to join the HJ. Due to some critical statements he had made, the businessman was back in the sights of the Gestapo and had again been summoned for interrogation.

The situation for Paul and his family seemed to be so volatile that he even applied to join the Party. Because of his membership in a Masonic Lodge, his application was denied. It was clear that his son would suffer from the consequences if he remained publicly defiant. Thus, Heinz took part in several HJ meetings, but he found these to be "deathly dull, trivial, and pointless."[8] A sympathetic doctor and friend of his parents finally declared him "unfit for duty"—despite the fact that he pursued competitive sports.

Heinz Drossel described his school, particularly his class and most of his teachers, as "non-political." However, after 1934, everything became "browner." Some teachers began coming to class in SA boots. The daily routine soon included the flag pledge and

Heinz Drossel's graduating class, Berlin 1936. Drossel, upper row, second from the right. Salomon Warmann to the right of him.

Hitler greeting. The "study of race" was now part of the curriculum. The biology teacher was a small, fat man who corresponded little with the Nazi racial ideal. He once expelled the only Jewish student, Salomon Warmann, from the room: "Warmann, you must now leave the room. Today we are talking about the Aryan people!" Heinz and several others felt ashamed, but Salomon smiled understandingly, grabbed his jacket, and left.

Heinz and Salomon were friends. After his graduation in 1936, the young Jew wanted to leave Germany. Prague was his goal. Both of the boys passed their exams. Salomon worked on the graduation newspaper, but he was already gone by the time of the graduation party. To say good-bye, the two young men met one more time. In a subdued mood, they went for a walk through the city. They could find nowhere to sit down. Everywhere there were signs: "Jews not welcome." Drossel made an effort and dragged Salomon into a restaurant, past just such a sign. They ordered two coffees, and as they waited to be served, the whispering started. Their coffees arrived, but before they could take a sip, a man in uniform materialized in front of them. He stared at Heinz and bellowed: "The Jew must leave!" Drossel remembered: "I was horribly ashamed." Both of them left the restaurant. On this day, Salomon's and Heinz's paths parted forever.

What would Heinz Drossel have seen if he had walked past Bischoff Street 23 on April 1, 1933? Here he would have found the business established by Kurt Sigismund Hirschfeld in 1932. Marianne Hirschfeld's father ran an impressive, large-scale fabric business. Giant bolts of damasks; fine, medium-fine, and coarse linens; striped satins; all qualities of cotton. These were primarily sold for the sewing of table and bed linens but also for shirts. The customers were composed of retailers who had certain products produced in the sewing shops, which were then sold in their shops. Heinz Drossel's father could have been a customer of the Hirschfeld company, since he offered all of these items for sale with a special focus on handmade shirts.

Exactly what happened on April 1, 1933, at Hirschfeld & Co. is unknown. All that is known is that after this date many of the Jewish businessman's customers fell away. Within one year of the first boycott, the company's profits dropped by half, when compared with the previous year's profits. The Hirschfelds were forced to give up their seven-room apartment at Heilbronn Street 13, Berlin-Wilmersdorf, in 1934 in exchange for a four-and-a-half-room apartment.

The business was liquidated in 1935. The Hirschfelds no longer had a source of regular income, and like most German Jews, they had to fight to merely survive. It was pretty much impossible to find a new job, since the bans on the hiring of Jews were already in force. In addition, the acquisition of only the bare necessities was a huge undertaking.

A native Berliner, Kurt Sigismund Hirschfeld had been actively involved in Hirschfeld, Sturmann & Co., a wholesale textile business, since 1931. He had invested 30,000 Reichsmarks in the business, a small fortune, which he had obtained in part through his position as general manager for South German Woven Goods, Inc., LLC. When he met his wife Rosa, née Lippmann, a native Pomeranian, she was working as a cutter in one of the firms with which Hirschfeld did business.

Kurt and Rosa Hirschfeld were married in 1909, and their first daughter, Ruth, was born soon afterward. After additional education as a merchant in the textile trade, Kurt earned a good living for the family. On December 12, 1912, the second daughter, Marianne, was born. Two years later, World War I broke out. Kurt Hirschfeld was drafted, and he served until 1918. After the war, he was fortunate to immediately be rehired as a merchant at his old company, Fraenkel Brothers, a wholesale textile company.

The Hirschfeld family belonged to the small number of those who were able to weather the confusing, hard postwar years well. In 1924, Kurt Hirschfeld joined South German Woven Goods, Inc., as a partner and general manager. Despite the hyperinflation, the family prospered financially. Their apartments were increasingly comfortable, and their furnishings became more dignified. Both daughters completed school at a relatively high level. The Hirschfelds were a typical Jewish family in Germany in the early twentieth century: middle-class liberals, assimilated, patriotic. On Christmas Eve, a Christmas tree stood in their salon, alongside a Hanukkah menorah. Their religion did not play a major role in their lives.

The youngest daughter of the business manager, Marianne, experienced firsthand the downfall of the very promising start-up company. She had been hired in 1932, the year of the company's founding, as head clerk in her father's firm. Marianne, a fun-loving, talented, pretty young woman, had completed her education as a foreign-language correspondent for French and English.

The older daughter, Ruth, had studied classical philology at Friedrich Wilhelm University. However, the political developments in Germany, specifically the growing antisemitism, caused Ruth to end her studies and leave her home country. According to family recollections, she was involved in the Zionist movement. She was a politically engaged woman, and the waiting and perseverance of her parents made no sense to her. In 1934, she went to England and later emigrated to Palestine.

The liberal mentality of Marianne's parents permitted her to pursue wholeheartedly her greatest passion: dance. It soon became more than a hobby for her. She was so talented that she danced competitively and was quite successful. Dance was also what led Marianne to her first husband, Adolf Albinus. With him as her dance partner, she won various medals and danced in competitions across Germany. It was an exciting, glamorous, gloriously untroubled time.

On March 23, 1932, Marianne and Adolf got married. He came from the Lorraine region and was one year older than her. In the early 1930s, the two of them planned to open a dance school in Düsseldorf. However, nothing came of this. Later, Marianne told her youngest daughter, who inherited her mother's dance talent, that the failure of this dream was tied to her Jewish ethnicity. She said nothing more than this.

"The Large Concentration Camp, Known as Germany"

Berlin, Kurfürstendamm, November 9, 1938
The law student Heinz Drossel saw it with his own eyes: columns of smoke over Berlin on the morning of November 10, 1938. He was riding the street car to his law exam tutor. Near Kurfürstendamm, he observed how the police and fire departments had broadly cordoned off the burning synagogue instead of rescuing the sacred building.

During the so-called Night of Broken Glass, hundreds of synagogues across the German Reich were destroyed. Countless Jewish businesses and residences were plundered and demolished. In Berlin alone, over 1,000 Jews were arrested and deported, mostly to the Oranienburg Concentration Camp. Dozens of people died over the course of the night. The focused actions were predominantly directed and initiated by the SS. SA men dressed in plain clothes played the parts of irate common people and wrecked indescribable havoc. The terror of that night was justified as "the people's rage against world Judaism," which was supposedly guilty of the downfall of the German people. The catalyst for this was the fatal attack on

Ernst vom Rath, secretary to the German ambassador, by the young student, Herschel Grynszpan.

Grynszpan was of Polish extraction. The news about the deportation of thousands of Polish Jews out of Germany, including his own family, drove him to this act of despair. The Germans confiscated the official papers of the Jewish families, and the Polish government hesitated to permit the people into Poland. Under horrific conditions, the families sat for weeks on end in No Man's Land between the two countries' borders.

Heinz Drossel was unsettled and appalled by the scenes he saw on Berlin's streets. As usual, his tutor, whom he visited that morning, initially adopted a neutral stance. However, he then changed the daily program, and without batting an eye, dealt with the criminal offense of arson. Suddenly he turned from his students, looked out the window, and ended the session: "Gentlemen, today one must be ashamed to be German!" And, "Now go, gentlemen! Perhaps you will still find a couple of Jewish diamonds."

At the very latest, this was the moment that Drossel regretted returning to Germany. In July 1938, the young man had accepted an invitation from his Aunt Betty to visit her in San Remo, Italy. He was finding the political circumstances in Germany to be increasingly oppressive and dangerous. Hitler's marching on Austria in March 1938 and the outcome of the national referendum for the annexation of Austria were events that secured Heinz's critical position against the government. Heinz Drossel was one of the few who risked using the anonymous election booth to vote No to "Greater Germany," thus avoiding the watchful gaze of the uniformed election helpers, the Party members, and the SA men.

In his memoirs, he described that experience: "I placed my X in the No circle and inserted the sheet into the appropriate envelope. I walked across the hall to the ballot box, watched by ten or twelve waiting voters and Party members. I gave my ballot to the SA man at the box, and he stuck it in. Done! I had voted. None of the waiting voters followed me. All of them obediently marked Yes at the table. I think my negative vote was one of the only 17 negative votes from among the 600 or 700 votes possible [in the district]."[9]

Already as a 10th grader, Heinz Drossel had indicated a spirit of resistance, even in the small things. Together with several other boys, including his best friend Poldi (Luitpold) Hagen, Heinz started a literary club in Spring 1933. In and of itself, this was nothing unusual for teenagers; however, this group had adopted a particular goal. They were intentionally only going to read and discuss authors whose books had been burned during the May 10, 1933, book burnings. These books were, henceforth, included on a list of "un-German," banned literary works. In later years, the possession of some of these books would result in serious punishment. Heinz Drossel would have had to destroy two-thirds of his personal library if he had followed the Nazis' decree. Many of his fellow Germans did just that, and thousands upon thousands of books were burned in bonfires across the Reich.

In late 1934, the 18-year-old Drossel became familiar with the spaces of the Berlin secret police force on the Alexanderplatz. Unlike others, he was not dragged here, but he willingly entered the den of the lion. The Drossel family maintained close contact with similarly minded Berliners, individuals who were just as critical and negative about the "new times." Mr. and Mrs. Dettbarn were among this group. The Dettbarns belonged to the very small circle of those who chose not to acquire a swastika flag. One morning, Mrs. Dettbarn stood in front of the Drossel shop, upset. She was almost in tears, and she explained that her husband had not returned the night before. She was sure that something had happened to him. Father Drossel tried to calm her down and advised her to wait.

After another night of anxious waiting, Paul Drossel telephoned various hospitals. No success. Mrs. Dettbarn was turned away from the district police office, since it was yet too early to file a missing person's report. Drossel Junior could no longer withstand the lady's worries. He promised to help her and immediately made his way to Berlin's central police station on the Alexanderplatz. No one could help him in the general missing person's office. Then, in passing, a policeman whispered a tip to Heinz: "Try up on the fifth floor!"

Here, the young man found a barred door, on which a sign hung, announcing "Secret State Police" (*Geheime Staatspolizei*, or Gestapo). He did not spend long considering this. He rang the bell. An SS man came to the door and asked him what he wanted. His answer: he wanted to ask about a missing person. This resulted in an astonished look from the SS man, but Heinz was allowed to enter. He had to wait and was then shown into an office. A lamp shone in his face, and he had to wait again. Eventually, an SS officer spoke to him and asked what had caused him to think that Herr Dettbarn had been taken up by the Gestapo. "Is he an enemy of the state?" Heinz Drossel responded ingenuously: "No, but I thought the Gestapo knew everything." Later, his knees buckled; after he got back home, he could not say anything else. That evening, Mr. Dettbarn returned to his wife. He had actually been taken up by the Gestapo and interrogated.

As first semester university student, Heinz tried to join a Catholic association. However, his undertaking failed because the group's first meeting was broken up and banned by the SA. After that, the young men only risked private, sporadic meetings. Heinz would have gladly joined a resistance group, but that was not successful either. The caution and fear in such groups was too great. During this period, horrifying reports about the conditions in the Buchenwald, Oranienburg, and Sachsenhausen concentration camps were trickling into the public realm. These rumors were only discussed behind closed doors.

Nonetheless, in Summer 1939, only a few months before the start of the war, the Catholic law students who had stayed in contact over the years decided to take action. They wanted to copy and distribute a talk that had been given by the writer Ernst Wiechert, who had been declared an enemy of the state. In 1938, Wiechert had been interned for two months in the Buchenwald Camp, and after that, he was under constant Gestapo supervision. Two years before, in 1936, he had held a lecture at Heidelberg University, and he had openly explained his rejection of Nazism and the fascist system at large:

"Yes, it may be that a people can stop distinguishing between justice and injustice, and that every fight is justified. However, such a people stands on the edge of a precipitous slope, and its destruction has already been dictated . . . But the scales of justice have been raised over such a people, and the hand that writes in letters of fire has already appeared on every wall . . . I swear to you today that I will not seduce you to see only radiance and happiness where there is so much suffering. And I will never encourage you to keep silent if your conscience compels you to speak . . ."

Using a typewriter and typing paper, Heinz Drossel fabricated 32 copies of this speech, which he both handed out personally and left on the tables in the lecture halls to be collected. He hoped that many others "read and seriously considered what was in them."[10]

Heinz's increasing conviction that a war was unavoidable combined with the day-to-day harassment and the Nazis' unfettered control over all parts of German society inspired him to consider leaving his homeland. He drew up plans to emigrate to Argentina or Mexico, somewhere away from Germany where he saw no future for himself. And then, ideally timed, he received an invitation from his Aunt Betty to travel to Italy in Spring 1938. After a few complications, Heinz was able to obtain a travel visa that would allow him to travel through Switzerland and other necessary papers from the district defense commander. His father paid for his train ticket and gave him a small amount of travel money.

The time in San Remo with Aunt Betty, his father's fun-loving, unconventional sister, was two-sided. On the one hand, there was the sun, summer, and Italian lightheartedness. On the other, there was the depressing lack of certainty about what should come next. Compounding the problem were the various interactions with numerous German Jews, unwilling emigrants. Most of them were in fear of their lives. Drossel became friends with one particular young Jewish couple. The two of them offered to pay for his passage to America. He refused. Looking back, he explained: "It was never my way to have others pay for what I did. And the two of them needed the money much more than I did. That was clear to me."

Heinz Drossel in San Remo, 1938

On September 30, 1938, the Munich Accord was finalized. The German Reich signed the agreement with France, Great Britain, and Italy as a solution for the so-called Sudeten Crisis. With this step, the danger of war, which had been heightened by Hitler's territorial ultimatums on Czechoslovakia, was averted for the time being. Without consulting the Czechoslovakian government, France, Great Britain, and Italy mandated the transfer to Hitler of the border areas whose residents were predominantly ethnically German. Back home, Hitler had himself celebrated as a diplomat and keeper of the peace. The other European powers deluded themselves into thinking that this was the means of satisfying Hitler's aspirations for power without any bloodshed.

Heinz Drossel was not nearly so naive, but he now concluded that he had enough time to complete his degree before war would break out. As he crossed the border at Basel in October 1938, he told himself, *Now you go back into the world's largest concentration camp, which is called Germany, you stupid dog.*

By this time, Marianne Hirschfeld had already learned firsthand what it meant to be in a concentration camp. On June 14, 1938, her father was arrested and imprisoned in the Buchenwald concentration camp. The *Arbeitscheu Reich* police action had been implemented the day before under the leadership of SS General Reinhard Heydrich. Over 10,000 people were arrested and interned in forced labor camps. So-called asocial Germans, which for Heydrich included vagrants, beggars, Gypsies, and pimps, were to be eliminated, "since criminality is rooted in asocial behaviors."[11] In his "strictly confidential" memorandum, Heydrich added that "all Jewish males" should be arrested as a "police preventative measure." Within this group, any minor offense was enough of a reason for the police to take action. That June, hundreds of Jews were arrested in Berlin alone.

Regardless of a legal conviction or lack thereof, the flimsiest of justifications was all that was needed. Sometimes it was only a ridiculous traffic violation, such as jaywalking, that resulted in an arrest.[12]

Kurt Sigismund Hirschfeld became Prisoner, Number 5290. He was categorized as "reluctant to work, Reich" and as "Jewish." He was seriously tortured and worked under inhuman conditions for the two and a half months he was in Buchenwald. Ironically, the camp's entrance gate was emblazoned with the words, "To Each His Own." At the age of 56, weakened by the preceding years of deprivation and worries, Hirschfeld was of little use to the Nazis as a slave. He was released on August 31. As a result of his mistreatment, Kurt Sigismund Hirschfeld died on November 29, 1938, in the Berlin Jewish Hospital.

Despairingly, Marianne had sought to rescue her father from the concentration camp. She did not have many options. Perhaps she tried to emphasize his military service during World War I, since some Jewish veterans were spared the harshest of treatments upon occasion. Perhaps she hoped that her Aunt Dorothea Hirschfeld's former political acquaintances could help. Aunt Thea had been a Social Democrat, which meant she was now viewed as an enemy of the Nazis. Furthermore she was Jewish and had been forced to retire from her position, but she had been a well-known personality during the Weimar Republic and had been in contact with many influential people.

After the Night of Broken Glass, Marianne had been forced to leave her parents' apartment. She was "permitted" to sell the furniture, good pieces purchased during better times, for ridiculously low prices. She was assigned a room in a "Jewish house," one of the buildings that the Nazis had seized from its Jewish owners. Here Jewish citizens were ghettoized. After the death of her father, Marianne found herself in a lonely, desperate situation. Her marriage with Adolf Albinus had ended in divorce on August 15, 1935, one month before the passing of the Nuremberg Law. Her sister had emigrated years earlier.

Even before her father's arrest in June 1938, Marianne's mother Rosa had slipped into a serious mental condition. Since late March 1936, Rosa had been in a private clinic for the mentally ill. In March 1938, she was moved to the Wittenau Clinic, a state psychiatric facility. After the war, Marianne wrote: "During the interim [between Hitler's coming to power and Kurt Hirschfeld's arrest in June 1938], my mother had a total psychological breakdown. I was responsible for her treatment and her accommodation." Marianne was the most important contact person for Rosa, and she was also responsible for one other person—her son.

William "Billy" Albinus was born on February 2, 1936, in Berlin. It is not known if his father, Adolf Albinus, saw him as an infant. The divorce predated Billy's birth by six months. Since 1933, when the Nazi persecution began, Marianne's menstrual cycle had been irregular. It could be that she first learned that she was pregnant shortly after her divorce. Perhaps Adolf never knew that his wife, whose family was in dire straits, was expecting his child. One can only guess if he might have handled things differently if he had known. According to Marianne's personal writings, it is clear that he was the one who wanted the divorce due to "his fear of being personally disadvantaged."

Already by 1933, long before the banning of such marriages under the Racial Law, the ending of so-called mixed marriages was much easier than the ending of "pure Aryan marriages." In 1938, a clause was added to the marital legislation that allowed race to be used as a justification for divorce. According to the Nazis' racial ideology, the mixing of "German blood" with the blood of others was to be completely discouraged.

Whenever possible, the existing German-Jewish marriages were to be dissolved. However, no legislation requiring the ending of such marriages was ever passed during the Nazi period. There were concerns that such a measure would create turmoil among and be rejected by the "purely German" population. After all, every German wife of a Jewish man had an "Aryan" family, and every "Aryan" husband had German relatives.

Political calculations prevented a final decision on this issue. The authorities demanded the ending of mixed marriages, providing incentive through the repressive measures that the "Aryan" spouses had to suffer under as well. At the same time, the Jewish spouses of "Aryans" (and their children) remained for a long time relatively spared from the government's annihilation policies. For many Jews, divorce was synonymous with a death sentence. In the immediate aftermath of the German surrender, approximately 8,000 Jews lived in Berlin. About 4,000 of them had "Aryan" spouses. At least 1,700 Jews who had gone into hiding in Berlin experienced the liberation of the city.[13]

Merely considering financial issues, Marianne was negatively impacted by the divorce from Adolf Albinus. Of course, she searched for work since there was no financial support from her parents. Marianne had excellent credentials, but she had no chances of employment because she was Jewish. Only Jews were allowed to hire Jewish employees, and the few who at this time were still running businesses were fighting for their own survival. There was no money left for employees. The search for work was grueling and frustrating. And then the day arrived when Marianne learned that she was pregnant. The confirmation of this must have been a serious shock. How would she be able to raise a child in these times?

For every divorced, single mother in the 1930s, life was very hard. For a Jewish woman in this situation, it was a complete catastrophe. Marianne could still live with her parents, where she took care of running the household. By Spring 1936, right after Billy's birth, her mother Rosa was already suffering from severe depression. She was physically wasting away and could use any possible help. Still at liberty in 1936, Kurt tried to reactivate some of his old connections to earn at least enough to cover the staples they needed to live. During this time, he worked sporadically as a sales representative, a humiliating situation for a former company director.

Starting in 1938, the government instituted a food rationing program. What constituted rationing for "Aryans" translated as hunger for Jewish families. The allotments for them were usually only half of what "members of the nation" received. However, material concerns were not the only things that complicated the lives of Marianne and her fellow sufferers. The unrelenting fear, the marginalization, and the daily harassment—bans of all kinds, including the limited access to public transportation—made "normal life" impossible. Every morning, one awoke to questions about whether there was enough food to eat, if any acquaintances had vanished during the night, or if the Gestapo will come for "a visit."

Nonetheless, little Billy flourished, easily learning to talk and walk. He was a cute, cheerful boy with an enchanting smile. The company of the child must have brought comfort and joy even in the midst of all the worries and fears about the future and survival. And Marianne made a concerted effort to create a lighthearted environment for her little boy.

She did everything that young mothers do with their children. She played with Billy, let him splash around and frolic in the garden, and went for walks with him whenever the weather allowed. On one sunny November day in 1938, mother and son went for a walk through the streets of Tempelhof. Billy was two and a half years old, trotting along in short steps beside his mother. He had just found a rock that he was holding in his small fist.

Marianne and Billy, Berlin, ca. 1938

The little one was anything but shy, and his treasure seemed so wonderful to him that he wanted to share it with someone. He held his rock out to the next person who passed him. It was a young man, a student, who was hurrying to finish his preparations for his first state law exam. Before the war broke out, which he had long expected, he wanted to at least have something to show for his years of study.

Heinz Drossel described this meeting in his memoirs: "In order to muddle through, I went for a long walk every day. During one of the first ones I took, I made a small friend. I was walking through the New Tempelhof neighborhood when a little boy no older than two or three jumped out at me. He handed me a very pretty, little rock. And then the little man started talking a blue streak. Finally, his Mama intervened—a lovely, young woman. We exchanged a few words, but then duty called. I felt like I did not have an hour to lose."[14]

III. An Unwilling Officer (1939–1942)

More Than a Formality

Berlin, March 1939

Germany demanded the annexation of Danzig onto the Reich. Poland refused. England and France sided with Poland, and formulated a "declaration of guarantee," which referred back to the Versailles Treaty's protection of the Polish borders. In response, Hitler terminated the Polish-German non-aggression pact and the German-British naval agreement. France and Great Britain reacted in concern but remained passive. Danzig was far away, and the German army had grown quite strong.

Already long ago, Hitler had discarded various sections of the Versailles Treaty. He reinstituted compulsory military service in 1935 and had rebuilt the armament industry. The slogan "People Without Space" was spread through Joseph Goebbels's propaganda machine, and many Germans were convinced by its message. In August, the German Reich and the Soviet Union signed a non-aggression treaty, which contained a secret protocol that stipulated which country would control various nations and areas. These included Poland, the Baltic states, Ukraine, and Finland.

The Drossel family and other anti-Nazis were depressed by the announcement of the German-Soviet non-aggression treaty. It was now clear to them that war was about to start, quite soon. The hope of a short two-front war in which the Nazis would be quickly defeated was now dashed. The Drossels and other like-minded Germans were convinced that only a lost war would bring the hated regime to an end. Now that the Soviet Union to the East had become an ally of Germany, and France and England in the West had showed their unwillingness to stand up to Germany despite all of Hitler's violations, such as the annexation of the Czechoslovakian territory, the possibility of this seemed to be shrinking.

On September 1, 1939, the German army invaded Poland. The Polish troops were hardly able to react in time to offer a defense. On September 17, the Red Army marched from the East to Poland. The country was forced to capitulate. The Soviets and the Germans divided the territory. Hitler, and many Germans as well, reveled in the triumph. Others feared that this maneuver only marked the beginning of something much bigger.

"Since 5:45 a.m., shots have been returned." This report reached the German nation via radio. Hitler represented his violation against a sovereign state as a defensive measure by fabricating a blatant lie about the Poles staging an attack in the border area.

Born in 1910, journalist Erich Kuby was an anti-Nazi. Distanced in tone, he observed the political and social developments in Germany. In a letter from September 1, 1939, he wrote: "Now we have a real mess. Did you hear the radio? Just don't listen too much, or it will warp the connections and make you stupid. I don't listen to any of it. Read the newspaper to stay up to date, the local one and the one from Frankfurt, which only gives its opinion three days later, or what one would like to call an opinion. Gunshots are fired, but it is still not really a war. Will it become one? The Englishmen say that they did not know anything about it. The Italians say nothing at all."[15] Shortly after he wrote this, Kuby was called up, and he spent the duration of the war as a private.

In his diaries, Victor Klemperer described the first day of World War II: "On Friday morning, September 1, the young butcher boy came by and announced that the radio had reported that we already held Danzig and the Danzig Corridor. The war with Poland had begun. England and France were staying neutral. I said to Eva [Victor's "Aryan" wife] that a morphine shot or something like that would be the best for us, so we could end our lives. And then we both told each other that things could not possibly be so bad. After all, the boy had frequently told us other harebrained things . . . For Eva's birthday, Annemarie brought over two bottles of sparkling wine. We drank the one and decided to save the other one for the day the English declared war on Germany. We have now made it to today [September 4, 1939]. All day long I was full of hope. Now I am depressed again."[16]

On September 4, 1939, Heinz Drossel took his first state exam. In reality, he was still missing one semester of his studies, but because he had long been afraid of the war beginning, he had intensified his efforts. In November 1939, Drossel passed his first exam with a mark of "satisfactory." The next step in his effort to become a fully qualified lawyer was a clerkship. It was his only hope of avoiding military service. He applied for a position in the Supreme Court. Drossel was called to meet the Chief Justice. The government official skimmed through his documents, murmuring in satisfaction. He then told the young man that everything looked great, and he would definitely receive a position in short order.

Drossel thought he could leave, but then the Chief Justice cleared his throat: "All that is missing is the document proving your social and political engagement. Anyway, bring it by tomorrow. Today we will file the papers to defer your military service." This was just a formality for the Chief Justice.

For Heinz Drossel, it was not. He had never joined any party organization, to say nothing of being active. He had managed to avoid being caught up in the gleichschaltung of German society until now. He had nothing to support his political engagement, which he revealed to the Chief Justice bluntly: "What? You aren't a member of any party organization?" The Chief Justice's joviality slipped some, but he made one final offer: "By tomorrow morning, bring me proof of your membership in the Nazi Party. I advise the NSKK."[17] The *Nationalsozialistische Kraftfahrkorps* (The Nazi Motor Vehicle Corps) was a Nazi paramilitary organization, but at this time, it was considered a harmless leisure society, although this perception was not actually justified. Like a shot, Drossel's response was delivered in formally correct Prussian manner: "I am sorry, Your Honor, but I am not in a position to do so." The man hesitated and then shoved Drossel's personal papers away from him. Tersely, he declared: "Well, then, as you want. Your application for a position is declined."

Twenty-four hours later, Drossel received an express letter calling him up for military service.

As an old man, he recalled: "I did not act very cleverly at the time, but I could not do anything else." Drossel had resisted the Nazis' assimilation efforts for so long that he could not, even in this situation, give in to them. Did he later regret his decision? What came next was five years of military service in the war, and even after the end of the war, his hesitation to yield to this "formality" had negative consequences for his career. But no, he did not regret it, "not in the least."

On December 1, 1939, new recruit Drossel reported to a barrack in Spandau-Ruhleben. He was assigned to the Grenadier Guard Regiment Graf 9 in Potsdam. His basic training began on December 10 in Fort Hahneberg. From the very beginning, he found military life to be bleak. At his regiment's swearing-in in a gymnasium, Heinz Drossel refused to utter his oath or raise his hand to do so. It was a silent gesture of nonacceptance noticed by absolutely no one.

After one weekend leave, Drossel's regiment was unexpectedly commanded to the West on February 19, 1940. The 23-year-old traveled by train, the first of many forms of transportation he'd take during the war through Cologne into the Eifel region. The regiment went through weeks of combat training, and then in March, they were again ordered to move west to the Luxemburg border. In the meantime, Drossel had found his place in the company. With careful calculation, talent, and luck, he had managed to escape the worst drudgery and to win the respect of his fellow soldiers. The "service" on the Luxemburg border was pretty quiet; most of the time, the soldiers just sat around, talking about God and the world.

In April 1940, Hitler's troops began to occupy all of Denmark and most of Norway. The long-planned western offensive began on May 10, and the Netherlands and Belgium were quickly taken. Both countries capitulated in a matter of days. With the heavy bombardment of Rotterdam on May 14, the German military leadership set an example for how German citizens would end up living through the later portion of the war.

On April 12, Heinz Drossel became a runner. On the one hand, the position was more dangerous than most since he had only himself to rely on and had to run back and forth between the lines. On the other hand, Drossel was pleased with his post because it decreased the likelihood that he would have to use his weapon. In essence, he was not prepared to shoot at other people. His faith and his humanistic convictions forbade him from that, regardless of the war. However, he was not naive enough to claim that he would not defend himself in a life-threatening situation. He decided to make a decision first when the need arose and to not think too much about it.

Heinz Drossel as a runner in France, 1940

And to help ensure that he would not be faced with this need, he did everything he could to avoid this situation.

Drossel and his regiment crossed the Luxemburg border on May 10 at 3:28 a.m. Marching through the next two days, the troops reached Belgium and approached the French front. The muck, the hardship, the lack of sleep, and the torturous experience rendered the young man insensible, as it did so many others. He registered little except thirst, hunger, and weariness. And then the first true battle came. For the first time ever, Heinz Drossel felt actual fear. During the engagement, a lower officer died and several soldiers were wounded. Drossel thanked his lack of injuries to his survival instinct which convinced him to ignore the order to attack. Instead of charging at the enemy, he ran across the field to another troop in his unit. During the following days and weeks, Drossel witnessed several heavy battles. He saw dead animals, destroyed villages, and mutilated corpses. Above everything hung the smell of decay.

On June 14, the French capital was surrendered to the German troops without a fight. The Armistice at Compiègne went into effect eight days later. The country was divided henceforth between the unoccupied South under the Vichy government, which agreed to cooperate with Hitler's Germany, and an occupied zone. Hitler triumphed. Having already reached Burgundy, Heinz Drossel and several others were promoted to lance corporals on June 26, 1940.

The Germans' victory provided a much-needed rest for him and his troop. Slowly, the battalion moved back toward Germany. En route, the young men enjoyed the advantages of being victors: French women celebrated with them, the French wine flowed freely. The German soldiers were just happy to still be alive.

"Murder and Fire"

Dagda, July 9, 1941

In the middle of the night, the orders came to move, this time east: through Heidelberg, Berlin, and Bromberg (Bydgoszcz) to Leslau (Włocławek) on the Weichsel River. "A different world" awaited Corporal Drossel and his comrades in this Polish metropolis. It was "the first hint at tragic developments . . . an eastern world," as recalled by Drossel in his memoirs. "A large square stretched out in front of the low-stretching train station, covered in medieval cobblestones. Grass was pushing up between them. Humble wooden cottages. Simple horse-drawn wagons with typical eastern harnesses. Men with long beards. Women with dark head handkerchiefs. Everything seemed to be filled with fear. Many German soldiers."[18]

German soldiers were forbidden from entering the Jewish ghetto, but no one cared about that. Drossel observed the active trade between the Jewish residents and the German occupiers. Women took care of the soldiers' laundry in exchange for bread and other foods. Services of a more physical nature were also offered.

Drossel felt uncomfortable when Jewish residents left the sidewalk whenever a German soldier came their way. They were under orders to do so. "I felt personally ashamed when the first of them moved out of my way. After that, I walked on the rough roadway. One soldier tapped an ancient man wearing a kaftan and slippers on the shoulder: 'Old man, stop acting so ridiculous!'—'Pan, you are a good person. Why should I take the risk?' Thoughtfully, I left the ghetto. What will this lead to? Then I ate in the German House Hotel, pan-fried potatoes with eggs and bacon. Life is bitter."[19]

The subsequent months were relatively calm for Corporal Drossel. He was made a clerk, and later he supervised telephone communication. The work was not stressful, and he had free access to the military radio receivers. Secretly, he listened to broadcasts from Radio London. Between late September and late October and again at Christmas 1940, he was given leave to go home.

Drossel went to a birthday party with friends while bombs were falling outside. He toasted Churchill. With increasing intensity, the British were bombing Berlin, and the friends began to hope for help from the outside world against the Nazis. In April 1941, Drossel received orders to take part in a Russian interpreter training course. During his college years, he had spent two years studying the language, and as a result, he made good progress in the course. He also quickly learned how to handle and ride horses. Both of these skills would serve him in good stead.

In May 1941, Drossel's troop again marched east, through East Prussia to the Lithuanian border. During the night of June 22, his unit crossed the Scheschuppe River.

Heinz wrote a letter to his parents on the evening of June 21:

"Dear Ones,

We are only a few hours away from the attack. I am completely calm and go into this attack with great confidence. Please stay calm and go into the future with peace.

We will see each other again! The Lord is with us. He never abandons His own, and even in these hard times, He is with us.

He gives us the strength to endure everything and to persevere . . . A lovely evening is coming to an end. A wonderful summer day is now dwindling. I now need to close . . .

Auf Wiedersehen!

Heinz"

At this point, there was still no declaration of war against the Soviet Union, who was still officially an ally of Germany. Drossel took the order to attack to his company's officer, along with the command to "take no prisoners."

The river was crossed with no resistance. Then what? "There— Soviets! I ran forward: 'Ruky wjerch!—Hands up!' . . . I thought about the order . . . I will bring them to the company officer! 'Here, you have prisoners!' He looked straight through me, and the silence stretched out over minutes. All of the soldiers stopped stock-still and looked over. Now, I saw it, felt it, blind obedience had won. He turned to the prisoners, pointed ahead and yelled: 'Get out of here! Run!' They hesitated and then understood. They were already racing across the damp field to the woods 150 meters off.

"They were 15 or 20 meters away, when W. [the company officer] hollered hoarsely: 'Fire!' I sped behind the prisoners, like a dodging rabbit, trying to take the field of fire. Two or three shots were fired high over our heads. I stopped still. They were running for their lives. They reached the edge of the forest and vanished. The soldiers looked around without understanding. Some of them were trembling. Standing in front of W., I shook in rage and snarled at him: 'That would have been murder, Lieutenant, base murder!' He stood motionless for a moment and then turned to the company:

'Now, march!' . . . Did I do the right thing? Maybe they will later kill some of us. I had to do what I did—there was no other option."[20]

Shortly after the "release" of the Soviet prisoners, Drossel saw for the first time at close proximity the harsh mistreatment of a Jewish man. He saw it while he was walking by. The head of an old man was hanging out of a shed window. His sidelocks and his long white beard had been lashed to the wooden door. A uniformed German was cursing the old man in the worst possible way. The entire company mutely passed by this horrible example of debasement. No comments were made, and some soldiers turned their heads away. Heinz Drossel also went on. He was ashamed, but he knew that this time there was nothing he could do without putting himself in serious difficulties. At least, this is what he believed. Sixty years later, Heinz was still wondering if he could have, should have, intervened somehow. He could never let the scene go, and in hindsight, he knew that here was the turning point in his attitude toward Nazism. If he had previously felt scorn toward the regime, that scorn had now turned to hatred.

At the same time, he was increasingly suffering from his experiences. He never became immune to the violence. He was greatly troubled by what took place around him, as reflected in a letter from July 7, 1941:

"Dear Parents. As is always the case, my thoughts turn to you today. During the hard hours, my thoughts of you renew my strength and help me persevere. As in France, I have put my trust in our Lord, and until now, all danger has passed me by . . . Believe me that those things that I have had to go through here, especially in the spiritual sense, are things that I cannot describe to anyone."

Lance Corporal Kuby, who like Drossel stayed involuntarily in the Soviet Union, also suffered from mental stress. He was revolted by the behavior of the men, his so-called comrades, against the local populace. His powerlessness against the atrocities depressed him: "Seeing a mounted farmer ride up, they yell at him that he should dismount. Shouting, one of the drunken men leaps on the pony; another one gets on behind him. The farmer stood there. Despair, fear, scorn, rage in his eyes. After ten minutes, he got his horse back and

The second page of a letter to Heinz Drossel's parents,
June 21, 1941

went on to work. An act of nonsense! But still, the horrible feeling that came from watching this was not caused by the event itself, but by the fact that our common uniforms made me an accomplice and prevented me from doing anything against it. When do you reach the point at which complicity has to end, immediately and without consideration of the consequences? Are the crimes that I do not see not my own crimes simply because I do not witness them?"[21]

At about this same time, Heinz Drossel had to ask himself the same question. On July 9, 1941, not far from the small Lithuanian city of Dagda, the corporal left his troop, which had set up camp here. He wanted to get away from the noise, the stink, and he wanted to be alone again. So, he entered a small, nearby stretch of woods. His hatred for the Nazis, their politics, and their inhumane sensibilities were about to be made all the more acute in a most heinous way.

Instead of quiet, seclusion, and contemplation, he discovered a mass grave in a small valley about 30 or 50 meters below him. There were dead men, women, and children, and the shooting was not yet over. He witnessed the murder of a six-year-old boy who was then kicked into the ditch. Drossel was so horrified and shocked he could not cry out. He could only manage to shriek out an inarticulate sound, attracting the attention of an MP guard, who was also standing up on the edge of the valley rim close to a tree, only about 49 feet (15 meters) away from Drossel. The execution commando unit was composed of SS men or men from one of the infamous police battalions. The guards were simple soldiers. The guard close to Drossel shooed him off threateningly and called behind him: "Get out of here, and hold your tongue!"

Heinz Drossel fled. He felt ill and dizzy. He ran for his life, sobbing. He was totally aghast. There had always been rumors about the execution commandos and the massacres of civilians. There were also whispers that claimed this was only enemy propaganda. Nonetheless, the critical souls among the soldiers suspected that there was something behind the rumors. And now Drossel had been an eyewitness of one of the horrifying crimes, which had absolutely nothing to do with a "decent" war or a "fight for the Fatherland." Drossel recognized what it was: murder, "the violent dominion of the devil."[22]

A short time later, he was able to resist this system of violence. During a skirmish with Soviet fighters, a Soviet commissar was taken prisoner by his company. The notorious commissar order, which had come down from the army headquarters in June 1941, required the execution of any such officer who was taken. The order was very clear: "In this fight, the sparing of such elements [commissars] or the consideration of their human rights is quite wrong. They are a danger to your personal safety and to the quick pacification of the conquered areas . . . Whenever they are seized in either battle or in resistance, they are to be immediately shot."[23]

However, since Heinz Drossel was the one instructed to bring the commissar to the battalion, things did not go quite as the high command wished: "I let him precede me by two steps with arms raised up, and I held my revolver at my right hip, loaded and cocked . . . I ordered: 'To the left!' I was speaking to him in Russian . . . 'Hands down! Turn around!' He dropped his hands and turned around. We stood about two meters away from each other. He did not move. I smiled at him and dropped my weapon. I said in Russian: 'Don't be afraid! I am not a murderer, I am a human being. Run down that path. There are no German soldiers down there. Now run!' He took a step toward me and stretched his hand out to shake mine . . . I was alone in the middle of the Soviet forest. Slowly I returned, satisfied with myself. Here, two 'enemy' soldiers had ended the war!"[24]

Drossel was not in the least worried that the freed commissar would harm German soldiers in the future, as he had been concerned with the Soviet soldiers he had protected only one month before. To the contrary: "I believe this was my life's finest hour—and I am convinced that if he ever met any German prisoners of war, he saw and treated them with human eyes."

Of course, he never learned if this actually was the case, just like he never knew if his commanding officer had entrusted him with the delivery of the commissar specifically because he knew how Drossel would react in this situation. After all, the company officer had witnessed how Drossel had responded to the experience with the prisoners during their march to the Soviet Union. When he returned to his company, he neglected to file an implementation report. His commanding officer never asked about it. Especially from this situation, Drossel learned what all could be accomplished if you sought to stay human in this inhumane war, one that he increasingly loathed. On August 14, he penned a poem:

> Why am I standing here in distant Russia,
> I do not want to conquer or acquire anything—
> And yet I spread murder and fire.
> For that, must my comrades die?
>
> Thus, my thoughts are tangled
> And I quarrel with my fate.
> I will go mad—

And all I want is to go back!

And so I stand here in distant Russia,
A little star falls here below;
In my thoughts, I stretch my hand to you
And beg God for peace!

"Russian Night," the first stanzas. The poem was dated August 14 and was written during the night watch. Heinz Drossel sent it to his parents with a letter he wrote two days later.

For the young man, God was a solid fixture in these times, as was clear in a letter he wrote his parents on August 16, 1941: "There is horror in front of and behind me—next to me, the endless street . . . At the moment, I am experiencing the hardest time I ever have in my life. I can only thank my Lord that I am staying true to myself and that I am mentally calm and almost joyful. He has never abandoned me, and he gives me the power and strength to persevere through everything . . . Those who have brought a God with them are the truly fortunate ones."

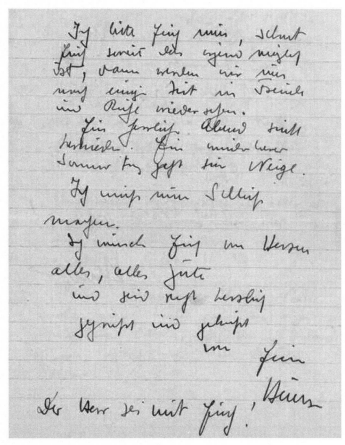

The third page of the letter to the parents, August 16, 1943

At the end of August, for the first time as a soldier, Drossel was called on to make use of his legal education. He was appointed as a defense lawyer for a court martial. The case involved a soldier who left his company without leave, a serious offense. Drossel felt uncertain and uncomfortable, and he would have gladly refused to serve, but this was impossible. Nonetheless, the process was handled fairly, in his opinion, and he was satisfied with the case's outcome, as was the defendant.

After the evidentiary hearing, the presiding judge took Drossel to the side and informed him of what kind of penalty was under consideration. Drossel carefully pointed to extenuating circumstances and requested a less serious penalty. Then, the judge cautioned him that if he set the punishment too light, there was a danger of harm being brought to the defendant. If Drossel requested a high penalty, the court could come in under this mark and impose a probationary punishment. The delinquent would have to spend time in a probationary battalion, but this would be better than an army prison. Drossel informed the defendant of this plan, and the latter agreed; Drossel took the advice of the judge.

Over the following weeks, the German soldiers marched through rough countryside, through forests and swamps. They were pressing deeper into Soviet territory and were engaged in serious battles and in an increasing number of hand-to-hand combats. Two of Heinz Drossel's closest comrades and many others died. They would move forward several miles and then be pushed back again. The fighting around small villages, woods, and fields was horrible, arduous, and exhausting. Drossel's division was growing appreciably smaller.

Drossel spent his 25th birthday in a foxhole under heavy fire. Like everyone else, he had no choice but to relieve himself in this hole that he could not leave. He had to stay there for hours on end, trying to ignore the unrelenting din in order to keep himself from going crazy out of fear. On the next day, he received a glass of Schnaps and an Iron Cross II from his commander. The break in the attack was brief. Drossel and his comrades were under fire by the Soviet artillery, MGs, grenades, and panzer tanks for several days. The losses were enormous.

Kuby believed that a paradox existed in that the direct contact with danger caused one to be less afraid. He theorized that those who experienced suffering in their own lives felt less miserable than those who only witnessed suffering. All the same, he fought to keep his mental balance during this war: "The contention with danger is child's play in comparison with the analysis of the circumstances that have given rise to this danger . . . However caught in the middle, the war has helped me deal with my internal war. Against the feeling of disgust, like sewage, in which I drown. Whenever we, Bertram and I, stroll through the star shine on the other side of the birches and I tell him about what is going through my mind, such as this, he is very disconcerted. In the deepest part of his good heart, he cannot believe that this loathing represents our last grasp on humanity and that those who do not feel this have ceased to act like humans . . . The squalor of our thoughts and feelings is revealed in the way they connect with that which is estimated as subhuman and is too often actually called that. Although things are quite a bit different now than they were in 1940."[25]

During Christmastime 1941, the situation for Heinz Drossel had grown worse than it had been three months before. His division was quartered for the winter in Salessje, a small village near Seliger Lake. The entire battalion was stationed around the lake. A short time later the so-called cauldron battle of Demjansk took place here. The connection with supply troops, about seven miles away, could only be maintained with great difficulty during December. Mail was rarely delivered. The soldiers experienced cold temperatures which reached -20, -30, and even -40 degrees Celsius. They suffered from freezing conditions, but the temperatures had one advantage: the bugs that had been a real plague in the fall had vanished without a trace.

The noose tightened, and the munitions started running low. Major Albert von der Goltz, whom Drossel respected because of his prudence and friendliness, applied to the army's main headquarters for permission to retreat. Declined. The Führer demanded that the position be held to the last man. Shortly later, Goltz allowed his men to withdraw, even without permission from Berlin. The connection to other battalions was broken off, and the supply lines collapsed. Over the preceding days, hundreds of men had died.

Von der Goltz ordered the start of the retreat for the night of January 13. The withdrawal was disastrous; of the 360 men involved, only 37 survived. Drossel crawled under the bodies of his fallen comrades in the rescuing cover of the thick forest. The dead offered the only cover from fire for the few survivors.

Silence reigned as the sun rose. The Soviets had ceased their bombardment. The few survivors gathered together, freezing at -40 degrees Celsius and stunned. The enemy could be lurking anywhere, and the woods were becoming brighter and brighter: "We were standing there on the edge of the forest at Samoschenka, about 200 yards from a village located on a rise. The land first fell steeply before it climbed up to the town, which was situated somewhat higher than we were. Across the way, we saw positions that had to be our baggage train. There were hillside elevations all around the village. We soon ascertained that the Soviet MGs had taken over all these positions. Time and again, a few shots or MG salvos were fired into the village. The stretch in front of us was white and empty—with no cover."[26]

The soldiers were overwhelmed by the cold, and the time seemed to pass so slowly. By dusk, they would all be frozen. The sky was strikingly blue, clear except for one small cloud high over the hill on which the village sat. "The Count [Major Albert von der Goltz] was just on the point of giving the order to storm toward the village—at least as far as our strength would take us—when something unbelievable happened! The little cloud sank relatively fast over the village. It grew larger and thicker. After several minutes, a thick fog settled over everything, and you could not see ten yards in front of you."

The little company made good use of the peculiar natural phenomenon. The men ran as fast as they could. Without a single shot being fired, they reached the German positions. For the first time, they were safe again. They were given tea and blankets, and they could sleep where it was dry and warm. Soon, the little cloud that had spread out like a fog collected itself and took itself back up into the sky, as if nothing had happened.

The situation was still tense. The Russian tanks threatened the German position, and during the night, the German soldiers entrenched themselves in hurriedly dug bunkers under the houses. All told, about 95,000 German soldiers were caught around Demjansk in an area of about 1,800 square miles. They could only be supplied by air transport.

On February, 3, 1942, Drossel received the Iron Cross, First Class, for his engagement in the retreat from Salessje. He was also promoted to officer status and was notified that he was being sent to Potsdam as a reserve officer. "That was not my ambition. I wanted nothing to do with a career as a military officer. However, we were caught in a mouse trap. The Count explained to us that the entire 16th Army was encircled. Except for an injury, it [the officer training school] was the only way, at the moment, to get out of this alive."[27]

IV. Persecuted, Betrayed, Hidden
(1939–1945)

Mail from Poland

Berlin-Lankwitz, March 13, 1940

Since 1933, Germany's antisemitic legislation was based on the exclusion of the Jews from the classification of ethnic Germans. The goal was to make their daily lives as hard as possible, in order to expel them from the country. There were countless, extremely detailed bans: from the tending of pets to the purchase of flowers, from the levying of taxes on all electronic appliances, gramophones, and lamps (metal), to curfews on the times one could be in public. There were always new edicts, the observance of which was increasingly difficult and the rejection of which brought welcome excuses to beat, to imprison, and to even kill.

At the Wannsee Conference on January 20, 1942, the Final Solution was designed: A small number of German politicians condemned millions of people to death. Already in an edict from January 3, the following was announced: "Considering the almost complete final solution for the Jewish Question, the emigration of Jews of German citizenship, as well as those without any citizenship at all, from the German Reich is prohibited . . ."[28]

The Nazis had now adopted a goal of annihilating the Jewish people, all Jewish people. They were no longer to vanish, but rather to die. As perverse as this plan was, its implementation was just as rigorously and systematically arranged. The decision made at the Wannsee Conference was the start of the open liquidation policy. There had been a few concentration camps in place in the early years of the Nazi regime. These were internment camps in which innocent individuals—Jews, Communists, homosexuals, and Gypsies, as well as anyone who was a nonconformist—suffered and died. After the Wannsee Conference, the death camps were constructed. Death became systematized.

In order to gain full access to the "enemies of the people," the Nazis used the administrative framework of the Jewish community. The community administrators had to register the addresses of its members and to later deliver the summons for deportation. Often the community's communal spaces were used as gathering points for those being transported to their deaths.

The "Law for the Rental Arrangements for Jews" was passed on April 30, 1939. It dictated that the Jews had to vacate their rental apartments and to move into spaces in the so-called Jewish Houses. The property belonging to Jews was confiscated, and even former property owners had to now reside in the Jewish Houses. Marianne Hirschfeld was among those forced to move into a Jewish House in 1939. The ridiculously low amount she was given for the forced sale of her parents' property after the bloody pogrom of 1938 did not last long. The black market prices for groceries were astronomical, and Marianne had to provide food for both herself and her young son. Her mother's mental condition had continued to deteriorate after Hitler's rise to power, and now she needed permanent care.

Rosa Hirschfeld experienced a serious nervous breakdown. According to the intake book and the register of residents, she arrived at the Wittenau Clinic on March 9, 1938. Her medical records no longer exist. According to the few documented references, such as Marianne's written notation about a "nervous decline," Rosa suffered from serious post-traumatic stress disorder and depression.[29]

In 1933, the Wittenau Clinic (relocated to Berlin-Reinickendorf and renamed the Karl Bonhoeffer Nerve Clinic in 1957) received a new medical director. Gustav Adolf Waetzholdt succeeded the 65-year-old Emil Bratz. On October 1, Waetzholdt transferred to his new position from the Hospital Department of the Main Health Office. He was not a psychologist but rather an administrative specialist. That same year, between 30 and 40 clinic employees were fired due to the new law for the "Re-establishment of the Professional Civil Service."[30]

As the oldest and most renowned medical and therapeutic care clinic in the capital city, Wittenau was quite modern, and between 1918 and 1933, it helped generate new medical theories. The occupational therapy practices pursued here were highly respected and replicated. Against the background of Nazi ideology and its biological views, the progress of clinics such as this one was predictable. Patient handling and care, in addition to the supply of food and medicines, rapidly declined. Critical resources were not to be spent on "those unworthy to live." As in Germany's other mental clinics, forced sterilizations were part of daily life after 1933. The Wittenau Clinic was no longer a place for recuperation, but rather a collecting station for those who had forfeited their right to live.

As early as 1935, Hitler had argued that a euthanasia program should be launched as soon as the war broke out.[31] The program began with the murdering of handicapped children, followed by the killing of handicapped adults. Both programs were kept secret and were directed by the Führer's Chancellory. Later, the murder of the adults was known as *Aktion T4*.[32]

Those who were supposed to heal and help now supported the murderous regime. Some of them even engaged in murder itself. At Wittenau, the death rate after 1939 rose dramatically and continuously. Between 1939 and 1945, 15,000 patients entered the clinic. About 5,000 of these were transferred to death or interim stations. During this same period, 4,607 patients died at Wittenau.

An above-average number of foreign and Jewish patients were among those who died. Frequently, "heart or circulation weakness" was given as the cause of death. It is likely that these patients died of hunger or from poisoned medicines.[33]

Doctors and nurses at the clinic were active in the T4 program. Several nurses were sent from Wittenau to the Hadamar Euthanasia Center; their salaries continued to be paid by the Wittenau Clinic. Over 200,000 victims were sacrificed to Hitler's euthanasia program, and its significance cannot be overestimated.[34] It functioned as a kind of gruesome dress rehearsal for the organized, factory-like murders of millions of people.[35]

Almost two years after entering Wittenau, Rosa Hirschfeld was sent to Berlin-Lankwitz on March 13, 1940. The family was informed that Rosa, "after improvement," had been transferred to a home on Priesterweg. The "home on Priesterweg" would turn out to be another way station on the path to death. According to a Red Cross memorandum, the official address was that of the former Sanatorium Berolinum.

At that time, the Berolinum was located at Leonorenstrasse 14–16, and it was mentioned in a publication about the patients in the Wittenau Clinic: "Description: founded for the mentally ill and those in need of recuperation, for Jewish patients, only for the upper social classes . . . In 1942, the new owner or renter was Elektrolux, Inc. In September 1939, at the very latest, the clinic was closed. According to a notarized document from December 10, 1940, the clinic was sold by the Fraenkel and Oliven families to a SS enterprise."[36]

Since its establishment, the sanatorium in Lankwitz had had an outstanding reputation. The furnishings and comfort were considered excellent, and internationally renowned experts were employed here. The most modern treatment methods were applied, including psychoanalysis. By the time of Rosa's arrival, none of these specialists were there anymore. Like every other Jewish institution, the hospital was a thorn in the eye of the Nazis and was shut down.

The discrepancy between the supposed closure date ("September 1939, at the latest") and Rosa Hirschfeld's admission at Lankwitz (March 13, 1940) is impossible to explain. Most likely, the clinic was officially closed in September, and the clearing and settlement of the sale took some time. Then, it is probable that the clinic's spaces were used through 1940 as a holding area for those psychologically troubled and handicapped individuals who had been slated to be killed. It could also be the case that the address was simply a cover address and that the sick were accommodated in "dependencies," such as the aforementioned home on Priesterweg.

Starting in the winter of 1939–40, the murder of "those unworthy of living" had already been organized to run smoothly. For the Nazis, this category included both physically and mentally handicapped people ("crippled" and "weak-minded"), as well as those deemed "mentally ill," such as those suffering from depression, schizophrenia, and other psychological disorders. Being Jewish and psychologically troubled resulted in a definite death sentence at this time.

The public therapeutic and care clinics were ordered to send the registration forms on their patients to the newly created euthanasia authorities at Berlin Tiergartenstrasse 4. By the end of 1940, the information on about 6,000 patients had been recorded. Most of these individuals were murdered that same year. One goal of the organizers was thus achieved. The therapeutic and care clinics could now fulfill other functions, such as being transformed to military hospitals.

Perhaps Marianne tried to visit her mother but could not locate her. This was the case for many relatives of psychiatric patients in Berlin during Summer 1940: "Having never been notified, the relatives would come on Sundays to visit and would be confused. The nurses could provide no information. Finally, they were told the following: the Berlin facilities had to be completely vacated, and the sick had been relocated to provincial clinics."[37]

By moving the patients from their original clinics to interim stations and from there to the euthanasia centers, usually without notification of the new destination or with only the words "location unknown," all traces of the actual course of events were erased. The medical records were destroyed. Later the relatives receive a death notice with a falsified sender and an invented cause of death.

The letter to Marianne Hirschfeld was sent from Cholm/Chaim via the city of Lublin, Poland. In reality, the staff of the Berlin T4 Division had written the note. A courier had taken the notification to Lublin, where it was actually postmarked.[38] This duplicity served as a distraction from the actual murder center in Germany itself. The families were to be kept from further researching the burial site of their loved ones. None of them were actually allowed to bury the murdered remains of their relatives. The corpses were incinerated and then disposed of like trash.

Marianne's letter was short, and no actual death date was given. Supposed cause of death: periarteritis. Thousands of relatives received similar notes on loved ones who suffered the same fate as Rosa Hirschfeld. After the war, her daughters recalled that Rosa had been taken to the Buch Mental Hospital near Berlin. That was the last report that they received during their mother's lifetime.

On July 12, 1940, the Presiding President of the Mark Brandenburg Province had ordered, by express mail, the concentration of all Jewish patients in the Berlin/Brandenburg region into the Buch Therapeutic and Care Clinic. From Summer 1940 until its closure on October 31, Buch was the gathering location for Jewish patients until they were murdered in the Brandenburg Penitentiary. Between February and September 1940, 9,772 people were killed in this penitentiary's gas chambers.[39] Rosa Hirschfeld was most likely one of these victims. Her daughters never received official confirmation of this, but they were certain that their mother had been murdered.

"With Deep Pain"

Jewish Hospital Berlin, August 23, 1942
"Today [May 30, 1942] we discussed over breakfast the unbelievable ability of people to endure and become accustomed to things. The fairytale abominations of your existence: fear every time the bell rings, mistreatment, humiliation, life-threatening danger, hunger (true hunger), new bans, abject slavery, daily progress toward the danger of death, new victims around us day to day, absolute helplessness. And yet there are always the hours of comfort, of reading aloud, of work, of decent meals. And then you always vegetate and start to hope again."[40]

Victor Klemperer and his wife Eva were in their early 60s, when the philology professor wrote these lines. At the beginning of the war, Marianne Albinus, nee Hirschfeld, was 27 years old. She turned 30 in 1942, as the repression, persecution, and annihilation measures were intensified. The glamorous period of the dance competitions was not that far in the past. She had grown up with wealth and had led a sheltered life during her early years. She was a vigorous, lively woman. Even now, the stresses and hardships of day-to-day living usually left no time to feel afraid.

Everything was regimented: the times to be out in public and to go shopping, the use of (or ban from) public transportation. You could only get a new toothbrush if you gave up the old one. Jews were strictly forbidden from purchasing flowers. The regulations were arbitrary and vast. Survivors reported that sheer exhaustion led to a kind of indifference that functioned as a protective measure. On the one hand, there were always new moments of confidence, even if these seemed to exist for no clear reason. Marianne, like the Klemperers, hoped time and time again. And sometimes she searched for and found forgetfulness.

After November 12, 1938, Jews were forbidden to visit "theaters, cinemas, concerts, exhibitions, etc."[41] In addition, meetings between Jews and "Aryans" in private rooms were forbidden, as were meetings between so-called mixed bloods and "Aryans." Not everyone followed these regulations, but to a large part, the Nazis succeeded in isolating the Jews. Even the non-religious Jews found themselves forced to spend more and more time with other Jews. They adapted to the circumstances. Sometimes they even broke the laws that were meant to oppress them. They secretly went to the movies and sneaked into restaurants. Primarily, though, they increasingly withdrew into the private realm.

This retreat led to the deepening of existing friendships with other Jews and the formation of new relationships. The marginalized recognized each other. They shared the same fate and felt bound together. People tried to create relaxed atmospheres and sought a little distance and forgetfulness. However, this was not always possible, as one eyewitness revealed: "Even if we found ourselves in a group of Jews, this did not mean that you relaxed even in the slightest, because each of us had our own unpleasant experiences to relate or knew of a Job-like story to tell about someone else."[42]

Margot Hass, the daughter of an upper class Jewish family in Berlin, regularly invited friends and acquaintances to her house. There were certainly anxious conversations and fearful moments. However, there was also dancing, joking, laughter, and good times. The young people who gathered in the Hass house were in their early 20s, and they yearned for a different life beyond daily difficulties, beyond trepidation and fear of the future. In late 1940 or early 1941, Marianne Hirschfeld entered this circle through a common acquaintance. Marianne was almost ten years older than most of the clique's members, but this did not matter to anyone.

In 1943, Margot and her parents along with Günter Fontheim, the son of an attorney, went underground. On December 24, 1942, Günter's entire family had been removed from their residence by the Gestapo, before his very eyes. As a forced laborer, the young man was not affected at this time by the deportation. He told his family farewell without knowing that he would never see them again. On January 12, 1943, the attorney and notary Dr. Georg Fontheim and his wife Charlotte, along with Günter's 15-year-old sister Eva Irene, were deported to Auschwitz.

In late 1939, Marianne received notification from the Jewish Employment Office that she had been called up for forced labor by the provincial cable works. This, at least, brought her some money. However, a new problem arose: care for her small son. As Marianne's slave labor started, the boy was not quite four. Most of Marianne's relatives either had been killed or had emigrated. She only had two aunts yet in Berlin. Marianne had no contact with her ex-husband by this point. She could sometimes ask a neighbor or a friend to watch over the child, but every day brought a new fight to find a way to care for the little boy.

For a while, Billy lived in a Lutheran children's home, and Marianne regularly visited him here. All of the documents from here have been lost. Later mementos were also lost, such as photos from Billy's matriculation into school or any records from Billy's elementary school years. There are no childhood drawings or hardly any actual written evidence related to the life of this boy. He himself could not be asked anything, since he had died twenty years before the writing of this book.

William Albinus's child identification card

Only a few fragmented stories, undated and unspecific, have survived to date. One scene: mother and son in a shop, Marianne violating regulations by not wearing a star. Billy was not required to wear the star. There was a crowd at the cash register. Marianne had only unmarked Marks with her. These Marks had not been marked with a "J" [for Jew], which was supposed to indicate which items she was not allowed to purchase. For one week, no fat, then no eggs, and later no sugar. The coveted Marks had perhaps been a gift from some decent people or had been exchanged for some of the hard-earned cash. Possibly, these were the result of a black market transaction, a piece of family silver traded for Marks to buy vegetables.

It was very dangerous for Jews to possess unmarked Marks: "If the Gestapo found a Jew with Marks without the J on them, the Marks were torn up, and the Jew was, in the best of cases, beaten and spit on. In the worst cases, he was 'asked to accompany' the policeman and even 'detained.' When buying bread, change for larger J Marks was often given in smaller bills without the J. Yesterday, this happened to Mrs. Ida Kreidl. She tore out the lining of her purse and hid the forbidden notes in the interior of the bag, until she could exchange them with Eva [Klemperer's Aryan wife]."[43]

Marianne had pockets full of forbidden Marks. In the store, people were pressing all around. Inspection. Two Gestapo men stood behind the counter, blocking the exit. They demanded to see the customers' identification cards and looked through their shopping bags. *It is over now*, Marianne thought, and she grabbed her son's small hand.

She could not get out, but what about the boy? Should she send him out alone? But where to? The cashier was 100 percent politically correct. And she had known the Hirschfelds for a long time. Marianne cursed. Why had she not gone somewhere else? The line moved forward. The men in their long coats looked sullenly over the crowd coming toward them. The mood was tense. An occasional testy murmur, otherwise silence.

Marianne reached the counter, and the Gestapo officers were just inspecting the papers of another customer. She packed up her modest purchases with shaking hands. Then one of them turned to her: "Identification!" Desperately, Marianne searched through her bag. Billy stood next to her, holding tightly to her jacket. His dark eyes glanced from one man to the other.

Then the cashier interjected, "Everything is fine with her," raising her chin in Marianne's direction. Just then, the grumbling from the waiting crowd grew louder. The Gestapo men looked at each other and shrugged. "Get out of here!" one of them said. Marianne grabbed her child's hand and left the store. Not running, not looking over her shoulder. Billy was too slow, and she had to keep herself from yelling at him. She was trembling. Billy was quiet. He had learned early on that a quiet child was a good child.

The altercation at the store was one of the few stories that Marianne told later in life. This occurred during the time that she was no longer "privileged" and was required to wear a star. This began after February 1943. If she had been found out, she could have been charged with two violations. First of all, she was not wearing a star. Secondly, she was using Marks that were forbidden to her. According to Nazi regulations, both of these violations carried stiff penalties.

The work for the provincial cable works was quite physically difficult. The metal cables had to be turned by hand. Foreign language correspondent Hirschfeld often came away from work with bloody fingers. The requisite wooden clogs covered her feet with scratches. However, her training proved to be of some use in this context, since she worked alongside French and Belgian forced laborers with whom she could communicate, thanks to her foreign language abilities. She made new, valuable contacts, and she got to know some friendly people.

While working for the provincial cable works, Marianne met the Belgian forced laborer Luis. They became a couple. They took great risks to live out their love.

In early 1942, Marianne became pregnant. She again first discovered the pregnancy relatively late. Her physical well-being had not improved over the course of 1941. The food situation was worse than ever before, and the physical labor took its toll. Furthermore, there was the ongoing need to remain silent about the unrelenting fears—for her son, for Luis, for herself, for the few relatives and friends who had not yet been deported.

As was the case for many women who lived under constant stress during the war, Marianne's menstrual cycle had long stopped being regular. She never thought that it would be possible for her to become pregnant. As her situation became apparent, she would have discussed the future with Luis. Perhaps they had made plans to flee together. Flight would have been the only possibility to have even a small chance at survival. Nothing came of this.

From this time with Luis, a black and white photo of Marianne with Billy still exists. The boy was perhaps five or six years old. The studio photo shows mother and son looking seriously into the distance. Written in French on the back side of the photo is the following note: "My little darling, I am sending this photo back to you in deep sadness. For the life of your darling. Luis, adieu."

The tenderness of these lines along with the fact that Marianne kept this final greeting over the years indicates that the two of them parted on good terms. Marianne also said that this was the case later in life. The paternity of the Aryan forced laborer had to be kept secret at all costs. According to the law against "racial defilement," Jewish-Aryan couples could be harshly punished, sometimes even with the death penalty.

On August 23, 1942, at 1:29 p.m., Marianne Sara Albinus, nee Hirschfeld, gave birth to a daughter in the Jewish Hospital Berlin. Judis Hirschfeld was born prematurely, and she weighed only 3.9 pounds and measured 18.5 inches long. The birth threatened the lives of both mother and child. The labor lasted 14 hours, but Marianne seems to have left the hospital shortly after the delivery. In the birth register, there is an illegible entry near the release date. It could be the word *Hauswöchnerin* (a woman who has just given birth and has gone home). However, Marianne's daughter stayed at the hospital, since she required special medical care. On the birth certificate, Marianne provided a false name for her father: Abraham, Martin.

The last of the staff at the Jewish Hospital, which as of 1942 was the last functioning Jewish hospital in all of the German Reich, certainly did not ask about the father. Dr. Segall, the doctor on call who delivered Judis, and Sister Rosa, the assisting midwife, could have known more. Perhaps Marianne trusted them with her secret. Both of these employees, as well as all of the other workers at the Jewish Hospital, no longer cared about the past, nor did they think much about the future. What concerned them was the present. Under the current conditions, caring for a premature baby was a very difficult task.

Completely Hopeless

Theresienstadt, October 14, 1942

The weeks following Judis's birth robbed Marianne of the final remnants of her vigor and will to live. In October 1942, her Aunt Dorothea Hirschfeld, the sister of Marianne's father, received the dreaded letter in its oblong envelope. It informed her that she was slated for Transport 1/71 to Theresienstadt and was required to report at a certain time at the intended collecting point.

Marianne had first taken refuge with her Tante Thea after the November 1938 pogrom. Thea had been a seasoned Social Democrat, and in 1919, she became the first woman to be appointed to an elevated position in the new Weimar government.[44] Coming out of the field of social welfare, Undersecretary Hirschfeld had achieved an impressive career in government administration despite her lack of a college education. She was a talented woman, but this was definitely an exception to the normal course of government positions.

Thea was born on February 26, 1877, into a prosperous family in Berlin. The family still remembers her as a "true original." She was pragmatic, boisterous, and outspoken. Thea Hirschfeld devoted herself completely to her work. For many years, she was active in the Workers' Welfare Association and was later engaged in soldiers' dependents' welfare. After that, she became a civil servant.

Already as early as November 27, 1930, her incredibly high position in the government (in the interim, she had become the Director for the Federal Office for Work Placement and Unemployment Insurance, which she had personally established) became the focus of a parliamentary inquiry. The Nazi Party Representative Wilhelm Frick and others asked if the government intended to "immediately remove Undersecretary Hirschfeld from her position with the welfare program for wounded veterans or to at least limit her work to citizens of the Jewish race." Incensed, Federal Minister of Labor Adam Stegerwald (Center Party) rejected the demand and fully endorsed Dorothea Hirschfeld. Less than three years later, there was no one left to speak up for her. Justified by the "Re-establishment of the Professional Civil Service" legislation from April 1933, Thea Hirschfeld was placed in "provisional retirement" at the age of 56.

Together with her sister Pauline, Thea lived in a small house on Manfred von Richthofen Street in the Berlin Tempelhof neighborhood. Very little is known about Pauline Hirschfeld's life. Around 1910, she was a college student in Berlin in the fields of Mathematics and Physics. The State of Prussia had only first granted women the right to university matriculation in 1908. Even a century later, the Hirschfeld family recalls that Tante Paula was "so clever that she could not even walk." She dedicated her intelligence to service to the state, becoming a teacher in 1920. On October 25, 1942, Pauline Hirschfeld committed suicide.

Together with 947 other Berlin Jews, her sister Thea had been deported to Theresienstadt on October 3, 1942. Thea Hirschfeld's relative fame might have been the reason that she was placed in the "showpiece ghetto." It was not until the liberation that the cynical facade of this model ghetto was revealed. Of course, there really was a library there. Several, in fact. However, it was just as true that in 1943 this area, which had been initially planned to hold 10,000 individuals, actually contained 430,000 people.[45] The prisoners suffered from hunger, and countless numbers of them starved to death. The hygienic conditions were deplorable. Illnesses and epidemics cost numerous people their lives. In addition, trains were soon traveling daily between Theresienstadt and Auschwitz, taking prisoners to certain death. The majority of the inmates died of hunger, disease, or abuse, or they were transported to the extermination camps. On October 14, 1942, Dorothea Hirschfeld was delivered to the Theresienstadt Ghetto by the Berlin Gestapo. Category: Jewess.

During the Wannsee Conference, where the "Final Solution of the Jewish Question" was discussed in detail, the first official reference was made to the establishment of a "Seniors' Ghetto" at Theresienstadt. This was on January 20, 1942. Besides Jews over 65 years old, "severely injured Jewish veterans and Jews who had received military honors" were to be kept here, so that "with one stroke, the numerous interventions could be cut off."[46] In addition, a large number of prominent Jews—politicians, economists, artists—were kept at Theresienstadt, the only entirely Jewish concentration camp.

Several foreign delegations and representatives of various humanitarian organizations were permitted access to Theresienstadt, after extensive preparations were made to the "Jewish City." This permission was intended to convince these visitors that the conditions here were in accord with the Geneva Convention and that everything was in good order. Several new streets were laid. Bushes were planted. Houses were repainted. The better nourished children were collected to present to the officials. Seemingly healthy adults received decent clothes and instructions on how they were to behave themselves. If anyone betrayed the actual conditions at Theresienstadt, they would be punished. The threat of no longer receiving the subsistence food packets frightened everyone.[47] The cynical masquerade came off without a hitch. The Nazi propaganda presented Theresienstadt as a Jewish paradise, and at the same time, it tried to deflect attention from the rumors about the horrible, unspeakable cruelties that were happening.

In October 1942, as Tante Thea was being "sent away," a Nazi euphemism that even those affected by the deportations used, the birth of Marianne's daughter lay two months in the past. Marianne had once again lost someone on whom she relied. There were fewer and fewer of these people in her life. Her situation was completely hopeless and lonely.

She could not fetch her daughter, who thanks to the care at the Jewish Hospital was still alive. She did not know how to feed the child, since she could hardly provide for just herself and her son. On the one hand, it seemed that the baby was in the best possible hands at the hospital. On the other, Gestapo men were now on continuous patrol at the hospital. For this reason, Marianne did not risk going back there. As the mother of a fully Jewish child, she was afraid to attract the attention of the hunters. She would endanger both of her children if she did that.

In the case of her daughter Judis, Marianne decided, like so many other parents did with heavy hearts, to hand the child over to the good will of other people. Thousands of sons and daughters were either hidden or sent abroad. They survived the Holocaust because their parents made the difficult decision to separate themselves from them. Judis Hirschfeld spent the first two years of her life under the care of staff at the Jewish Hospital. Later, she was sent to a children's home and then transferred to Palestine.

By late 1942, Marianne was still classified as "privileged," which meant she did not have to wear a star. This status made daily existence a little easier and provided a degree of protection; Marianne did not want to lose this. This privileged status was the result of the fact that Marianne had a son whom the Nazis considered a "mixed blood" due to his Aryan father. In 1940, William Albinus was baptized in the Lutheran church at the age of four. This was a kind of life insurance for his mother. Of course, Billy was first born after the divorce was final, however his paternity was officially recognized. Thus, he was categorized in the Nazi racial system as a "mixed blood of the first degree."

In the case of children who had German and Jewish parents, the Nazi race ideology created problems for the persecutors: "The complexity of the regulations is curious. The Nazis were not in a position to clearly define and isolate the Jews. Instead, they created an elaborate system full of ambiguities."[48] The extermination of children from German-Jewish relationships would have meant that "Aryan blood" would have also been spilled. Furthermore, the Jews with "Aryan" spouses had access to a network of relationships to other "Aryans," whose disapproval the Nazis feared.[49] The discussion about "mixed blood" Germans of the first degree and the second degree, as well as those legally considered Jews and others, and how they should be treated filled entire files: "The ministries of Justice and the Interior argued that in the instances of single parenthood or overwhelming guilt [in cases of divorce], custody should be given to the 'German-blooded' parent. However, the Nazi Party/StdF was of the opinion that 'mixed bloods of the first degree' (referred to as 'legal Jews') should generally be given over to the Jewish parent . . .

Behind this argument was the not-so-secret intent to ascribe the 'mixed bloods' to the Jews. Ignored in these discussions, about which they presumably knew nothing, were the Jewish women who were protected from deportation, through late 1944, by their under-aged children (at least, until these reached a certain age)."[50]

In 1942, Marianne and her son lived in a room at Knesebeck Street 79 in Berlin-Charlottenburg, which they sublet from Mr. and Mrs. Fleischer in one of the so-called Jewish Houses. They got along well with the Fleischers. They provided mutual support to each other whenever possible, and they trusted one another. They even planned to flee together at the end of the year.

Marianne had been able to rescue some pieces of jewelry from her parents' home. By doing that, she violated one of the countless regulations. On February 24, 1939, a decree was made that "Jewish jewels and jewelry pieces" were to be sold. The Jews had to accept any offer that was made to them, and they could do nothing to influence the price assigned to their valuable items. The fact that Marianne still possessed jewelry in late 1942 was a punishable offense. The sale of these items would have been understandably delicate. She took the greatest care in turning diamond rings and a pearl necklace into cash, without which flight would be impossible. She needed this money to procure falsified papers. Through her French friends, she had the necessary contacts, but she did not have enough money.

The stretches between the deportation transports to the East were growing shorter and shorter. By this time, most of the Jewish people in Germany knew about these and feared the worst. Although most of them could never have imagined the gas chambers, it was clear that "the East" was synonymous with "death." More and more relatives, friends, neighbors, and acquaintances were disappearing. The Fleischers did not want to wait any longer. They told Marianne good-bye without telling her their exact travel plans, and they asked her to delay the news of their departure as long as possible.

The prospect of fleeing had reinvigorated Marianne over the preceding weeks. As her last living relative in Germany, Aunt Thea's deportation had been a hard blow. Marianne had helped her pack and had taken her to the collecting area. She choked back the tears; this was the least she could do. Aunt Paula had taken her life. Now the Fleischers were gone. The ration cards had all been turned in, and she was once again suffering from horrible migraine headaches. She did not want to go on. She had not wanted to go on for a very long time, but now she absolutely could not keep on living. She was sure of this.

Welcome in Case of Emergency

Jungfern Bridge, Berlin, November 1942
It was cold and dark, and the street was totally empty. Marianne Albinus, nee Hirschfeld, tried to take her own life. She wanted to jump from the Jungfern Bridge into the Spree River. However, she was prevented from doing so by a Wehrmacht officer. She might have thought, *Now it is over*, as she saw the man in uniform. It is more likely, though, that she thought about nothing. After all, what does a person in such a situation think? The man spoke quietly, kindly: "Are you Jewish?"

What followed was like a rush of warmth and friendliness. Heinz Drossel took Marianne to his apartment on Berliner Street. He placed her in a chair and made her some coffee. He commented: "We know each other, don't we?" She had noted that as well. They had met each other once and had chatted pleasantly. Billy was only two years old at the time. Everything had been awful already in 1938, but it had been a very different life. "Now, tell me what happened." And she told some things but not everything by far. There was not time for this. He believed her. He actually seemed to understand, and he wanted to help. She sensed that right away. Then he left her alone for a short time.

He returned in the company of his friends Poldi and Charlott. They were good, friendly people to whom she did not have to explain everything. There were still such individuals. She was given something to eat, and a bed was made up for her. The four of them decided that Charlott would keep her company during the night.

The Jungfern Bridge, Berlin 1929

The two men went back to Poldi's apartment and spent hours discussing what they should do to rescue this woman—and her son, of course. Because this is what Drossel insisted on doing. The involuntary officer had an idea. He was going to give the Jewess his entire savings, 6,000 Reichsmarks. With this, she could try to get the necessary falsified papers, and the sum should also cover other expenses. Furthermore, he decided to give her all of the photography equipment that he had intended to use for his own emigration effort. Poldi had to help. Heinz would give him the money, organize a few details, and then leave Berlin. His leave was over. Luitpold "Poldi" Hagen, his childhood friend, was ready to do his part.

Before his departure, Heinz contacted his Uncle Oscar, the black sheep of the family, to tell him of his plan and to get his permission to give Marianne his address as a possible future hiding place. Uncle Oscar, a very talented tailor with an unfortunate gambling addiction, already had one secret "subtenant," a young Jewish woman. Heinz supposedly did not know the nature of her relationship with his Uncle Oscar. However, despite the gambling addiction and the questionable nature of his romantic affairs, Uncle Oscar could be relied on. Marianne would be welcome here in case of emergency.

Berlin Will Be "Free of Jews"

Knesebeck Street 76, Berlin, December 27, 1942
The concern and helpfulness of Heinz Drossel and his friends gave Marianne a little hope again. She remained in contact with Luitpold "Poldi" Hagen and his girlfriend Charlott. Heinz traveled back to France the morning after her rescue. From the 6,000 Reichsmarks that Heinz had given her via Poldi, she paid for the falsified papers. She sewed the remaining money into various pieces of clothing. This was the same way she had hidden the rest of the jewelry that she had not yet sold. The suitcases were packed. It was only a question of days until their departure. Marianne continued to go to work at the cable works to prevent any suspicion arising.

She was waiting on the papers, and each day was terrifying. Christmas 1942 was bitterly cold, and Berlin lay in ruins already. Marianne's hopes hung completely on the flight. Marianne and her six-year-old son Billy were both at home at Knesebeck Street 76 when the Gestapo arrived. It was early in the morning and still dark as fists pounded on the door. Open up, Gestapo! The dreaded call struck fear in her heart.

Quickly, it was supposed to go quickly. She could leave her things behind, and they would be fetched when the time came. Marianne was allowed to bring along "a small case with only the bare essentials."

Later, Marianne wrote out a description of her imprisonment which served after the war as source material for a report on "persecution-related health damages." "On December 27, 1942, I was arrested in the course of a large-scale action, and along with my six-year-old son, I was brought to the Grosse Hamburger Street camp. Besides the worst of lodging conditions and insufficient food, we were also subjected to constant interrogations and mental abuse. This was caused by doubt about the legitimacy of my status."

The "mental abuse" consisted of threats to deport her and her little daughter. Her son was to be given over to his father. The civil servants wanted Marianne to tell them where her Aryan ex-husband was living. They clearly suspected that she was in contact with him. The baby was registered as "a full Jew," but perhaps this was a lie. Perhaps this had been an attempt to cover up a "racial defilement." It could be, though, that Marianne's persecutors did not need a reason to beat and humiliate her. Maybe this simply seemed normal to them since they constantly terrorized helpless, defenseless people without any cause.

Marianne remembered: "At the last interrogation in the presence of two men in civilian clothes (one of which was the main interrogator, Duberkel), a third man struck me hard in the face and brutally hit me in my torso. I was accused of lying about being in contact with my ex-husband (although this was the actual truth)."

It is hard to imagine what this situation meant for young Billy. Whenever his mother was fetched for interrogation, he had to sit alone in an over-filled, stuffy room full of unknown, fearful people, hungry, tired, and afraid. When his mother returned, she was in a horrible condition. She shook, sometimes she cried, she would not speak. Sometimes she was bleeding from wounds in her face.

Walter Dobberke, 1939

The interrogator that Marianne mentioned, Duberkel, must have been the director of the Grosse Hamburger Street camp, SS master sergeant Walter Dobberke (1906–1946).[51] This former criminal assistant officer with the vice squad obviously made an impression on Marianne. At one point, she described him as a "Gestapo chief." She attributed her final release from the Schul Street camp to his authority.

SS official Dobberke was indeed a powerful man in his field of influence. He was in charge of drafting the lists for the large transports (up to 1,000 individuals sometimes) to "the East," to certain death. He was also the director of Gestapo's Search Service stationed at the Grosse Hamburger Street camp. The "searchers" were Jewish women and men. Many of them hoped to save themselves and their loved ones by serving as spies for the Gestapo. Dobberke was responsible for the recruitment and deployment of these "takers," and they delivered their reports directly to him.

Dobberke was the one who decided that Marianne had to wear a star from then on. The birth of her daughter, whom she had registered as a full Jew, resulted in the suspension of her privileged status. At least, this was the justification given for the decision. It was a miracle that the threat to deport her along with her little daughter never turned into reality. Apparently, the existence of her son Billy, born of an Aryan father, played a roll in this. The unsettled question of how to handle the "mixed bloods" crippled the extermination apparatus; there were no clear regulations and no defined procedures for what to do in such cases. However, the boy could have been placed in a home. Then there would no longer have been a reason to spare the full Jewess and her fully Jewish baby. For the time being, though, Gestapo official Dobberke decided differently.

On February 17, 1943, after 52 days in prison, Marianne's incarceration ended. Upon arriving at her room in the Knesebeck Street, she discovered that the room had been sealed by the police. All of her belongings were behind this sealed door—the sewed-up money, the valuable jewelry, everything. She did not risk breaking the seal. Exhausted, she made her way to Poldi to ask his advice. Practical and rational as ever, he told her that she should go to the police. Her release papers were in order, and she should not be afraid. He would go with her.

Poldi waited outside the police station, and he did not go along into the building when a policeman accompanied her to the apartment. But it was a consolation to know that someone was there. The policeman broke the seal and opened the door. The shock could not have been greater. The suitcase that contained the clothing with the concealed money and jewelry was gone, as were the photography equipment and all other items of value. In one blow, Marianne had lost everything. Flight was once again impossible. There was only one explanation. The Gestapo men were thieves. When they had led Marianne away, no one had sealed the door, so this had to have been done later. This knowledge was of absolutely no use to Marianne, since she was in no position to file a complaint with the police.

Only ten days later, Marianne was again arrested. This time she was a victim of the "Key Action Berlin Jews," which started on February 27, 1943. The initiative was also called the "Great Factory Action," because people were primarily arrested in their places of employment. During the first wave of arrests, about 5,000 Jews were taken by the Gestapo.[52] A large number of these people were "mixed bloods" or were Jews who were married to "Aryans," a "privileged" group that had not been deported before now due to fears of protests by Aryan relatives and domestic policy difficulties.

Before the initiative was launched, the question of how to procedurally handle this group of Jews had led to arguments at the highest levels of the Nazi regime. On the one side, Minister of Propaganda Joseph Goebbels wanted to avoid anything that could cause the German public to turn against Hitler. On the other side, senior Nazi functionaries in the Reich Security Office wanted to finally see the racial laws systematically implemented. Reichsführer-SS Heinrich Himmler was operationally in charge of the "Final Solution," and he constantly argued for a radical solution of the mixed blood issue. Goebbels's tactical considerations went against the grain for Himmler. Hitler switched sides from time to time, taking first one side and then the other. Hitler might be the one directly responsible for the October 1941 directive to initially not deport the "mixed bloods" and the Jews living with German spouses.[53]

In late 1942, the Nazis decided to arrest and deport the last of the Jews living in Berlin, regardless of their status. The "Key Action

Berlin Jews" had long been in the works. Transport trucks located in and around Berlin were confiscated, and the holding centers were prepared. The arrests began during the early morning hours of February 27, 1943. Hitler's SS bodyguard unit was in charge of the arrests at the factories. Gestapo men and uniformed policemen seized individuals in their residences or on the streets.

Marianne and other Jewish forced laborers at the provincial cable works were transported in trucks. The first stop for hundreds of prisoners was the Hermann Göring Barracks. They were packed tightly together here without either light or water. They were forced to spend the cold winter night on the bare concrete floor of the barracks. The following morning, the SS men divided the people into two groups: one for those who had German spouses and the other for everyone else. The latter stayed in the barracks, while the individuals in "mixed marriages" were taken to Rosenstrasse 2-4, the address of a welfare office for the Jewish community.

Over the following days, what American historian Nathan Stolzfus enthusiastically hailed as "a resistance of the heart" developed. Other contemporary historians classify this more sedately as a private initiative. The relatives of the Jews kept in the Rosenstrasse, most of whom were wives, positioned themselves in front of the building. Day and night, they watched what went on there. They brought packages and letters. Ultimately they started to make loud demands: Give us our men back! This was the first and only public demonstration against the Nazis in the 12-year span of the violent regime. Whether motivated by civil courage or by personal concerns, the women achieved their goal. Their Jewish husbands were released.

The other group remained in prison. Marianne was taken to a camp on Levetzow Street. Her son Billy was not with her. He was permitted to stay with the new landlord, Ms. Bäcker, at Lietzenburger Street 8. Marianne would have known nothing about the unprecedented events on the Rosenstrasse. She also had no one who could speak up for her. However, her guards probably knew about the women's demonstrations and sensed the nervousness of their superiors. It was not intended that the victims would cause a fuss, but less so that they receive help and support.

For Marianne, only ten days had passed since her release from persecution and imprisonment, and her suicide attempt had been a mere three months earlier. She spoke with her guards. She wanted to escape, she wanted to go to her son, she did not want to die. On March 1 "with the help of a policeman," she secretly slipped out of the Levetzow Street camp. This she described in one of the numerous protocols recorded in the context of her post-war retribution process. Why did he help her? Was Marianne able to convince the officer on duty, who was under pressure because of the Rosenstrasse demonstrations, that she too had a special status? Did she show him her son's papers in order to give weight to her claims? Perhaps this was not necessary. Maybe this nameless policeman simply had pity on the young lady who begged him to let her go, and then a favorable moment arose.

After this large-scale crackdown and the latest mass transports to the extermination camps, Minister of Propaganda Joseph Goebbels declared Berlin to be "free of Jews" in July 1943. At this time, over a thousand Jewish persecutees had already vanished "underground." They called themselves *U-Boote* (submarines) and attempted to escape from their murderers. According to estimates, up to 5,000 people violated Nazi law and illegally vanished within Germany. Among these were about 1,400 Jews who survived in Berlin.[54]

Marianne also increasingly retreated from the control and reach of the Nazis. On April 16, 1943, she began work as a night shift forced laborer for the BVG [transportation service], washing cars. During the day, she no longer stayed at her registered address. This was an absolutely forbidden decision. There were strict rules about when Jews could move about on the streets.

Excepting these periods, they were supposed to stay in their residences where they were reachable by the authorities at all times. The times that they could go out were limited to a few hours, which had to be used to go shopping. That is, if there was enough money and food ration cards to allow this.[55]

For the first few weeks after Marianne's imprisonment in the Levetzow Street camp, this did not seem to cause many problems: "During the time afterward (after the imprisonment), it was possible for me to receive my food Marks. The director of the rations office on Knesebeck Street, which was the office I had to use, liked me and she always gave me my food Marks without any difficulty."[56] This information is relatively disconnected to the rest of the text in Marianne's report. It is probably a hint that her access to food Marks and to food in general became much more difficult.

The food situation had become increasingly catastrophic over the course of 1942. This was even the case for "Aryan" citizens, as Klemperer indicated using his wife as an example: "Eva has now reached the end of her nerves. The unsuccessful hunt for food has pretty much destroyed her. And now there has been a string of days of abject hunger . . . Eva no longer has any fat ration Marks, because she cannot swap them for the J Marks any more. At home, I live almost exclusively on bread. For the past few days, the garden shops have been permitted to give away a portion of their vegetables to the public for free. Eva spent over an hour in line, but she only received very few or none at all."[57]

Marianne described her time living "illegally": "I met my current husband Heinz Drossel in 1938, and in Spring 1944, he came to Berlin on an official visit. He advised me to immediately start living illegally, because he was convinced that within a short time span something was going to happen politically. He believed that the authorities would soon start another action against the Jews. On June 12, 1944, I began to live underground. To help with this, my current husband gave me the key to his apartment in Tempelhof at Berliner Street 76."[58] This description was specially formulated, in part, to provide the authorities with a reasonable account of the events that led to her "illegality." In any case, this depiction of the events that resulted in her existence as a "submarine" would seem to indicate this intention. The reality was actually much more chaotic.

For example, Heinz Drossel could have only personally given Marianne Hirschfeld the key to his apartment in November 1942.

In Spring 1944, Heinz Drossel was not in Berlin. It is extremely unlikely that during the war years the two of them saw each other again outside of the dramatic night on the Jungfern Bridge. It is more likely that Luitpold "Poldi" Hagen, Heinz's best friend, was in possession of the key. If Marianne actually stayed in the Berlin Street 76 apartment between Summer and Winter 1944, it was through Poldi's intervention. Perhaps she simply mixed up the memories of her stay in Drossel's apartment in November 1942 with the tense period as a "submarine."

Only one thing is clear: she must have stayed in various locations while she was in hiding. She would have only stayed in these places during the day, since during the nights she continued to work at the BVG to earn at least a small amount of money. According to current estimates, up to ten helpers were necessary to help a single Nazi-persecuted individual living illegally escape the reach of the authorities. The hiding places had to be constantly changed. Food had to be procured, transported, and delivered.

The person in hiding required not only nourishment but also clothing, shoes, and hygienic articles.

Beginning in July 1944, it was likely that Marianne stayed for a while with Heinz's Uncle Oskar, who enjoyed gambling and who already had a Jewish girlfriend in 1942. In Fall 1944, Uncle Oskar died in a bomb attack. Occasionally, Marianne stayed with Poldi and with "Eva F." in Tempelhof. She stayed there through the end of 1944. That is, she spent the days there, when she did not have to work, and her little Billy stayed there as well.

It is unclear where the boy otherwise stayed during the six months of moving around and hiding. He was eight years old by this point. In 1944, many Berlin children of his age were sent away on children transports, out of the reach of the Allied bombs. William Albinus spent his entire childhood under a hail of bombs at the side of his hunted, severely physically and mentally compromised mother, who would vanish time and time again for days or even weeks at a time.

V. Two Times to Russia and Back
(1942–1945)
From Heinz Drossel's Memoirs

"Where Are Germany's Psychologists?"

Demjansk, July 1942

Drossel's ticket out of the mousetrap that was Demjansk came in the form of his officer's promotion. However, the reserve officer candidate still had to actually find a way to get away from the region. No one else took care of this. There were no plans and no instructions about how Heinz Drossel was to reach the officer training institute in Potsdam.

Drossel forged his way through woods and swamps to the airport in Demjansk. He never forgot this flight, the first one he had ever taken. Besides his fascination as the giant Ju 52 skimmed the tops of the trees, he long remembered the impact of Russian machine gun rounds in the airplane's fuselage. The flight took Drossel over Riga and Königsberg all the way to Berlin. His parents could hardly believe their eyes when their son stood at their door. After one night at home, Drossel traveled to the war academy in Potsdam.

He found the training to be "varied," and he especially enjoyed the weekend trips home to Tempelhof, although these "were increasingly affected by the air attacks."[59] The first of the Allied attacks on Berlin took place in 1940. During the night of August 25–26, British and American bombers attacked the neighborhoods of Reinickendorf, Pankow, Malchow, and Wartenberg. Three days later, the British succeeded in pushing as far as Kreuzberg. During the night of August 29, 1940, the first 12 Berliners lost their lives in the bombings.[60] The material damages were, at first, relatively low. Then the frequency and the precision of the bombardments increased.

With the new use of fire bombs as the main type of weapon, the attacks on Lübeck on March 29 and on Cologne in late

May 1942 marked the beginning of a new era in air warfare. Extreme damage was the intent of these massive attacks, such as the one against Cologne when over 1,000 bombers were used in a single concerted attack. The goal was to kill as many civilians as possible and to finally end the war. However, this strategy, developed by the British to demoralize the civilian population and to incite it against its own government, was not successful.[61] The German populace reacted like the British had to the German night air raids, with hatred toward the enemy and an increased will to fight.

At the end of Drossel's officer training at the war academy in Potsdam, the Führer was personally on hand to bid farewell to the freshly minted officer at the Sportpalast venue. From Drossel's memoirs: "His screaming and rage was meaningless and could hardly be understood. At the end, he walked along the first row, and I had the opportunity to confirm my belief that 'Greater Germany' was being ruled by a madman. Outstretched head, face like a mask, bulging eyes related to Grave's Disease. His ridiculous mustache trembled from cramps and excitement. His right arm was cocked upward in his special version of the 'German Greeting.' And his gaze caused one to shudder. This revealed his focused, fanatic will for extermination. It was evil incarnate. Where were Germany's psychologists and psychiatrists?"[62]

In early June 1942, Lieutenant Drossel arrived at a relief battalion

Petty Officer Heinz Drossel, 1942

in Landsberg. What followed was an "elegant time full of deprivation."[63] The young lieutenants sat in the elegant officers' mess, but they often did not get any food because as soon as the ranking officers, who were served first, were done eating, the table would be cleared. Drossel was given the command of a company. During the morning, he led their training on the field, and he received riding training in the afternoon.

Soon, the next push toward the East began. On July 15, Drossel arrived in Dnjepropetrowsk, Ukraine. This time he traveled second class on upholstered seats. The German officer was lodged in the house of a woman in her mid-40s and her daughter. Her husband was at the front. This period passed relatively comfortably. "The rides out into the area surrounding Dnjepropetrowsk, with its endless sunflower and wheat fields, have stayed with me all these years. It was easy service, and I had no problems with my military staff. My striker, Günter Busch, became the tailor for the battalion. You could always talk easily with him; his brother was in a concentration camp. He made my life easier whenever he could."[64]

The German advance on Stalingrad took its course. Drossel's unit was also commanded to move. The first order was to join up with the 6th Army, which was locked in fierce fighting near the Don River west of Stalingrad. Despite the resistance of part of his general staff, Hitler had chosen an attack strategy against Stalingrad that was to parallel the southern offensive against the Caucasus. On August 23, 1942, hundreds of airplanes began a bombing strike on the city. This was the same day that Judis Hirschfeld was born in distant Berlin.

German tanks reached several of Stalingrad's outer districts. Through bitter street and house-to-house fighting, the Germans gradually increased their occupation area. However, the Germans never succeeded in totally capturing the city. August saw the start of what a few months later became the siege of Stalingrad, which resulted in hundreds of thousands of German soldiers being killed, wounded, or taken prisoner.

In late August, Drossel was once again traveling by train. He rode through Brest, Belarus, and Oppeln until he finally reached a troop training camp in Breslau. Most of the time, none of the men knew where and for what reason they were being transported across war-torn Europe. And, then, suddenly it was clear that their train was "back in the Reich." However, there was no pause. Faster and faster, the miles sped by: Liegnitz, Cottbus, Berlin, Magdeburg, Kassel. France. The trip temporarily ended at a bleak troop training camp near Épernay. Slowly the information trickled down that this "load" of soldiers was being mobilized to serve as reserve troops for the strengthening of the Atlantic wall.

· The men made their way to the French military harbor at Brest, which now served as a German naval base. The men were quartered in Saint Renan, a village with less than 3,000 residents. The officers were accommodated in a confiscated hotel. There was cake at the bakery across the way and meat dishes at the bistro—everything was unmarked. "The woman prepared excellent roast rabbit, delicately fixed, and seasoned differently day to day. One day this too was over. When asked, the woman answered: 'Gentlemen—this is horrible— but there are no more cats far and wide.' We drowned this shock with red wine."[65]

On September 21, Heinz Drossel turned 26 years old. A noisy party was thrown for him. It began in the morning with a rich breakfast and a carriage ride, and it ended at 4:00 a.m. with glasses of Cognac. In between, there were lobsters and champagne. It was hard to believe that only one year before, the birthday boy had spent his day in a foxhole under strong fire, deathly afraid.

One week after this example of high living, Heinz Drossel came down with a serious case of hepatitis. He was taken to a military hospital. It was located in a cloister, where nuns cared for the sick and injured. He enjoyed the quiet and security of this spiritual location. Fourteen days after his arrival, he was allowed to stand up for the first time. Autumn flowers were blooming in the cloister garden. Heinz remained here for another two weeks, after which he was deemed cured. Shortly thereafter, the company was relocated to the north to enforce the Atlantic wall.

The Woman on the Jungfern Bridge

Jungfern Bridge, Berlin, November 1942
Prior to his deployment, Drossel was able to travel home on leave in November 1942. This was his first trip home since becoming an officer.

Almost 1,000 miles separated the Atlantic coast and Berlin. Although the population was suffering from hunger and the natural resources were slowly running out, transportation across bombed Europe at this time still functioned fairly well. Lieutenant Drossel enjoyed his stay in Berlin. He spent the evenings with his former classmate and "like-minded soul" Poldi Hagen and Poldi's girlfriend Charlott, visited relatives, and took walks through his beloved hometown.

On his final evening, it happened. He saw a woman on the Jungfern Bridge: "She wanted to jump over the railing. I grabbed her and spun her around to face me. One look, and I stared in amazement. Here was the young woman from New Tempelhof. When was that? 1938—an eternity ago . . . I thought about the child—about her child and the one in the ditch near Dagda . . . 'Poldi, do what you can with this money to bring her to safety.' I went back to my apartment and told her good-bye. Her name was Marianne . . . Now I had to make my way back to France."[66]

Heinz Drossel's memories of this night and the following day, of the things that he had to take care of, and of his parting from Marianne were oddly weak. This was a time of excitement, and he must have been quite tense. However, whenever he spoke of this encounter, whether as an eyewitness in front of schoolchildren or in a private conversation, he would tell this story within a span of only a few sentences. Even if one asked for more details, there was nothing more for him to tell. In hindsight, everything seemed to be concentrated on one point. And this point was the meeting on the bridge: the look of this woman as she wanted to jump over the railing, the memory of her son, the little boy with the rock, and the memory of the boy from Dagda who was murdered before Heinz Drossel's very eyes.

This concentration of impressions, thoughts, and images inspired him then to do what he did. He took care of the unknown woman, assumed responsibility for her, and put himself in danger. According to his own statements, Drossel did not hesitate "one second." It was "simply clear" to him that he had to do something, that he had to intervene. In some ways, his handling of the situation seemed to be more of a reflex reaction than a decision. This may explain his initial impulse, which caused him to not only hold Marianne Hirschfeld back from jumping into the water but also to take her home with him. The fact that he offered a secure place for her to spend the night could also be interpreted as a reactionary impulse. However, what followed was obviously a decision, rational and the result of mature considerations. Drossel closed out his savings account and instructed his friend Poldi to give the persecuted woman his 6,000 Reichsmarks. She, along with her son (this was important to Drossel), were to leave Germany, if possible. In addition, he provided contact between her and his Uncle Oskar, who could hide her as needed.

Thus, November 1942 began for a couple of people in Berlin with a share of hope and humanity. On the other hand, all hope was lost that November for the German soldiers in and around Stalingrad. On November 19, the Soviet counteroffensive was launched. Three days later, the 220,000 men of the 6th Army found themselves trapped in Stalingrad. Commanding General Friedrich Paulus recommended to Hitler that an attempted escape should be made. Hitler forbade him to bring his soldiers to safety. None of these initial reports reached the public.

Drossel and other anti-Nazis and realists no longer believed in the possibility of German victory. What at the beginning of the war had been a doubtful hope was now certainty. Hitler's army was not undefeatable. Instead, it was relatively poorly prepared and provisioned.

The condition of the "Atlantic Wall," which was primarily meant to discourage the Americans from making a landing in Europe, confirmed Drossel's estimations. He described the ditches, dugouts, and tank traps that he saw as "poor" and "shoddy." The Atlantic wall was a "bluff." "The entire thing was quite comfortable as long as peace reigned. In the case of an attack, the area could only have been held for a couple of hours. Furthermore, there was no artillery anywhere nearby."[67]

On January 31, 1943, the 6th Army at Stalingrad was defeated. General Paulus and thousands of German soldiers were taken prisoner by the Soviets. The militarily nonsensical decision to hold out in a hopeless situation had been very costly. Over 200,000 German soldiers had lost their lives, and on the Soviet side, over 1 million people had died.

For the growing number of war-weary Germans, especially for the persecutees and other anti-Nazis, this defeat was a cause for joy and hope for a swift end to the war and the regime: *"January 27; Wednesday evening . . .* The mood in the synagogue was more positive. The reports from the front were truly catastrophic. (Even today's were, as well.) In Stalingrad, the entire army, the 6th, along with Romanian and Croatian armies, have admittedly been lost. We are retreating all across the eastern front. In Africa, there are no longer any Italian colonies. Only Tunis is still held and, in that case, only at bay."[68]

The lost battle for Stalingrad held great symbolic value. Many anti-Nazis hoped this meant the beginning of the end for the Nazi regime. Sophie and Hans Scholl did not only want to hope and yearn for this. They wanted to do something. They tried to instigate their fellow citizens to resist the Nazis. Through the revelation of the scandalous circumstances of this battle, the Germans were supposed to change their opinions about Hitler. On the morning of February 19, 1943, at the University of Munich, the Scholl siblings distributed the sixth and final flier produced by the White Rose resistance group:

"Fellow students! Fellow students! Our people have been shaken by the defeat of our men at Stalingrad. Through the ingenious strategy of our World War Private First Class [Hitler], 330,000 German men have been irresponsibly and wastefully driven to their doom and their deaths. Führer, we thank you for this! The German people are seething. Do we want to trust a dilettante with the fate of our armies? Do we want to sacrifice the rest of the German youth to the base power instincts of a political clique? The day of reckoning has arrived, the reckoning of our German youth against the most abominable tyranny our people has ever experienced. In the name of Germany's youth, we demand from Adolf Hitler's state the return of our personal freedom, the most precious property of the German people. He has betrayed us in the most wretched possible way . . . The German name will always be a shameful one, if the German youth do not finally stand up to both avenge and expiate itself. It must shatter its tormenters and create a new, moral Europe."

While distributing the fliers, Sophie and Hans Scholl were discovered and imprisoned. Four days later, accused of "subversion of the war effort," "aiding the enemy," and "intent of high treason," the People's Court sentenced the siblings to death by hanging. The leaflet, which had been composed by their resistance comrade Karl Huber, was smuggled out of the country, and by the end of 1943, British pilots were dropping copies of it all across Germany.

Within a few hours of the arrest of the Scholl siblings, Joseph Goebbels held his famous Sportpalast address. The minister asked his audience: Do you want total war? And the people cheered, Yes!

A New Dimension

Bretagne, February 1943

As time passed, Drossel's reserve company could increasingly sense the animosity of the natives in Brittany. This was hardly any surprise to the Berliner. It was known that this area was a stronghold of the Résistance movement. The resistance fighters were well organized and were strongly backed by the local residents. Even children assisted the freedom fighters. In Drossel's district, a 10-year-old boy was caught trying to steal munitions. Drossel took the child to his father, a craftsman, and he explained that such activities were life-threatening. At this time, the SS was known to frequently execute partisan hostages. Drossel cautioned that the SS were unscrupulous enough to even kill children. "Before I left, I quietly said something in passing: 'If you happen to be in touch with the Maquis, I would be interested in talking to someone in authority—but only me personally. I could promise safe conduct.' He looked at me hard for a moment and then nodded. A hand shake, then I left."[69]

Several days later, Drossel received by mail secret documents about the location of mine obstacles in his region—German mine obstacles. The leader of the regional resistance group, the Maquis, was demonstrating his power by showing that he could steal such documents and have them secretly delivered to the German occupiers. Drossel stayed quiet about what happened and carefully returned the maps to their original files. Shortly thereafter, the German officer was visited by a bearded man in a Basque cap, who invited him to go for a walk.

For most of the walk, the Frenchman was silent. Drossel talked about his loathing of the Nazi regime and this war. He assured his companion that he respected the right of the French people to resist and that he wanted to avoid the spilling of any innocent blood. If anything happened to German soldiers, the SS retaliated quickly and brutally. He had no influence on this. Drossel also said that he was convinced that Germany would lose the war. This statement seemed to move the Maquis fighter and to convince him of the integrity of the man at his side.

Only one week later, a young Frenchman invited the occupiers to join a game of soccer: the village against the soldiers. Drossel convinced his battalion commander to permit the game, but at the end, his heart was beating hard: "Ten minutes before the end of the game the victory goal was shot for the French youth— thank God!"[70]

After this, it was quiet for a while. The atmosphere was noticeably more relaxed. Drossel often had the opportunity to go riding. He was fascinated by the landscape, and he took various excursions out into it. He spent the evenings playing cards and drinking wine in the officers' mess. However, he was troubled by haunting thoughts: "I would have liked to enjoy this glorious country as a guest. As it was, by rights, I was a hated foreigner who deserved the contempt of the entire world—and my own. However, in this self-loathing, I was alone—completely alone. What would be changed if I tried to help them? Even if I was able to reach one or the other of them, I did not belong with them. And if it came to it, would they treat me like all the rest? Despite this—I struggled with this demon—were these thoughts comforting?"[71]

In the end, these considerations did not provide much comfort. Drossel found himself increasingly despondent and lonely. One day, he once again rode out to the dunes. He dismounted and sat down in the sand. He pulled his pistol out of its holster. Staring out to sea, he cocked the gun. Without giving it any further thought, he placed the weapon against his temple and pulled the trigger. The gun had always been reliable during shooting practice, but this time it jammed. Drossel started to shake. He did not pull the trigger a second time.

By this point, the war had reached a new dimension. The signs of "Greater Germany's" inferiority were more and more apparent. The defeat at Stalingrad was one of the most visible indications. The disaster in the Soviet Union may well have been the reason behind the destination assigned to Drossel's next mobilization orders, which he received in February 1943. He traveled through France, Germany, Poland, and Belarus, until he reached the same spot he had been six months before: Dnjepropetrowsk, Ukraine. Since he had last been there, the land and the type of war being waged had changed drastically. The Soviet troops now seemed to be everywhere, and they were much better armed at this point. They had a distinct advantage over the Germans through greater manpower, a larger number of tanks, and above all, more positive morale.

Nonetheless, the first few weeks were relatively quiet. Drossel and his men were situated in the area between the Dnjepr and Donez rivers, on the banks of the Donez. After bitter fighting, they relieved the SS "Viking" division, and a meeting between Drossel and the division commander caused the former to react in horror and anger: "Here I met an impertinent, conceited member of the 'master race'—we were of secondary importance. During the relief process, our soldiers were treated like dirt. I saw free and clear what would happen if this scum ended up victorious. Even the Germans themselves would end up being treated as badly as the Poles and Czechs. Germany would turn into a giant concentration camp with a tiered class system."[72]

The company got organized. Ditches were dug, and shelters were built. The headquarters was located a little to the side in tents and bunkers. On the other side of the river, about 100 yards away, the Soviet enemy was encamped. Drossel spent much of his time near the front lines with the soldiers in the ditches. And he was confused; days and nights passed without a single shot being fired. After a while, the officer discovered the reason for this unusual calm. The Germans and the Soviets were carrying on a lively trade with each other. The latter loved their enemies' watches and offered to swap for them decent boots. Some of the soldiers played chess with the enemy troops, and there was even a small tournament in which Drossel and several Soviet officers participated. The men, who had come to this desolate location to kill each other, toasted the Soviets in their chess victory with vodka and cognac.

This unique idyll soon ended. The Soviets retreated a little, and the Germans received an official order to not engage in combat, due to insufficient munitions. Drossel's men sought accommodation in the abandoned village. They observed their enemies building a bridge, but they could do nothing about it. Later, thanks to his journal entries, Drossel recalled how on August 17, 1943, the Soviets completed their bridge across the river. And then the barrage started.

Hour after hour, the earth shook, and the village was soon reduced to ashes and rubble. Along with others, Drossel waited in one of the simple bunkers. At night, it was quieter, but then come morning, it all began again. Finally, the Germans fled from the village. In vain, Drossel called for assistance from the outside. He was told that the few remaining tanks had to be spared. That same evening, the German soldiers stormed the pathetic remains of the former village, which they had already once abandoned. Drossel believed that it was the courage of despair that gave them the strength to do this: the terrifying image of spending the night in the open air without any protection catalyzed their final burst of strength.

In late August, Lieutenant Drossel was again given leave to go home. He spent several peaceful days with his parents, who had previously moved to their summer cottage in Senzig, about 20 miles southeast of Berlin near Königs Wusterhausen. The shop had been closed in early 1943 after the Gestapo required its liquidation. His parents felt somewhat safer here in Senzig, farther away from the British air attacks on the capital. The frequency and intensity of these attacks were constantly increasing. Heinz Drossel sensed this when he visited his friends Poldi and Charlott in Tempelhof.

The two of them gave him news about Marianne, the woman from the Jungfern Bridge, with whom they had been in touch a few times. They told Heinz that she had received the money but that she had been unable to escape. She had been arrested twice. Poldi and Charlott had only learned about the second imprisonment at Levetzow Street from someone else. Since then, there had been no news about Marianne. Heinz was quite dejected when he returned to his unit at the front in mid-September.

After arriving in Ukraine, he learned that his company had retreated from the Donez area. Now he had to "search" for his regiment. Someone told him the general direction that the unit had taken; otherwise, he was all on his own. Trains were still traveling, but there was chaos everywhere. Everything was pushing westward: people, animals, goods. Villages were burning all over the place, torched by Wehrmacht soldiers following orders to leave behind "burnt earth." Drossel boarded a transport train going in the opposite direction. About 30 or 40 other soldiers traveled with him. They were also looking for their units. It was quite cold, and after a while, Drossel vacated his protected spot in the brake house located directly behind the locomotive. Two other soldiers, who were inadequately clothed for the weather, gratefully took his place. Drossel huddled in one of the train cars toward the back of the train with the other men. Not long after this, the train hit a mine. The locomotive and the first few cars were completely destroyed.

Drossel's battalion was scattered to the four winds. In an absurd turn of events, he ended up leading a baggage platoon through the night to a rendezvous point, a maneuvering area, where other platoons had been gathered so that they could travel together to the West. During the night march, the German platoon almost got mixed up with a troop of Russian soldiers who were also heading west. Outfitted with a long Russian coat, a share of Chutzpa, and his Russian language skills, Drossel was able to disentangle the two groups. The enemies separated at a fork in the road without a single shot being fired.

The Battle of Dnjepr had begun on August 26, 1943. It quickly became clear that the Germans had no chance of winning. What the military imagined as an "orderly withdrawal" became "in reality, a full-blown battle."[73] Drossel's battalion took a temporary position in a village situated on a bluff high over the Dnjepr River. The only people left in the village were women. "The position was actually ideal for defense . . . However, nothing had been prepared. There were no emplacements, no supply lines. Nonetheless, the brilliant 'Führer' had declared there was no going back, so there were no back-up positions or other precautionary measures in place. It was the crime of an insane 'Führer' against not only foreign people and races, but against his own people."[74]

The orders to retreat finally arrived in mid-October. Everything was packed and loaded in a great hurry. One evening, after marching for several days, the soldiers set up camp. They were surrounded by Russian troops. The Germans quickly dug emergency ditches, and

Heinz Drossel near Isjum, Ukraine, 1943

the men tried to find a halfway safe position on a small rise. The commander sent the soldiers out against the Soviet assailants with the order that this position must be held at all cost. That night, the soldiers engaged in bitter fighting, and many were killed, especially among the Germans. Drossel watched as several of his comrades died close to him. He was at the end of his strength: "P. lie in front of me, his eyes open, unseeing and astonished. I could hear Russian curses two or three meters to my right. I hurriedly moved back, but I could still only hear Russian nearby. Then, a moment of quiet, overwhelming depression—I did not want to go on."[75]

The young man found himself in the middle of a Soviet nowhere, surrounded by victory—and vodka-intoxicated Soviets. At this point, Drossel made an equally desperate and risky decision: he shot himself in his lower arm. The medical care in the immediate vicinity was less than adequate. The punishment for self-inflicted wounds was usually draconian and could even result in the execution of the guilty party. In the eyes of the military, such a man was on par with a deserter.

Drossel was lucky. After he reported to his commander, who did not hide his disdain for the "paltry" wound, Drossel made his way to the field hospital. A Russian farmer with a small wagon gave him a ride there. Drossel had to wait at the hospital since there were many seriously wounded men who needed care; he saw a tub full of amputated legs and arms. For the first time, he began to wonder if perhaps he might lose his arm. The waiting seemed to stretch on forever. Then he heard that the hospital was being dismantled. The Soviets were heading this way. A medic finally took a look at him.

The medical aid gave Drossel's wound a rudimentary dressing and advised him to go to the train station from which the hospital trains would depart. The aid filled out a transport form for Drossel, which became his rescue document. Then with a smile, he informed Drossel that a pistol needed to be held out at a distance of at least 12 in. (30 cm) when firing: "the burn marks betray everything."[76] The man was a Catholic chaplain, so denouncing Drossel never came into question for him.

In order to reach an airplane heading to Düsseldorf, Drossel had to travel with an overfilled medical train, by foot, in a horse-drawn wagon, and finally by streetcar in Odessa. The flight had to make a stop in Silesia due to bomber attacks in central Germany. Drossel located a Luftwaffe hospital near the airfield, which gladly provided medical care to him and another Berliner whom he had met during the course of his journey. What followed was three weeks of ideal circumstances: de-loused and bathed, wrapped in white sheets, Drossel was able to recuperate his strength. There were delectable meals, sparkling wine, and walks in the park. The doctors kept both men in the hospital as long as they possibly could. In early December 1943, the men were released and ordered to report to a Berlin medical hospital.

Drossel was received much less enthusiastically at the Tempelhof Garrison hospital. The accusation of shirking of duties hung in the air. He immediately received his travel papers and orders to join up with a relief unit. The following day, he reported for duty in Landsberg. There he was ordered on recuperative leave, and he traveled directly to his parents' house. The mood there was depressed. The increasingly severe attacks, the acute reduction in food supplies, and the uncertainty of how long the hated regime would still be in power dominated the thoughts of those closest to Heinz Drossel. Unfortunately, there were fewer such individuals than there had been two years before. Too many school friends or acquaintances had died on one front or the other. His close friends Poldi and Charlott were still alive though. As a long-distance communication technician, Poldi Hagen, who had so selflessly helped Marianne Hirschfeld—and whom Drossel believed had aided other Jewish victims—was "important to the war effort" and was never called up.

Christmas 1943 was a joyless celebration with his parents. Heinz spent New Year's, another subdued holiday, with Poldi and Charlott. The young people were plagued by anxious questions they could not answer: "Will 1944 bring the end to the war? Freedom? Freedom could only be achieved through a complete defeat of Hitler's Germany. Will we survive the coming year? What will the new world look like?"[77]

Between Hope and Depression

Drossell exceeded his leave. His new orders directed him to report as a specially appointed legal officer (*Gerichtsoffizier*) to Infantry Battalion 561. He was supposed to report to this probationary unit in the northern Soviet Union on December 30, but he only first left his parents' house on January 2, 1944. The trip took longer than usual since the transportation networks hardly functioned any longer. The trains were stopped for hours or were forced to take detours. Regardless, no one seemed to notice that Drossel arrived at his post late. His first task was to organize the battalion, and Drossel gladly turned his attention to this new duty. He felt that he finally had a sensible goal to pursue, and he hoped he could help the soldiers, who were here to perform their service "on probation," to rehabilitate and to survive.

At the top of the battalion were officers and petty officers who had been gathered together from various units. The actual troop itself was composed of Wehrmacht soldiers who had been found guilty of punishable offenses. The most common offenses were going AWOL, theft from comrades, and rape. In his memoirs, Drossel noted that among the probationary battalion's demoted officers there were numerous rapists. For their misdeeds, the soldiers were sentenced to probation. This meant that instead of being put in prison, they were sent to the front. Their service in a probationary battalion was expressly not to be punitive in nature.

Those individuals accused of political or civil law crimes were placed into either Battalion "999" or in the Dirlewanger unit. The SS Dirlewanger unit was made up of former concentration camp or prison inmates. The members of this brigade had nothing more to lose. Named for the notorious sex offender Waffen-SS officer Oskar Dirlewanger, the brigade was primarily used to fight against partisans or revolutionaries, and it was known for its brutality. Even civilians were not spared this cruelty, and it cost thousands their lives.

Drossel held one of the leadership positions in the new organization of the Infantry Battalion 561, which had previously been scattered in the fighting and had been decimated in combat. Later, he was put in charge of a supply train, in addition to his work as a contact person for the soldiers and his responsibility for the administration of the personnel files. His most important task was to prepare and submit appeals for clemency. The Lieutenant enjoyed his new situation; he quickly found a way to connect with the men, he valued the trust they placed in him, and he enthusiastically pursued his duties. Soon after his arrival, the most glaring organizational problems were resolved. The troop was quickly arranged properly. Drossel lived with the baggage train about ten miles behind the front line. The relative calm at this location surely helped to heighten his increasingly stabilized frame of mind.

From his memoirs: "Soon I felt quite comfortable among the 'criminals.' Over time, almost all of them came to me with their worries and cares, some of which were very personal. I . . . made no secret of my own views. Fortunately, there were very few, if any, real Nazis here. Each person had had his own set of experiences. . . . Thank God that nothing truly punitive took place here. . . . This was work with people who needed you and who were grateful to be treated as human beings, people who had almost all felt the hell that was a Wehrmacht prison."[78]

Drossel used the trust that was soon established between him and the probationary soldiers in order to explain bluntly the high risks of flight to those who admitted that they were considering trying to escape. Partisan revenge or prisoner-of-war camps on the one hand, and certain death after re-capture on the other. As the war grew more desperate as time passed, deserters were handled by the Nazi authorities mercilessly. Drossel argued that at least as long as one was in this battalion, there was the possibility that one would be pardoned or be sent to a medical hospital if wounded. He was clearly a convincing orator, since he later reported the following: "After a conversation over cigarettes and wine, all of them decided to stay. I hope they never regretted this."[79]

His argumentation skills were less successful in connection with two convicted soldiers who he fetched from a Wehrmacht prison in Riga in order to bring them to the battalion. They escaped, and Drossel never heard from them again. During his trip to Riga, he had the opportunity to visit the officers' mess in the city. This offered a glimpse into a very different world than he had yet seen: "An opulent building with glittering lights shining inside. Giant chandeliers, a large hall. Numerous officers and paymasters, civil servants, and everything that belongs to this class of individual. Almost all of them were accompanied by their 'ladies' in rich garments from the Soviet Union, Lithuania, the Baltic area, and Germany. A three-course meal, a small orchestra, the babble of voices. Was I dreaming? At first glance, I was incensed. So this is how the rear echelon lives it up in Riga. But then I calmed down. Could it be that they were justified in this? What was yet before us—before them? On the other hand, out there hundreds of thousands were bleeding to death for them. Was there an answer for this? I could not find it. I ate my three-course meal—it did not taste right—and I left."[80]

Soon after this, Drossel was called on to exercise his skills as military attorney: "My first task for the division was a defense, a delicate situation indeed. A senior physician was charged with cowardice toward the enemy. It was a simple issue of was he or was he not . . . I was on the go for days pursuing research on site and interviewing witnesses . . . I could verify that during the time in question my client had been located in a bunker at the very front lines and had taken care of the wounded there . . . I wrote everything down on a map and plead for a not guilty verdict 'due to proven innocence' . . . The verdict was as expected . . . From time to time, other more minor cases came up. Prosecution of negligence during guard duty, defense of unauthorized leave from the company. I achieved numerous acquittals and a few minor punishments."[81]

The months passed, and the battalion was sent back to Russia, this time to a position east of Düneburg. On April 15, 1944, Heinz Drossel wrote a letter to his parents: "Once again, a glorious spring day lays across the land. There is still a little snow, but it is quickly disappearing. In only a few days, true spring will be upon us. Nonetheless, everything is still barren, although the first buds are now coming out." The lieutenant described the actual situation briefly: "Everything is quiet where we are. Whatever else is going on in the world, we are currently not experiencing any of it. However, at home there must be all sorts of things going on. Over the past ten days, we have received no mail from Berlin, and it has been even longer since mail has arrived from anywhere west of there." The relatively calm situation was increasingly overshadowed by dark signs: "Last night, he [the Russians] must have again been pursuing something major. The rumble [of the planes] lasted all through the night—like when we were the ones making the attacks. Riga must have been the destination. Well, soon both of them [the Russians and the British] will be able to shake hands in the air."

One day, Heinz Drossel searched for "Major K." in order to talk to him about something, and he surprised him while listening to an English radio broadcast. Both of them nonchalantly passed over this occurrence. They simply understood each other. The major, whom Drossel believed was one of the men involved in the July 20 conspiracy to assassinate Hitler, explained that he had prevented the sending of a Nazi secret service controller to the battalion. He was supposed to have come to require the soldiers to renew their oath to the Führer.

The rumors of an Allied invasion of France increased as the weeks passed. "Major K." instructed Drossel to talk to the soldiers. Drossel handled this fairly casually: "I called the company together to make a political statement. If an invasion occurred, it could be repulsed. If only the Allies could gain a solid hold in France, but that had not happened yet. However, if it did, then the war would finally be lost."[82] Drossel's "political lesson" took place on June 2. On June 6, 1944, the Allied troops landed at Normandy, and it was soon obvious that the Allies were strong and had struck decisively. They could overpower the German troops.

On June 22, 1944, two weeks after D-Day, Drossel and all of the men with him were faced with the start of another nightmare: the great Russian offensive. The barrage shook the earth for hours on end, even miles behind the actual frontlines. For all intents and purposes, the German army fractured: what began as an organized retreat quickly turned into total chaos. The German officers had to draw their pistols on their own soldiers to prevent them from fleeing in front of the Russian tanks. All sense of order and orientation was lost.

Some of the German army corps were completely destroyed during this offensive. A large hole existed between the Central Army Group and the Northern Army Group, and the Russian army forged straight through it toward the west. Drossel's unit was located in the northern part of the sector. Weeks later, it joined up with the other part of the battalion and moved farther north. However, it was still located within Russia's borders. This was the situation when Drossel heard about the failed assassination attempt against Hitler. It was the evening of July 20. "We had been marching all day. Around 9:00 p.m., we made camp in a small wooded area. There we received the first news about the attack on Hitler. By this time, everything was over. Hitler was still alive. There was nothing especially interesting about this report. The men were tired and hungry, and all of them were disinterested in anything having to do with politics. Furthermore, the assassination had failed. Here and there, you could see mild regret in the faces around you. There were no other reactions . . . On the eastern front, this was a day just like any other day."[83]

With his entourage, Drossel traveled to Latvia. In late August, he received news that they would again be broken off from the rest of their unit because the Russians had succeeded in reaching the Baltic Sea between Libau (Liepāja) and Heydekrug County. Starting in October, rumors about a "Kurland Army" began to circulate, similar to earlier talks about a "Stalingrad Army." The Kurland Army was only first dissolved with the capitulation on May 8, 1945. The soldiers were effectively surrounded here, and through the end of the war, they functioned as the only large group of German Wehrmacht units outside the borders of the German Reich that was not defeated. They were engaged in bitter battles, and tens of thousands of German and Russian soldiers lost their lives here.

During the Fall of 1944, Drossel's emotional state swung between hope and deep depression. His letters home were full of nature descriptions that were both gloomy and optimistic: "Like these times, today it was stormy. Dense clouds rolled in from the sea . . . Only the trees stand bleak and empty in the pale starshine. They stretch their limbs up threateningly against the pitch black sky . . . Let the storms rage, let the violence run rampant. After all the storms pass, a white veil will lay across the earth and a new spring will herald a new awakening."[84]

In December 1944, Drossel found himself in a Latvian forester's house when he once again came down with hepatitis. He was unable to comply with the marching orders that were given at just this time because of his high fever combined with pronounced nausea and weakness. He was sent to the field hospital near Libau: "Despite my lethargy, my impressions of the field hospital were strong. It was truly a merry prison. There were all sorts of people without arms and legs, covered in scratches and shot up, who had only one goal: to get out of this mess."[85]

However, this was nearly impossible. One commanding physician confirmed that Drossel was suffering from severe hepatitis compounded with jaundice. He explained that it was absolutely critical that he be sent to a real hospital back home where he could receive proper medical care. Then in the same breath, he stated his regret that he could not give him travel papers to do just that: only the severely injured, not the sick, could be given permission to return home. The controls in Libau were extremely strict. The commanding physician reported that several mildly ill soldiers had even been shot when they tried to board a transport train. The doctor explained bluntly that for Field Marshall Schörner illness was almost the equivalent of cowardice.[86]

Drossel spent New Year's in the field hospital. The mood there was simultaneously ghastly, excited, and depressed. The officers in Drossel's 20-bed room vehemently refused to listen to the Führer's

New Year's radio address: "'Medic, kick your Führer in the ass, and shut the door!' That was from a major in the Luftwaffe. The staff sergeant remained stubborn: 'The door stays open.' Already a jackboot was flying through the room—from someone who wore only one—and the sergeant had only just enough time to move out of the way. The boot struck the loudspeaker, which rattled and clanged. Then there was silence. The Führer is not wanted here, at least not any more."[87]

With the aid of the commanding physician, Drossel was able to obtain his transport papers after New Year's. Things became a little dicey at the boarding in the Libau harbor. The surgeon general checking papers at the ship did not want to allow Drossel on board because he was "only sick." Eventually, the potential danger of infection caused by Drossel's hepatitis finally convinced the man to let Drossel on board. He did not want to risk infection among the still-healthy soldiers at the front. Obviously the wounded on board the ship were not of much concern to him. The old, dilapidated ship was hopelessly over-filled. It stank of vomit, urine, and pus, and inadequately tended wounded, many suffering from amputations, groaned in pain.

At Königsberg, Drossel and the other wounded were placed on a train headed for the hospital at Stuhm, East Prussia. The Wehrmacht could no longer hold off the invasion of the Soviet army. However, the civilian population was strictly forbidden from fleeing. The civilians had only themselves to rely on, and they lived in constant fear. Despite the threat of punishment, many began to march westward. After several days, horrifying news of attacks and rapes in nearby areas reached the hospital. The head physician decided to close the hospital. Drossel was asked to lead all of the mobile patients to Marienburg (Malbork). He organized these arrangements with an assisting doctor who was in charge of the bedridden patients. They were to meet at the train station in the small city. The march through the ice-cold night, about nine miles, lasted several hours.

There was not even the least bit of Prussian orderliness left in Marienburg. Drunken soldiers lingered in the alleys, no one was running the train station. Nevertheless, Drossel was able to put together a train, although initially without a locomotive. He settled the almost 150 people for whom he felt responsible into the train cars: "We waited, but nothing happened. I had already given up hope, when a transport train chugged into the station from the south. It halted beside us. The assisting doctor threw his arms around me."[88] With the help of this physician, whom Drossel never named, the group of men was able to reach the Baltic Sea via Neumünster.

Drossel was not the only one to profit from the amazing organizational talents and courage of this one man. He singlehandedly scraped together a train car full of sparking wine, sweets, and schnaps, which was critical to the hiring of a locomotive driver and boilermen. En route to Stettin (Szczecin), where chaos had not yet broken out, numerous refugees were able to be taken on board the train as well.

Together, Drossel and the assisting doctor were also able to "confiscate" a commissary from a rigidly loyal manager who would have preferred to dynamite the supplies. Drossel called the commissary and pretended to be a General von Alvensleben, and the assisting physician managed to deceive the manager during a face-to-face meeting. Thus, supplies for the desperate travelers on the train from Marienburg were secured.

After many hours of travel, the train covered the final leg of the 190-mile trip to Stettin. There were several stops along the way to unload the dead and to arrange for the seriously wounded to be transported to nearby field hospitals. The Stettin train station was patroled by SS men, who were searching the cars for deserters. Drossel presented his travel authorization papers from Libau with a nervous fluttering in his stomach. However, the documents fulfilled their purpose. After some back and forth discussions— the SS men wanted the refugees to be unloaded in Stettin—the train was allowed to head farther west the following morning. The assisting physician had argued doggedly to be allowed to accompany the wounded to their destination. His father was a surgeon general in Neumünster in Schleswig, and this is where the assisting doctor wanted to bring the wounded—and himself. Drossel received orders to report to a field hospital in Travemünde, where he spent almost three weeks.

His experiences in Travemünde were similar to the ones he had had in Libau. The officers in his hospital room were open in expressing their rejection of and contempt for the Führer. They also were united in their unwillingness to listen to a Hitler speech broadcast on the radio. This happened on January 30, 1945. On the following day, all seven officers found their release papers signed by the commanding physician next to their breakfast plates. The captain, who had acted as the leader of the small mutiny the day before, took care of things such that there was a delay before these men had to report to their new relief troops. All of them were granted 14 days of leave.

"They Are All Pigs"

Senzig, February 1945

Drossel arrived in Berlin via train. The trip was arduous and dangerous. British bombers controlled the entire area, and at night, bombs fell from the skies. The train halted so the passengers could crouch behind the railroad embankments. Finally, after numerous difficulties, Drossel reached Senzig, where his parents were at least halfway safe. He met their neighbors this time: Mr. and Mrs. Hesse and their 20-year-old daughter. There was even a young man living with them, as Drossel soon learned. The four of them had been bombed out in Berlin, and for the past two years, they had been living in a summerhouse located on the property next door to his parents. It was actually strange that the young man was not in the military. However, Drossel did not give this any thought at the time.

During the evenings, the three Hesses came over to listen to the radio. The program of choice was the BBC London, and the Drossels and the Hesses listened eagerly for news. Both of the older

Jack and Lucie Hass, 1951

men openly discussed their opinions. What bound these individuals together was their desire to have the war end quickly with Nazi Germany's defeat. The young woman seemed to be very skeptical of Heinz Drossel. He noticed how she would watch him distrustfully. During his visit, he wore his officer's uniform. He did not talk much, but sat in the living room with his parents and listened to the "enemy program."

Drossel hoped that the war would end while he was still in Senzig. However, the news did not bode well. The Allies had been halted by the Ardenne offensive. Drossel's leave was coming to an end. The local doctor was understanding, and he prescribed an additional week of leave. Huge US air force squadrons flew overhead toward Berlin. Drossel watched the formations with a mixture of amazement, fascination, and hope.

Margot Hass, ca. 1946

During another visit from the Hesses, the mood was subdued. The three Hesses did not stay long. However, Mr. Hesse asked Heinz Drossel to accompany them back home. Heinz was introduced to the young man staying with the Hesses. His name was Günter. The three men initially sat in silence around a garden table in the pathetic summerhouse the four Berliners had been living in for the past two years. The older man finally broke the silence. He admitted that they were living under false names. Their real name was Hass. Of course, Heinz had no idea that the younger of the two Hass women, Margot, had been friends with Marianne, the woman from the Jungfern Bridge. Mr. Hass continued: "Mr. Drossel, we are Jews, and we are living here illegally. We have received news that we have been betrayed. The Gestapo could show up here at any moment. We do not know what to do. Can you help us?"

Drossel, Jr., did not hesitate a moment. He stood up and told them that he could definitely help, but he wanted to talk to his parents first. The other two men nodded silently. Heinz Drossel informed his father of what had happened, and the older man reacted in support. His first question was: "Do you have a plan?" Yes, his son did. His first thought was to move the persecutees into his Tempelhof apartment. Together, the three Drossels went over to the summerhouse.

Over 60 years later, Günter Fontheim, the younger of the two men looking for help, described what happened: "It did not take long, but it seemed like forever to us. All three of the Drossels came over. And Mrs. Drossel slammed a basket full of food down on the table. She was incensed. She yelled at us! Why had we not told them sooner about our situation? What in the world were we thinking? If she had known sooner, she could have been helping us get supplies all along. She was very angry." This was a great relief for Fontheim and the others. The secret was finally out in the open, and they had been accepted. They had not been mistaken in trusting these people whom they had carefully gotten to know, these people who were their last hope in a horrible situation.

Together, the new allies packed various items of value into a crate. The Drossels later buried the box in their garden. The persecutees left their shelter and found a hiding place in the woods. That very night, Heinz Drossel observed how a black Mercedes drove up to the abandoned summerhouse. Men in long coats got out, approached the house, went inside, and quickly came back out again. They drove off empty-handed. The Gestapo found no additional victims in this house. Early the next morning, Heinz handed the persecutees the key to his rooms in Tempelhof. He gave them directions on how to find it. And he offered the older man a pistol. For self-defense. "I said: 'If someone should come by [before I get there], do not hesitate. Just shoot all of them—they are all pigs.'"[89]

Later, Heinz Drossel explained that he never considered the fact that his involvement with the Hesses could put him in danger. However, "the mere fact that he had given a Jewish family a pistol and bullets would have surely resulted in a death sentence."[90] In October 1942, General Rudolf Schmudt, head of the Army Personnel Office, drafted a secret decree that obligated all Wehrmacht officers to embrace antisemitism. The order included the following language: "An officer must . . . adopt a clear, completely uncompromising attitude toward the Jewish question. There is no difference between so-called decent Jews and others . . . Through his inner conviction, the officer must . . . reject Judaism and every possible connection to it. Whoever rejects this uncompromising position is no longer viable as an officer."[91] Of course, Lieutenant Drossel was aware of this order, however he chose to follow his conscience. Such an inhumane "decree" had no power over him.

Furthermore, Heinz Drossel took responsibility for erasing all traces of the four Berliners. Günter Fontheim had told him that he had made several phone calls to acquaintances in Berlin. The numbers that he had dialed had been registered in a list somewhere. Fontheim was afraid that this list could be used by the persecutors to locate other Jews living illegally.

As Fontheim confirmed in a 2011 interview, the telephone he used had belonged to a "Family G." In the second edition of his memoirs, Drossel explained how he deviously stole the book that contained the numbers. He described the situation as a minor escapade, and he was delighted to be able to help his friend this way. He was also proud that he had resolved the problem so cunningly.[92]

Subsequently, the "Hesse" family, Margot Hass and her parents Lucie and Jack, took refuge in an old horse stall at the Sanssouci Palace in Potsdam. Günter Fontheim stayed in Drossel's Tempelhof apartment in Berlin until the end of the war. Drossel told his landlord, a communist, that the young man was a deserter. The man was glad to hide him. Drossel assumed that if his landlord had known that the man was actually a Jew, he might not have been so willing to assist him. Both the family and Fontheim survived the war, and all of them emigrated to the United States after the war.

Ernest Günter Fontheim, 1955, Ann Arbor, Michigan

"Idiocy in the Extreme"

Near Olmütz, May 4, 1945

Drossel wanted to make good use of the ever-increasing chaos of March 1945. He tried to leave Berlin and head west. Actually, he was supposed to head east, but the reports trickling in from that direction were frightening. The Soviet army was getting closer and closer to Berlin. In their wake, the soldiers left a path of destruction. They were making their way through the areas that the Germans had destroyed, and as they approached Adolf Hitler's capital, they were increasingly vengeful. Deciding spontaneously, Drossel caught a train from the Anhalt train station heading toward the western front. From this moment on, he was a deserter. He almost immediately encountered a controller. He explained that he wanted to meet his unit in Kassel. The controller chastised him for his "confusion" and informed him that his relief unit was "somewhere in Bohemia." Drossel had no choice but to report to the closest headquarters. He claimed that he wanted to reach the front, and no one suspected what he actually was: a man who wanted to save his life by no longer fighting. A deserter.

As ordered, Drossel traveled through Dresden and Prague to Olomouc (Olmütz). Upon arrival, he was sent to the commander of the fortress there. This fort was composed of old walls and a sturdy tower. Instead of true windows, it had shooting slits in the walls, and the view from the ramparts of the surrounding area was striking. This is where Drossel was quartered. Everything was narrow, bare, and uncomfortable, but it was also peaceful.

The front seemed to be far away, and no gunfire could be heard. Like the other 150 men stationed here, Drossel had little to eat, but no one complained. Quiet reigned in this castle. During the nights and early mornings, Drossel wrote lyrical descriptions of the natural world: "The mountains stand tall in their seriousness, like the Norns [the Fates], secretive powers, through whose hands run the threads of this young day's fate. They carry joy and pain, happiness and suffering, triumph and defeat in their laps."[93]

There was never much time for poetry. During the night between April 18 and 19, 1945, the sound of artillery fire reached the fort from a distance. On April 20, the Führer's birthday, Drossel received orders to prepare to march. The men drove toward the front on board transport trucks and military utility vehicles. In the following days, Drossel came face to face with a new, horrifying side of the war. He became personally acquainted with true fanaticism and blind obedience.

In the early dawn of the following day, Drossel witnessed the arbitrary murder of several German soldiers by a "special commando" unit. Drossel's company reached its location, an old garrison, where an alarm unit had just been dissolved. The commanding officer, a man about the same age as Drossel, was at the absolute end of his rope. Out in the garrison's garden, two men in field gray uniforms were pointing their guns at two soldiers who were digging their own graves. The armed men claimed to be part of a special commando unit, and they maintained that the men had to be shot immediately. No one ever explained what crimes the soldiers had supposedly carried out. The "special commando" men, clearly Gestapo henchmen, threatened the unit officer with imprisonment if he did not follow their orders.

After hearing the story, Drossel only hesitated a moment before running down to the courtyard. The graves were already finished, and before his very eyes, the two men were shot in the back of the head. He froze in shock: "My entire body was wracked by tremors. I felt numb all over, and the words 'fill in the graves' came to me as if over a great distance, as did the sound of an approaching military utility vehicle . . . I could not move for a long time. I did not notice that I had been alone for quite a while. I had failed, and I was guilty." He wished that he had at least shot the murderers, and then he was immediately disgusted with himself. The change within himself upset him greatly: "It was unbelievable that the only alternative was to kill in turn. Once again, something shattered inside of me—deep inside. It could never be put together again. In the one hour of my life in which I had been required to act truly humanly, I had failed! I was complicit and could only hope for mercy."[94]

After setting up a cross for the murdered soldiers with the inscription "Here lay two unknown soldiers—murdered by the Gestapo," Drossel and his company continued their march. Scattered and wounded soldiers, a mass of men wildly thrown together, who only wanted to dissolve their company. Every one of them wanted to get as far away from the front line as possible.

In one village, Drossel met a captain and his lieutenant, who like him were desperately seeking a way to escape an inevitable encounter with the Russians. The captain explained that the region was swarming with SS men, and that that was why there was no escape toward Pilsen, where the American army had already set up camp. The men could not come up with an escape plan, and they parted ways. "We reached one location and stood around. No one knew what was going on . . . Everywhere, there were separate 'headquarters.' Some of them even had radio connections to some location or another. They were giving orders for the 'deployment' of these disorganized masses." Drossel's troop was sent to join up with an alarm battalion. This battalion seemed to be functioning relatively well, as it had both long-distance communication abilities and a field kitchen.

The next village was taken, and soon after that, another was lost. Drossel's unit lost all connection to the other parts of its troop and was on its own. At this point, Drossel gave the order to retreat. The Czech residents seemed to regret the departure of the German soldiers, since they feared the Russians even more. Although the Russians were close at hand, Drossel's company retreated from the village without any losses. It was only first after the retreat that Drossel realized that the battalion's command post had been abandoned without notifying him.

After marching for several hours, Drossel's company joined back up with the rest of the battalion. The major had set up quarters in an abandoned village located in a nearby ravine. This location was catastrophic from a strategic perspective, since the men here were caught in a narrow valley. The next morning, Drossel scanned the landscape with a telescope and discovered eight Russian tanks up on the rise that he and his men had descended just the day before when leaving the village. In vain, he tried to raise an alarm over a field telephone. The tanks began to fire. This was when Drossel found that the command post had been cleared out. Once again, the commanding officers had left him and the other men in a bind.

The flight this time was also successful, although several men were injured during the retreat. Most of them had time to grab their weapons, and they marched on. Three hours later they met up with the battalion's officers. Drossel was furious: "I wanted to scurry off just as much as the major, we all did, but it couldn't go that way. Even if was only by Hitler's grace, we were all officers now, and we were responsible for all of these people. Anyone could leave, if he wanted, but not at the price of betraying these men, at the price of their miserable deaths."[95]

At the very next opportunity, the major and his entire entourage vanished. As the company stumbled onto a village full of German soldiers and SS men, the commanding officers simply up and left without a word. That is also what about half of the 150 men under Drossel's command did as well. He was exhausted, and by this point, nothing much mattered to him any more. Even his suspicion that his adjutant, Staff Sergeant Weber, whom he greatly admired, also wanted to leave did not upset him. As soon as he found a spot, he fell asleep. However, when he woke up during the night, he discovered that Weber was sitting beside him and keeping watch. The sergeant had good news. He had found an escape route out of the village, and furthermore, he told Drossel that Hitler was dead.

The rumor of the Führer's death had been circulating for several weeks. Some of the stories were that he had "fallen near Berlin," while others claimed that he had shot himself. In actuality, Adolf Hitler, the Reichschancellor, supreme commander, and Nazi Party chief, shot himself in his right temple in the Führer Bunker in Berlin on April 30, 1945. Eva Braun, Hitler's longtime companion and wife of one day, died by taking a poison capsule. On May 1, Magda Goebbels poisoned her six children and then had herself shot by her husband, propaganda minister Joseph Goebbels. He then shot himself with the same gun. The bodies of Adolf Hitler and Eva Braun were burned on the grounds of the Reichschancellery building by the SS.

During the early hours of May 4, 1945, Weber and Drossel fled the village. By going through a non-operational fountain and a cave, the two of them managed to get out of the valley undiscovered. They traveled westward over farm fields. En route, they had to keep a look-out for low-flying fighter plans, but they were able to avoid the Russians. Instead, they ran straight into the arms of the Germans. "We had just crested a roadbed when we were surrounded by five or six watchdogs. They took us to a small house about 100 meters behind us. The officers were located here. A short question to me: 'What are you doing here?'"[96]

Drossel's answer was just as clever as it was jaded: "My alarm unit had scattered. As we were running, we had been attacked by Russian fighter planes and had lost our orientation. We had no maps of the region. Everything had been so badly organized." The interrogating officer "had a quiet conversation with the others and then returned: 'A short ways from here are about 150 men we have rounded up. Take over the leadership of them, and go straight down the road until you reach the main line of fighting. It is not far.' And then he added softly: 'Do not let yourself be seen around here again.' Well, what luck . . . I again was in charge of an alarm unit and one such as this to boot! You could rely on these fellows—travelers do not like to stay in one place. The guys did not have much with them, but most of them had their weapons."

One hour later, Drossel met up with his new troop at the same spot where he and Sergeant Weber had so cunningly escaped a short time earlier. Just as before, the alleys were full of men, hardly any soldiers, but numerous SS men. They were very busy. Trucks were being loaded, crates were being hauled, maps were being studied.

An SS man spoke to Drossel. He and his men were supposed to take up a position on the hillside and to secure the area. At first, Drossel hesitated since this seemed a very risky endeavor at best. He unwillingly set his men in motion and ordered them to take positions halfway up the hill. He thought that from this point, they would have a better chance of escaping should the Russians come over the top. From beneath them, the angry voice of the SS man reached Drossel. They were supposed to go all the way to the top and to be quick about it. As Drossel turned toward the screaming man, he saw that a machine gun was being brought into position. The SS man trained the machine gun on him and his company. His reaction was spontaneous, and without hesitation, he yelled an order at his men: "Turn both machine guns! Fire on the SS!" Only a few seconds lapsed, and then a barrage of bullets flew through the air.

Drossel called for a cease fire almost as soon as the firing started. He did not fear a counterattack by the SS since his position on the hillside was far enough away from the village down below. The hours passed, and in late afternoon, the trucks departed. The village slowly grew empty, and Drossel and his company descended the hill. An "excited and antsy major," who "had actually managed to pull together a military tribunal in the interim," was waiting for them. "That was the true legacy of the head of the SS. I was taken into custody and placed into a relatively intact house. I had to wait, but they left me my pistol. It made no difference to me. I was completely exhausted and was pretty much done with the adventures of these last few days. They had to wake me up when the high tribunal was convened."[97]

Drossel admitted to giving the order to fire. He explained the extreme emergency situation that existed at that point and argued before the court that since the death of the Führer, the SS had no legitimate power anymore. The presiding judge seemed confused. He did not address Drossel's arguments. After a short time, the judge passed the sentence on that May 4: death by firing squad. However, the actual execution of this sentence would be postponed until it could be confirmed by an actual authorized judge. Drossel assumed that he had the officers who were sitting as tribunal members to thank for this not insignificant detail. The entire situation left him strangely cold. He was simply too tired to feel any fear. The prisoner was locked in an empty rabbit hutch. He sank into the straw and immediately fell asleep.

A scratching at the hutch door woke him up again. His adjutant, Weber, had somehow found him, and he freed Drossel from his prison. During the past few hours, the village had been completely abandoned. Sergeant Weber had prepared for their flight as best he could. Two bicycles packed with supplies leaned against a nearby house wall. Drossel also contributed to the cause; somewhere he was able to steal two sets of authorized travel papers. Weber and Drossel could only amateurishly falsify the papers, but they felt better with them than without them. Before midnight, the two of them left the town.

Soon they stumbled across a rail line. They met German soldiers who were crouching on a transport train and waiting for it to continue on its course. Weber and Drossel joined this group. No one asked for any papers. Everyone was united in a common effort to not cross paths with "the Russians." All of them were fleeing. From a distance, they could observe troop movements, although it was not clear if the soldiers were Russian or German. No civilians could be seen anywhere. The trip ended in Bohemian Trübau, and here there was a waiting personnel train with an officer and enlisted sections. Presumably it was traveling toward the Reich.

"That night, we passed through Pardubitz [today, Pardubice (Czech Republic) on the Elbe River]. From one bridge, we could see a group of armed Czech militiamen in the street. We stopped at the station. Here, there was another militia, but they took no notice of us. On the tracks across from us stood two transport trains. These were guarded by two armed German soldiers. The cars contained highly valuable ordnance, but they could not be opened. Strict orders. In case of violence, the weapons were to be used. Good grief, violence—German delusions. A captain walked up to one of the guards and took his weapon away. One wave, and the cars were broken open. They were full of chocolate, chocolate cola, and other valuable provisions. German idiocy in its extreme. Armed Czech militiamen already patrolled the station, but two Hansels defended the best foodstuffs with guns in hand—against their own comrades."[98]

Better provisioned now, the train departed, but its trip ended sooner than expected. At Neu Kolin, a Czech major, who commanded a militia group of about 200 men, explained that the train could not travel any farther, because it was "not safe." Cluelessness and uncertainty ran rampant among the soldiers. Discussions and wild plans swirled around the possiblity of overrunning the militia. These were forged and abandoned in quick succession. At some point, Drossel simply had enough. He got off the train, and Sergeant Weber followed him. They surrendered their weapons to the Czech major and explained that they were placing themselves at his mercy. Gradually, the other men followed their example. The Czech officer declared them to be "free," and they could go wherever they wanted.

After some thoughtful discussions, Drossel and Weber made their decision. Their chances were clearly limited. They were facing advancing Soviet troops and vagabond SS groups who viewed any man who no longer believed in "Final Victory" as a deserter worthy of execution. The decision was not a difficult one for Drossel to make. "I gave the girl [someone he had spoken with previously] my medals, and then we returned to the train station. Since we had left, the building had grown pretty empty. Large piles of hand guns were scattered all over the place. I walked up to the major and told him that I wanted to be handled as a prisoner of war. He nodded and agreed that this was a smart solution . . . Two militiamen joined us, and we had to go with them along a small street . . . We were told to put our hands up, and the two men pressed their guns into our backs: 'Forward!' The place was well chosen, compliments to the major. We expected a shot in the back of the neck."[99]

However, none ever came. After several minutes of walking, the prisoners and their guards reached a camp with a field kitchen. The place was swarming with German soldiers of all grades: "The atmosphere was almost cheerful and relaxed. We were happy. We had survived. There were still a few idiots among us though. One lieutenant asked me: 'Have you seen? They are rounding us up!'"[100]

There truly were "idiots" through to the very end. Some of them believed that the reports of Hitler's death were only enemy propaganda, while others hoped hour to hour for the introduction of the ominous "miracle weapon" that was expected to singlehandedly reverse the course that the war had taken over the past three years and to bring Germany to "final victory." The tanks in which the deluded lieutenant placed his hope were actually Russian, and they were already being transported back home again.

"Wojna kaputt—War is Shit"

Ruhland, August 6, 1945

On May 6, 1945, the prisoner-of-war camp was taken over by Soviet troops. With that, a long march began. In seemingly unending columns that snaked across the land, the Russian soldiers taunted and robbed the German prisoners. Most of the time the treatment was coarse but good humored. "Mostly it was all a case of chance. Many of those who walked past did not pay us the least attention. Some of them would occasionally sock one of the men in the front in the jaw. They would laughingly comfort him with the words, 'You Sibirij!' Others would slap him cheerfully on the shoulder: 'You are heading out!' However, all of them confirmed: 'Wojna kaputt!'"[101]

More than anything else, the Russians wanted the Germans' wristwatches, but sometimes they also demanded that the defeated soldiers give up their shoes. One man tried to rescue his watch by sticking it into his boot, but he was discovered and immediately shot. Drossel willingly forfeited his Swiss watch and his boots. His sacrifice was short-lived. The new owner noted how small the shoes were and brought them back to Drossel. The guards of the prisoner procession did not engage in either theft or assault; stoically and silently, they accompanied the columns.

During this first phase of Heinz Drossel's march as a prisoner-of-war, Chief of the German General Staff Alfred Jodl signed Germany's unconditional surrender on May 7 in the American headquarters in Reims. At the request of the Soviets, the instruments of surrender were re-signed in Berlin-Karlshorst in the presence of Soviet Commanding General Georgi K. Schukow. This time Field Marshall Wilhelm Keitel signed the capitulation. The signing of the forms took place shortly after midnight on May 9, although the forms are dated May 8, 1945. World War II was officially over.

During this period, Drossel witnessed the severe mistreatment of German soldiers by the Czech victors. The Germans were chained together at their ankles and were forced to sweep the streets of various towns while being whipped. Of course, there had been collaborators in Czechoslovakia, which was one of the first victims to fall to Hitler's expansionist agenda. However, the cruelty, oppression, and humiliation practiced by the German occupiers had stoked a strong loathing of the Germans among the Czech populace. This hatred now ran unchecked.

At some point, someone tapped Drossel on the shoulder. It might be a good idea if the lieutenant removed his insignia. Drossel had not thought of this before. He followed the advice, and two hours later he was more than happy about this decision: "Three officers made their way along the line, checking each man and taking every officer into a nearby inn. We waited. After several minutes, we could hear shots coming from the cellar. . . ."[102]

The procession reached the edge of Prague on the evening of May 9. The prisoners had not yet heard about Germany's unconditional surrender on the day before. At least, Drossel did not mention anything about it in his memoirs. For a time, while located near Prague, Czech militiamen took command of the prisoners. The group moved north, and then the Russians took over and led the procession westward. The march was arduous, and the supplies were inadequate. In extreme cases, the hunger could only be suppressed by drinking water. Drossel deliberately avoided speaking a single word of Russian. He was too afraid of being mistaken as a spy.

During his march, he observed one other chilling occurrence: "Short rest. From behind, we could hear marched steps advancing toward us. Then they were upon us—a group of 60 SS men . . . their knapsacks were loaded with stones. They marched . . . in parade step, goose stepping mile after mile. They no longer noticed anything. We trotted after them and reached a town about an hour later. Here we ran into them again. They, too, were resting, six of them for eternity. These six were hanging from the lovely linden trees on the village square. We heard that in each village that they marched through, six more of them were hung. No one felt much sympathy. There were too many other things to deal with."[103]

The German prisoners of war were under the protection of the Russian soldiers, but this did not completely shield them from being the targets of upset and embittered Czech civilians. On the edge of one village, the commanding Russian officer, who spoke excellent German, brought the procession to a stop and divided the prisoners into groups of 80 men. He ordered them to march at a distance of 164 feet (50 meters) apart. "Over there is the village of Lidice—or what still remains of it. You know what that means?" the officer asked, waving in a general direction.

There was nothing left to see of Lidice. In June 1942, the Nazis had burned the entire village down to its foundations. This happened shortly after two Czech men assassinated Reinhard Heydrich, SS General, chief of the Reich Main Security Office, and Deputy Reich Director of Bohemia and Moravia. In retaliation, Gestapo and SS men killed all of the men living in Lidice who were over the age of 15: 172 men and boys. Almost 200 women were taken to the Ravensbrück Concentration Camp, of which over 50 of them were executed there. The majority of the village's approximately 90 children were gassed in another concentration camp. Today, a memorial stone commemorates the atrocity. After the war, a new village was established with the same name only a couple of miles away.

The German prisoners were forced to run the gauntlet as penance for the massacre. The alley selected for the gauntlet was about 110 yards long. The Russians neither could nor wanted to do anything to ameliorate the Czechs' thirst for revenge. The few survivors from Lidice stood along the alley with poles, clubs, and chains. Drossel came out at the other end without any wounds. Those who ran along the edges of the alley bore the brunt of the violence. Several of them were wounded. Drossel was not surprised in the least about the Czechs' pent-up fury: "This is the fruit of rage. Now we are harvesting what Hitler planted. I am affected—but I cannot condemn them."

The men grew hungrier. During one night encampment, Drossel knelt beside the camp's fence and begged for bread from those who walked by. Many passers-by had pity and gave him and the other starving soldiers what they could. Farther and farther on, toward Germany. Through Saxony and the Ore Mountains. Nights were spent in open fields surrounded by machine guns that periodically fired off rounds. The bullets lodged themselves low in the field furrows. It began to rain, and the ragamuffin group, tired and hungry, trudged across the land. Close to Pirna near Dresden, the men received bread for the first time in weeks. Since leaving Trübau, the men had covered almost 250 miles. Drossel and the other men were initially quartered in an old garrison that was already packed with prisoners of war.

Soldiers lay everywhere, on the floor, on tables, even on top of cupboards. The close quarters were not the only downside for the prisoners: "What we had to learn first was how to wash. Each of us had to stand naked in front of a watering hole and completely wash ourselves without even a small piece of soap. It would have been quite refreshing, if a female Russian doctor had not been standing nearby . . . here and there, you would see groping. Other soldiers, who had reached this spot before we had, were already occupied with the next task—cleaning out the latrines."[104] One must keep in mind that the experiences of Drossel and his companions were relatively mild. They did not have to suffer through sadistic terror or true, debilitating starvation. Many prisoners of war starved to death or were so badly mistreated that they died.

What had meant death only a few days before now became an advantage: the officers received preferential treatment. They were exempted from work details, having to shave their heads bald, and having to wash themselves under supervision. Furthermore, their quarters were more comfortable, and they received better provisions. Drossel decided to swap sides again, in the hope of avoiding the obligatory head shaving that was given to all of the lower soldiers. He succeeded in getting someone to listen to him. He acted a little arrogant, but told the truth about why he had temporarily lied about his officer status. In the end, he achieved his goal. He was taken to the separate officers' area in the camp and was re-registered there.

The officers' camp was self-regulated. Drossel became friends with a former lieutenant, a forester from the Spessart region by the name of Joachim L.[105] The provisions were ample, and the officers were even given a daily allotment of five cigarettes. However, L. warned his new roommate to treat the rest of the officers in the camp with great care. After ten days, the camp authorities made a request for volunteers to be transported out of the camp. Drossel had been able to recover sufficiently from the hardships of the march, so along with Joachim, he volunteered for the group that would be sent on.

They departed several days later. Again, on foot: "After about 15 miles, we got our first shocking glimpse of the Germany that had wanted total war. Or better said, of what was left of it. Dresden—we marched straight through the city. It was a wasteland, as far as the eye could see, only broken up by the ruins of the Zwinger Palace, one of the most beautiful buildings in all of Germany, and the cathedral. Otherwise, there were only mountains of rubble through which earthmovers and bulldozers cut 2- to 3-meter-wide swathes that ran through the entire city center. The sickeningly sweet smell of death hung over everything. A hundred thousand people had died! This is where the separation occurs—those who learn nothing from this will never learn anything. The columns trudged mutely through the rubble-bedecked graveyard, which had once been a glorious, lively city."[106]

What Drossel witnessed was the result of the firestorm that took place between February 13 and 15, 1945. The Allies dropped tons of incendiary and high explosive bombs onto the so-called Florence on the Elbe. No one knows for sure how many people were killed in the attack. Estimates usually fall between 18,000 and 25,000 victims. The city was destroyed. Even the Gestapo headquarters here was reduced to ashes. The planned deportation of the last of the Jews from Dresden never took place. Victor Klemperer was among those whose name had been included on the final deportation list. He had the bombs to thank for his survival.

Drossel's column stayed quiet for a long time, even after it had left the scene of devastation. They continued along the Elbe River Valley toward Senftenberg. After marching for several days, they finally reached the former Ruhland Reich work camp in the Upper Lusatia area: "Destination—or transit point? We had to go through the gate and be registered. The moment I crossed into the camp, it happened. My bowels emptied themselves into my pants, just as my nerves completely failed. I hauled myself onward. My first task at Ruhland was to wash my own underthings. It was the only time during the entire war that this happened to me."[107]

Once again Drossel was lodged with forester Joachim L. The camp was well maintained and administered. Drossel described the commander as "just and humane." All told, about 1,000 prisoners were kept here. This camp also organized its prisoners by officer status. The provisions were sufficient, although the hygiene here left much to be desired. The first cases of dysentery soon developed, but according to Drossel's estimation, the death rate was relatively low. A sick bay was set up. The camp commander even confiscated an empty dentist's office in the town. One of the prisoners was a dentist, and he treated the sick prisoners. Several musicians in the camp set up an ensemble, which played for the Russian officers. The officers were composed of members of an indigenous group of German-speaking Russians, who were feared for their brutality.

Drossel and his new friend Joachim L. soon discovered that their sleeping quarters was the source of their greatest fears. They learned quickly that one of their "roommates" was a former SS leader and concentration camp warden. Together with five other diehard Nazis, he was plotting an escape. Most of the others stayed quiet and tried to ignore the six plotters. However, L. and Drossel refused to hide their aversion to the Nazis. This would prove a costly choice. They experienced daily harassment, terrorization, and violence. The other men in the quarters were soon so afraid that they avoided helping Drossel when he was struck with an acute case of rheumatism and could not walk unaided. Only L. stood by him and helped him back and forth to the latrine.

August 6 was a day like any other day for the Ruhland prisoners. It was summery and warm. The low-ranking soldiers fulfilled their duties, while the officers, who had no work details, attempted to fill the hours as best they could. Lunch was the high point of the day. One day later, rumors began to circulate through the camp that the Russians wanted to disassemble everything they possibly could. They planned to load trucks with machines and building materials, and take off because the Americans were coming. The rumors subsided. What the prisoners did not know was that on August 6, the American air force had dropped an atom bomb on Hiroshima. By late December, approximately 140,000 people had been killed by the effects of the bomb.[108] Another bomb was dropped on Nagasaki on August 9.

Drossel regained his strength. A Russian doctor concocted a vitamin supplement that helped him to overcome the rheumatism. The "old fighters" in Drossel's barracks increased the expressions of their hatred toward the two men they viewed as "turncoats." Drossel was tipped off that the SS man wanted to murder them before he and the others escaped. L. and Drossel decided that they would sleep in shifts. The entire situation became unbearable. After yet another warning, Drossel finally turned to a Russian officer and explained that he was suspicious that one of the men in his barracks had been an SS man. Two days later, the SS man was interrogated by a Soviet commissar, and the former named his co-conspirators as additional members of SS. From this point on, Drossel and L. did not need to fear for their lives.

A few days later, news spread throughout the camp: work gangs had spent the entire day working on a long transport train. They had been instructed to construct small latrines in the cars and to secure the holes with barbed wire. It was clear to everyone what this meant. The Russians were preparing to transport the prisoners to Siberia. It was not long before the former Wehrmacht soldiers and officers were called up in front of a medical commission. They were examined for their fitness to work: "The soldiers stood in long lines, naked and quaking inside. At the front, there was a long table around which numerous civilians sat along with white-robed Soviet officers and secretaries. The doctors were almost all women. The people were examined. After a short discussion, the decision was made quickly: left or right. Those capable of labor were on the left, and those deemed incapable went to the right. Very few people were directed to the right."[109]

Drossel estimated that of the approximately 1,000 prisoners, only 50 or 60 were declared unfit for labor. They were released from captivity. A few days later, the 25 officers were brought out: "We only had to remove our shirts. We stood in a row in front of the chief doctor, and in the back were the camp commander and a secretary. There were no women here. We were divided into three groups: left unfit, middle fit, right special handling for SS men and those suspected of being such." The underside of the upper left arm was carefully examined. This was the location of the obligatory SS blood group tattoos, which some men had tried to have removed through relatively amateurish operations. Besides the already identified men from Drossel's barracks, several others were directed to the right. Only four men received the verdict of "unfit," a group that included Heinz Drossel and his friend Joachim.

Several days later, it was all over. Drossel received his release papers. He was a free man again and was allowed to leave the camp. The Russians were friendly and cheerful. They arranged for a hand cart and insisted that the rheumatic sufferer (who was actually almost healthy again) should sit in it and be taken to the train station. By this point, the camp had been almost completely dismantled. Heinz Drossel's departure corresponded with the annual local fair. The few musicians still in the camp picked up their instruments and played: "*Musi denn, musi denn, zum Städtele hinaus . . .*" as Joachim pulled the cart with Heinz in it to the train station. Joachim L. was released that day as well. At the train station, they parted ways forever. The train to Berlin was packed beyond capacity. People crouched right up next to each other in the cars. They were everywhere in the passageways, they stood in the steps, and they hung onto the doors. Refugees, returning soldiers, people who had fled their homes— all were trying to get back home. For the last stretch before his destination, Drossel had a special place in the train. With hooting and hollering, he was pulled through the window of the bathroom, which he shared with several other men. He disembarked at Königs Wusterhausen. He was almost there. Senzig was not far anymore, only a short walk. But he had mixed feelings. He did not know if his parents were still alive. He had had no contact with them since March. En route, he was stopped by a single Soviet soldier. Instead of the conflict he feared, there was a friendly, silent cigarette. When they were done smoking, the Soviet bid the German farewell: "Comrade, now you are home. War is shit."

Drossel did not think about much over the last few hundred yards to his parents' cottage. He was nervous. He rang the bell on the garden gate. The door opened quickly, and his mother looked out at him. And he experienced what so many other young Germans did in those days: his own mother did not recognize him. She studied him curiously with pity in her eyes. Then she turned back toward the house and called out to her husband: "Come here, Paul. There is a ragged soldier standing here. Perhaps he has heard something about Heinz."

VI. After the War (August 1945–1962)

"We Did Not Talk Long"

Berlin-Tempelhof, Fall 1945

Heinz Drossel spent only one night with his parents in Senzig. His father Paul insisted that he return to Berlin. The rationale was that in the anonymous city—or what remained of it—Heinz would be relatively safe from the Russians' hunger for revenge. The Soviet occupiers were reputedly "gathering up" random people and taking them into custody. They frequently patrolled Senzig and the surrounding area. Heinz's hard-earned freedom was not something to be placed at risk.

Drossel moved back into his room in Tempelhof and contacted his friend Poldi. He soon discovered other friends close

Residential permit for Heinz Drossel in Berlin-Tempelhof

to where his father's shop had once been located. The Hass family and Günter Fontheim were staying nearby. The four survivors had moved into a large Art Nouveau apartment that had been previously occupied by a Nazi and his family. Tailor Jack Hass had received permission from the Allies to open a clothing shop. Already as early as Summer 1945, Lucy Hass, his energetic, engaged wife, was providing an initial contact point for Jews coming out of hiding or the few returning from the concentration camps, all of whom had no money or anywhere to live. She did this all on her own at first, without any outside financial support. She established contact with the new regional authorities and later with the American liberators. In late July, the western Allies arrived in Berlin, and the city was divided into sectors. Tempelhof fell under the American administration.

During the first post-war months, the majority of the population was overwhelmed by existential questions, material needs, hunger, and "morale blues." Germany had lost the war, and the Nazi propaganda, which had through the end promised victory, was uncovered as a great lie. Few Germans actually felt "liberated." Of course, they were relieved that the war was over, but initially they were gripped by a kind of collective depression that prevented them from looking with optimism into the future. The people felt betrayed. Many of them were afraid that they would be punished. The future seemed bleak. Day-to-day life was overshadowed by the sad loss of relatives and property and by the search for food. Above all, the lives of millions of homeless people were shaped by exhaustion and resignation.[110]

However, in the Hass house, there was much to celebrate. The connections to the Americans quickly increased and were friendly in nature. Soon Heinz Drossel was spending every evening with the Hasses, who were always glad to have him over. Cigarettes by the box, alcohol, chocolate—nothing was lacking. After all of the fear, chaos, and anger, it was good to spend a few carefree hours together. Despite all of the suffering and concerns that they had gone through, now there was again reason to be happy. They were actually freed. They no longer had to hide. They had survived, and the cruelty was over.

Marianne and Heinz

Drossel was optimistic, although he had no idea what the future would bring. One evening, he again went over to his friends' apartment. He was looking forward to another evening spent with like-minded friends, a glass of whiskey, a couple of cigarettes. One of the Americans would call out: "Heinz, make a toast!" And Heinz would toss off a toast in English as well as in German, at which they would all raise their glasses and break into laughter after only one sip, just because it was so glorious to laugh again.

He entered the spacious living room that was full of people. Directly in front of the door, there was a large sofa. Five people were sitting on it that evening. In the middle, a delicate woman. She looked up into his eyes. He recognized her, and she recognized him. She jumped up—Marianne, the woman from the Jungfern Bridge, the woman whose survival had been so uncertain. She now stood in front of him, and they hugged each other. It was an intoxicating party. "We did not talk much," Heinz Drossel recalled of this moment decades later. Several hours later, Marianne accompanied her future husband to his apartment.

The Past Should Rest in Peace

Saarbrücken, June 1945

They spent as much time together as possible. This third meeting was overwhelming. They had to believe that they were meant to be together. They shared warmth, and in return, their intimacy gave them the feeling of being truly alive, of being human. The companionship in the here and now helped them to stop thinking about the past. Heinz did not ask many questions. This was good for Marianne in those days. She wanted to forget. Heinz, too, did not want to actively recall the horrible experiences he had been through during the war. The past should rest in peace.

How had Marianne survived? She fled from Berlin, leaving behind her two children. The small girl was still under the care of the hospital personnel, and the boy was living with an acquaintance. She did what seemed to make the most sense in her dire circumstances. No one can ever know how difficult this decision was. It could be that later in life she was ashamed of what she did, even though both children survived the war. Perhaps she felt guilty for leaving. Regardless, she never spoke of this.

Marianne Hirschfeld and Heinz Drossel in
the Hass family apartment, winter 1945–1946

Years later, a psychologist, who examined Marianne's daughter in Israel and only knew the child's history in bits and pieces from medical documents, diagnosed Marianne from a distance as a "serious psychotic," because she did not stay with her child. He did not mention in his evaluation the conditions under which German Jews were living during the first half of the 1940s.

Many survivors were faced with unarticulated speculations and negative suspicions. The question always was: if the murder apparatus was so perfect, how could anyone have survived it? Why did you survive? Many of those who found a way to escape the murderous machine asked themselves these same questions and suffered for the rest of their lives with feelings of guilt, regardless of whether they, in their adversity, actually had anything to feel guilty for.

By late January 1945, the Red Army had reached Breslau, about 220 miles from Berlin. It had advanced as far as Stettin by early February, a distance of only 90 miles from the capital city. War-weary Germans, anti-Nazis, and also Jews, such as Victor Klemperer, closely followed the army reports, hopeful of a swift end to the war: "Elevated and excited mood. According to yesterday's German army report, the Russians are northwest of Küstrin. The English reports claim that they are in Landsberg A.W. and Küstrin . . . Chaos in Berlin. Refugees and troops are jammed in the city, and they had a very severe bomb attack during our last alarm . . . ; the Russians are lined up along the Oder River for a frontal attack on Berlin . . ."[111]

Marianne left Berlin in February 1945. For a few weeks prior to her departure, she had vanished underground in a camp for French forced laborers, whom she knew from her time with the provincial cable works. The camp was located on Belzig Street. Her French was good enough that she did not awaken any curiosity, even from those who were not acquainted with her. She passed herself off as a French laborer. She either possessed falsified papers, or she claimed that her identification papers had been destroyed in one of the night air raids and received an authorized temporary pass.

In these days, people frequently lost everything except for what they wore on their very backs. No one had the time or the opportunity

126

to verify claims of loss. Some Jewish persecutees were bold enough to use this circumstance to their advantage. They would report to a refugee camp, tell of a bombing attack on the train they were traveling on from somewhere like East Prussia, and were then registered. Thus, they received papers, could stop living their underground existence, and could eventually leave the refugee camp for points west. Almost everyone wanted to head west at this point; fear of the Russians united Jews and Christians, Nazis and anti-Nazis.

Marianne and her friends decided to utilize the general chaos of the nighttime and daytime bombing raids, and the gradually crumbling political apparatus to vanish. They fled toward the west and the Allied troops located that direction. Despite the confusion, there was still a danger that they could be discovered, since German patrols were doggedly searching for deserters. The calls from the German army headquarters to keep fighting were of little avail. The number of deserters increased to the thousands. Captured deserters were hung along the roadsides as a means to discourage flight. They were often furnished with signs that read, "I am a traitorous pig."

The refugees ran during the night and hid during the day. The group was quite small, and Marianne was the only woman. After several days, they crossed paths with Allied soldiers, and they were taken to a holding camp for Frenchmen at Jeumont on the Belgian-French border. In her restitution protocol from December 6, 1951, Marianne explained what happened next: "After a careful examination of my case, I was allowed to travel to acquaintances living in Lille and Valenciennes. I stayed here until the end of the war."

According to Günter Fontheim, the friend of the Drossels, this is not the course of events that actually transpired. He recalled that Marianne left Berlin in the company of a particularly close friend within the group. She felt closely connected to him. Perhaps this person was Luis, the father of Marianne's daughter. After the end of the war, he was repatriated to France, and she wanted to go with him. However, she was not allowed to cross the border. A French civil servant refused to grant her permission to do so.

What is certain is that in June 1945, Marianne was staying in Saarbrücken. On June 23, the city's labor office granted her a "work card": Identification Number 2333 with the comment that she was "[a Jewess] initially freed from employment." From Saarbrücken, she returned to Berlin. Marianne was separated from her son and daughter for only a matter of a few months.

She went back to Tempelhof, her old neighborhood. She had heard of a branch office of the Jewish congregation that was offering aid and support. Here she once again met her friend Margot. The "congregational branch office" was actually the Hass family apartment. What joy and relief! The hope of again meeting acquaintances and friends grew.

Marianne neither attempted to establish contact with her daughter Judis nor did she ever explain why. Heinz either could not or did not wish to mention the issue. He remained non-committal when asked if, after her return, Marianne visited the Jewish hospital where Judis had been living the last time she had inquired: "She may have done so." It is unlikely that he simply refused to reveal what he knew. He gave the impression that the couple never openly discussed this or other aspects of the past.

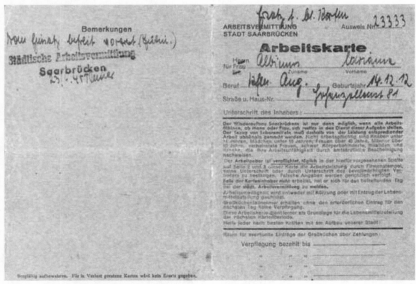

Marianne Albinus's work card, Saarbrücken, 1945

In August 1945, shortly before her third birthday, Judis was in Berlin. The girl was living in the Niederschönhausen Children's Home at Moltke Street 8/11. Her name was included on the membership roster for the Jewish congregation: "List III: List of the registered Jews in Berlin receiving care from the Allies, who were described as 'privileged' and not required to wear the Star of David and whose deportation . . . was postponed." The questionnaire was filled out and signed by Bernhard Baruch, the director of the children's home, on August 6, 1945. This means that Judis's name was included on a list of survivors available to the public.

Marianne had no problem finding her son Billy. A friend or acquaintance had hidden him and taken care of him. However, this was not Eva Fischer, the woman who had hidden Marianne for several weeks in late 1944 when she had lived in such great fear of the Gestapo. At that time, Marianne had still been working nights for the BVG.

For several months, an unnamed woman had taken care of Billy. "This woman," as Heinz called her—because he did not know her name and because she obviously ran a not entirely acceptable business—"also had contact with the Americans" after the war. Not much more could ever be found out about where Marianne's son lived. Several times, Heinz also stated that he was in a Lutheran children's home. No one ever said more about when and where this could have been. The childhood of this boy was primarily a shadow existence.

This "friend or whatever she was" had possibly been a prostitute during the war. It could be that after the war she searched for and found a protector, someone who made sure she had enough food— and the close relationship she provided to him was also beneficial for her. In any case, Heinz viewed her reputation as dubious at best. Later, the family did not maintain any contact with "this woman." Whenever Heinz spoke about the protectress of his stepson, his words carried a disparaging note. A quiet accusation was also present, an accusation that perhaps even Marianne herself sometimes felt.

However, the first months after the reunion were untroubled and full of hope. Only a few weeks passed before Heinz and Marianne moved in together. On May 4, 1946, exactly one year after Heinz had been sentenced to death and locked in a rabbit hutch in some small Bohemian village, they were married in the registry office in Tempelhof.

They shared a three-bedroom apartment in Tempelhof that was located near Tante Thea's apartment. Billy lived with them, and they were a real family. Marianne worked for American Joint, a charity organization that was dedicated to helping the survivors of the Holocaust. Later, she also worked for a bakery that was attached to a small café. Shortly after his return, Heinz filed an application to resume his legal clerkship in order to complete his legal studies.

Marianne and Heinz, wedding photo, May 4, 1946

In late 1946, Heinz received an invitation to the official ceremony that would begin his clerkship. In the Supreme Court, a civil servant welcomed him disconcertingly with the following order: he needed to "snap to attention." Heinz was stunned, and he turned on his heel and walked out. He had had enough of standing at attention and taking orders for the rest of his life. One week later, he received a new invitation from the President of the Supreme Court. This time the ceremony went off without a hitch. Because of his military service, his clerkship period was reduced from 36 months to 18 months.

However, he was not able to start his duties immediately because he quickly came down with a serious case of tuberculosis.

The Issue with Koschinski

In the meanwhile, Heinz Drossel's father Paul had become politically active in Senzig. He wanted to be involved with the reconstruction of a democratic state. The bourgeois-liberal salesman possessed the ability to sway his fellow citizens. In November 1946, in the state elections in the Soviet Occupation Zone (SOZ), which were the first elections in Germany since the end of the war, he was elected mayor. He was a member of the Liberal-Democratic Party (LDP). In Senzig, which today is a part of Königs Wusterhausen, a small city in Brandenburg, the Kremlin-controlled Socialist Unity Party (SUP) dominated the political decisions made here, as it did in other municipalities in the SOZ.

Paul Drossel, who had survived the Nazi dictatorship through inner determination, abhorred every form of totalitarian leadership. After the war, he made no attempt to hide his views. The catalyst for his and his family's personal catastrophe was not, however, public political confrontation but a kind of secretive intrigue.

In the early morning hours of March 11, 1948, the police arrested Paul Drossel in his apartment in Senzig. He was taken to the prison in Königs Wusterhausen. Initially, the family was not given any concrete reason for his arrest. Sometime later it came out that a complaint had been filed against Drossel and his son Heinz. They were accused of crimes against humanity.

Heinz Drossel described the background to this in a letter dated July 20, 1948, to his friend Günter Fontheim, who had emigrated to America in the interim: "Soon after the collapse [after the end of the war], 'Mr.' Koschinski came up with the idea of taking possession of my father's business. However, soon after that my father appeared in Tempelhof, and to K.'s irritation, I showed up there myself in September, too. In order to take us both out of the way, [K.] decided to file a complaint at the Communist Party headquarters. He accused my father of crimes against humanity and me of membership in the SA, as well as other things. As a basis for his accusation against my father, he claimed that in the final days of the war, my father had

Drossel family home in Senzig

tried to take him to a concentration camp. He also stated that my father had ordered Mrs. Koschinski to distribute fliers for the Nazi Party and other things."[112]

Plaintiff Koschinski was the caretaker and manager of the apartment house on Berliner Street in Tempelhof where the Drossel family lived until they were forced to leave. He was the man who had hidden Fontheim, believing him to be a deserter. His complaint against his former housemate first landed at the Tempelhof SUP State Office. For the time being, it was simply ignored. However, when Paul Drossel was elected as LDP mayor in Senzig, the complaint resurfaced at the Potsdam SUP State Office. It was a well-known fact that Drossel, Sr. was not willing to unconditionally subordinate himself to the wishes of the SUP.

As a witness, Koschinski had named a Mr. Röder, who provided a notarized statement about the alleged fascist activities of the Drossel father and son. As Heinz revealed to his friend in his letter, Röder had testified "that my father had, among other things, taken people to a concentration camp, and that, through the end of the war, I had been a big Nazi and had behaved just like my father."[113]

132

When Drossel, Jr. confronted Röder with these accusations, it turned out that he didn't even know the Drossel family. Without hesitation, Röder made an official sworn statement that he had never given this notarized claim against the Drossels.

Drossel sent a copy of this document to Potsdam and filed a penalty demand against Koschinski for libel. Later, in the pre-examination process, no mention was made about "crimes against humanity." The mayor of Senzig had in the meanwhile been removed from office, and he was accused of yet another infraction: the theft of a bicycle. Marianne Drossel called the entire affair a "grotesque, ridiculous thing."[114]

Paul Drossel was released after the election of a new mayor for the Senzig community. Shortly thereafter, the SUP filed a complaint against him for extortion, but the accusation was relatively quickly withdrawn. In Spring 1948, Drossel refused to take part in the "Referendum for the People's Decision about German Unity." This position was the one adopted by most of his LDP friends. However, on June 13, Drossel was picked up at his home. He was forced to cast his vote on the final day of the decision period. On August 4, Drossel vanished for a period of at least 11 days. Without just cause, the police had again detained him, keeping him at an unspecified location.

The SUP-initiated "People's Congress Movement for Unity and Fair Freedom" had organized and drafted the referendum. The SUP party leadership sent out invitations for a demonstration on November 26, 1947, which was to involve Germans from all of the occupation zones. The delegates were, in theory, supposed to represent all Germans, but none of the parties and unions from the western zones, except for the Communist Party, agreed to participate. On December 6 and 7, the First German People's Congress was convened. The 2,225 representatives, who were also involved with the Second German People's Congress, came from a variety of parties, unions, and cultural organizations. In the SOZ, the groups had been more or less integrated into the SUP-leadership apparatus, under the control of the USSR. 1,664 delegates traveled from the western zones, including representatives of the Socialist Democratic Party (SPD). The eastern zone Christian Democratic

Union (CDU) declined to be involved. Against the majority will of its members, the LDP chose to participate.

On June 3, 1948, the *Zeit* newspaper was emblazoned with the headline: "People's Referendum-People's Oppression." A long article was dedicated to coverage of the initiative. The following description was contained in it: "A 'control card' separated the signers from those who refused to sign . . . From the very start, there was no attempt to hide the secret voting pertaining to the 'referendum.' Rather, the official voting lists, organized by houses, districts, and neighborhoods, were publicly posted in thousands of restaurants and businesses. Every blank space was marked publicly as 'sabotage,' and those people were sometimes persecuted." Paul Drossel's public refusal to participate in the referendum seems to have been used as justification for treating him over the span of several years as a persona non grata.

In March 1948, the Second German People's Congress rejected the Marshall Plan that was being promoted by the western Allies, and it further rejected the recognition of the new border between Poland and Germany as it had been redrawn along the Oder and Neisse rivers. In addition, the Congress passed the referendum which demanded German unity.

Of course, the differences between the eastern and western Allies played a major role in the opinions expressed by and the initiatives proposed by the People's Congress. According to *Zeit*, "The occupying powers have spoken on the topic of the 'referendum.' This, too, reflects a politicized evaluation of Germany's prospects by the ruling powers, through which the 'referendum' has been completely moved into the tactical field of East-West tensions. In Berlin, the American and French military governments publicly explained their failure to collect the votes for the referendum because of their view of the endeavor representing a forced maneuvering by the Communists to meet non-German goals."

It was clear that in reality the referendum was directly linked to the ideological and political leadership goals of the occupying powers, and had little to do with the Germans' freedom to

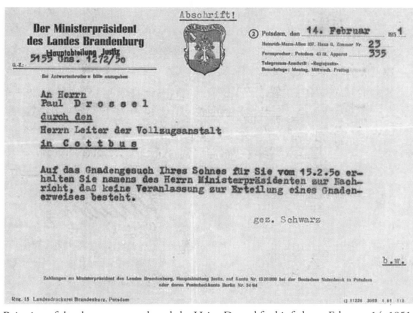

Rejection of the clemency appeal made by Heinz Drossel for his father—February 14, 1951

self-determine the shape of their future. In any case, the *Zeit* journalists bluntly criticized the proceedings: "At the behest of the host powers, the request was made to not discuss the content and boundaries of the demanded unity or the extension of the German territory. The calls for signature collections continue to go out, even as the eastern zone is throttled with a growing number of new control measures from the other zones."

The Allies continued to drift further and further apart. Their original collective goals—de-centralization, de-Nazification, democratization, breaking of the German industrial complex—for the creation of a new Germany could not be implemented because of differing ideological and political perspectives.[115] Starting in 1948, the USSR sought to establish a German state that could be influenced by Moscow. The western Allies set up the creation of the Federal Republic, which would belong to NATO. On May 23, 1949, the West German state was founded. The German Democratic Republic (GDR) was established on October 7.

In late 1948, Paul Drossel was sent to prison for three years for "economic offenses." According to the complaint, during his time as mayor, he supposedly misappropriated products harvested by the farmers in the Senzig area. He was accused of stealing, on a grand scale, bread, flour, potatoes, and such. Pleas for clemency were refused without any reasons being given. He sat in the Luckau Prison for the full duration of his sentence.

Already as early as Spring 1946, the authorities once again reduced the food ration quotas. A "normal" citizen in the British zone was supposed to receive 1,100 calories per day.[116] Although they were living in the American zone, Heinz and Marianne Drossel were among those who went hungry during the period right after the war. The situation improved for the young family over the course of 1947. They received support from various sources. Marianne's sister in Israel sent food to them. A family in America with which Heinz had corresponded as a schoolboy sent over packages. The Drossels also received support from the Jewish charity organization American Joint. Heinz Drossel described the situation as "almost luxurious" in a letter from January 1948 that he sent to his friend Günter Fontheim, who had emigrated to America in early 1947.

In all reality, there was no true luxury here. Both Marianne and Heinz were suffering from major health problems, and furthermore, they faced immense professional difficulties and a disastrous financial situation. In December 1947, Heinz Drossel enrolled in an interpreter course, which he completed as the best in his class. However, the prospect of a job with a US office quickly faded. The location of his parents' residence in the Soviet Zone was one primary reason for this. Heinz thought that the Americans feared that he could be potentially pressured by the Soviets. For example, they could threaten his father if he refused to provide them with information about his employer.

Besides the fears pertaining to the well-being of the father and husband, Paul's family was troubled by the incredible unfairness that he faced. His own emotional state was clearly reflected in a letter that he wrote after his first imprisonment:

136

"My dear Mr. Fontheim. It was not my intention to make you wait such a long time for a letter from me. But today's arrival of your surprises of chocolate and the savory canned fish have reminded me of my negligence. You must know, my dear Mr. Fontheim, how delighted we were with your gift and how sincerely we want to thank you for it. Above all, I am glad that you have not forgotten about us completely. I am sure you know, good Mr. Fontheim, how one can lose all faith in other people. This has especially been true after the recent events that we were put through over the past several months. As a result, you end up cutting yourself off from others more than you had done in the past. Now you know my mindset, but I must admit that I still regret that here there are so few individuals with whom one can truly build friendships. Despite the difficult times, it was so nice when you and the Hass family were living close to us. Yes, I miss even that . . . I am sure that Heinz has told you all about what has happened to us in the past few months . . . We have been through so much. There is not much more that I can say. Yes, this is what can happen to such a fanatic anti-fascist. And our enemies? We do not discuss them much, since there is no point. Be happy that you live over there, since here the difficulties just seem to get bigger all the time. Whenever one thinks about the rations, forgive me, I don't want to talk about food—it makes a bad impression."[117]

The proceedings against Drossel were obviously a farce, and the situation for the entire family soon became a nightmare. In prison, Paul Drossel did not receive enough food, and it was hard for his family to provide him with sufficient supplies. Periodically, his health suffered so badly that he was moved to a hospital. During this time, he was allowed to receive coffee. His son and his daughter-in-law shared this with him via their generous care packages from America.

At the time of his release in 1951, Paul Drossel was a sick, broken man. He died of cancer in Berlin-Tempelhof in November 1954. Soon after his incarceration, Elfriede Drossel reached the limits of her physical and emotional strengths. In August 1948, after the disappearance of her husband, she wanted to move into the city to be close to her son. She was scared, and she did not function well on her own. However, she never followed through on this plan. When her husband was convicted and put in prison, she was afraid that she would not be allowed to visit him if she moved to the western section of Berlin. During the year after Paul's release, the Drossels left Senzig and moved back to Tempelhof.

"Suddenly Poor"

Helmstedt, June 20, 1948

In January 1948, Heinz Drossel inquired about jobs through the Berlin company, Büttner & Co., which had just recently extended its activities into a new business endeavor. Büttner & Co. sent representatives into the barracks in the American Occupation Zone in order to offer the soldiers a specific service. They could commission oil portraits to be made for their loved ones back home. For this purpose, the company was employing artists of varying degrees of talent and English-speaking sales representatives to find new clients. Starting on February 15, 1948, Drossel was one of these new employees. He became the official company representative in southern Bavaria.

The first trip was scheduled for mid-March, and he traveled to Traunstein. He named his old friend Poldi as a reference in his search for lodging. The agent warned him that he would have a difficult time trying to find a place to stay considering how late in the day he arrived in the small city. In addition, the fact that he was "a Prussian" made the matter all the worse. Nonetheless, Drossel soon found suitable and accommodating lodging at a local inn.

He quickly learned that he was not a very effective salesman. However, his start on the morning after his arrival had seemed quite promising. Even the ease with which he gained access to the barracks seemed too easy. No one wanted to examine his identification papers or seemed even slightly concerned about the foreigner in civilian

138

clothes who was carrying around a large portfolio with him. Drossel asked for directions to the commander's office, the door of which was standing wide open.

After a short while, the commanding officer appeared, listened sympathetically to the German's intent, and recommended that he try his luck in the mess hall. The GIs were quite friendly, but the presentation by the short man in civilian clothes was not particularly convincing. He received very few orders. Looking back, Drossel recalled, "Others were more clever. They never returned home without two or three dozen orders." He laughed at himself: "I was too dumb. I was certainly no salesman." Regardless, Büttner & Co. still paid him a salary of 250 Reichsmarks for his three months of work.

Back in Berlin, Drossel submitted his contracts to Büttner, and the artists got to work creating authentic European artworks for the American soldiers. Two weeks later, the art handler traveled back to Traunstein to deliver the oil paintings. He was just in time to enjoy the arrival of spring: "I went for walks and spent very little time in the barracks," Drossel explained. During one of these walks, he came up with the idea of bringing his wife Marianne and stepson Billy on his next trip to scenic Bavaria.

"After 1,001 formalities (certificates, approvals, applications, forms, recommendations, public health forms, interzonal passes, appointments, tickets), the trip could finally start. After 32 hours of constant travel, we finally reached Traunstein. There was more than enough excitement here. No one wanted us here, because we were 1) Prussian and 2) Jewish. In the end, I was able to push hard enough that they 'tolerated' us there. Description: glorious landscape, wonderful air, insufficient supplies, bad treatment."[118] As Drossel told his friend, Marianne was just recovering from a three-week stay in a hospital due to an intestinal illness. She had gone through surgery, and as a result, she had lost quite a bit of weight. She weighed less than 90 pounds, and she was weak and delicate. The change of air must have been good for her.

For Drossel's wife and 12-year-old Billy, this was the first time that they had been able to leave the city that had been the context of their traumatic experiences. They could breathe more slowly and recuperate. In comparison with experiences of most other Germans at this time, this modest trip was like a small miracle. The daily fight for survival limited the day-to-day existence of most people.

On June 17, 1948, Drossel learned that the currency reform was ready to go into effect. The miracle was over. They left the next day on the early train through Munich to Hanover. Here they had to wait until June 19 to catch a train back to Berlin. As Drossel remembered: "It was early in the morning. Numerous people were traveling that day. The train traveling toward Helmstedt was full of workers. We pushed our way into the compartment, found a spot, and then I noticed the headline of the newspaper held by the person sitting across from me: 'Currency Reform at Midnight!'"

Announced to occur on Saturday, June 19, 1948, the quickly implemented currency reform surprised many Germans in the western sectors. The Reichsmark was no longer legal tender, and on Sunday morning, the distribution of the D-Mark began. Every adult received 40 Deutsche Marks. As of June 21, the D-Mark was the sole legal currency in the occupation zones of the western Allies.

Most of the people who experienced "Day X," that June 20 on which the new money was handed out, associated that momentous day with long lines. They stood in line for the new money that was to hail the advent of a new era, one without deprivation, ration cards, or ration coupons. The planning that led up to this reform had been carried out mostly in secret. Of course, rumors had run rampant during the days and weeks leading up to the reform, but they died down almost as quickly as they flared up. It was hard for people to actually imagine or accept the fact that such a radical change was being planned. They were concerned but hopeful. Many remained skeptical until the very last minute.

At first, the Drossels had other things to worry about. As Berliners, they were initially excluded from the currency reform. Outside of their hometown, they were officially "suddenly poor," and they fell "under the care of public welfare."[119] They had no ability to claim the money on the day of the reform. In a camp set up for individuals like themselves, they were provided with hot soup and lodging. They did not know that this was the situation that would be facing them until they arrived in Helmstedt. The train they were on was not permitted to travel any farther. At first, there were no trains that could be taken eastward. The Drossels could not proceed or go back. The situation seemed quite hopeless.

One option remained open to them. They could try to reach Tante Thea in Tempelhof. Dorothea Hirschfeld, the sister of Marianne Drossel's father, was a resolute woman who possessed influential contacts and a healthy sense of practical solutions. Heinz Drossel left his wife and stepson sitting on a bench, while he went to a post office to call the aunt.

Tante Thea had survived Theresienstadt. One Red Cross document described how she was "freed on May 8, 1945, by the Russian Army." On August 12, 1945, she was admitted to the Jewish Hospital in Berlin. Then, on May 18, 1946, she appeared again on the residential rosters for Berlin-Tempelhof. She did not resume possession of the house that had been confiscated by the Nazis, but financial restitution from the Federal Republic did help her out substantially. She rarely spoke about her time in Theresienstadt, limiting her tales to short ones about the theatrical evenings and the lending library.

The situation in Helmstedt proved to be too much for Marianne Drossel. Her weak nerves were unable to handle the arduous trip, the uncertainty, the exhaustion, and the stress. She broke down in tears. Her son Billy could do nothing but stand close by, unhappy and helpless. Then, a middle-aged woman approached them and asked what had happened. Marianne described the unfortunate impact that the approaching currency reform had had on the family from Berlin. Immediately, the woman offered to help.

Heinz Drossel returned from the post office to his wife and stepson, having failed in his attempt to reach Tante Thea.

His wife, however, shared with him the offer from the unknown local woman: the family had been invited to spend the night in her house. She had offered to feed them and give them lodging.

They would just have to wait and see what the next day brought. However, they should know one thing yet: her husband, as well as she herself, had been members of the Nazi party. Her husband had even held a party office.

Almost 60 years later, Drossel commented, "It was really very nice. She did not know what to expect of us, and she gave us a choice." Clearly, the former Nazi party member had guessed that Marianne was Jewish. Or she had recognized Billy's ethnicity. The Drossels did not spend much time considering their options. "We ignored our reservations, if we had any, and went with the woman," Drossel recalled.

The three of them spent the night in relative comfort. They had an ample breakfast the following morning, but then they had to acknowledge that the situation was still just as difficult as it had been the previous day. Drossel remembered that several Berliners, who were in the same situation as they were, asked the local authorities for assistance. In order to help these individuals as quickly as possible—or simply to get rid of them—an open-backed truck was made available to them. They would all be taken as far as the border. On foot, they would have a chance of getting over to the other side, and at the next train station in the "Eastern Zone," they could board a train to Berlin.

Billy found the drive on the truck powered by a wood gas generator to be an adventure. The adults had less positive things to say about it. At the border, Soviet soldiers forbade them entry. The group prepared itself to walk back to Helmstedt. A short time later, they met a couple of young men who offered to take them across the "green border." They wanted to be paid in "old money," which was still accepted in the SOZ. Heinz Drossel and a few others accepted their offer. One of the men presented himself as the leader of the group. About seven people followed him into the forest toward the border. As their leader stopped and told them that they had to go the final 300 yards on their own, only the Drossels and one old woman were willing to keep going. The leader described the route to them, collected his money, and left them to their fate.

A few minutes later, Billy announced that he had to go to the bathroom. His parents sent him behind a bush and waited. The old woman was too excited, so she kept going on her own. After Billy returned, they could hear shots being fired. "The bullets flew past us," Drossel described. "I threw myself onto the ground and called to the others: 'Get down! Get down!' The shooters had to be very close to us." After this attack, the Drossels had had enough of the green border. They hurried back the way they had come. As for the other woman, Drossel never knew what happened to her. She simply vanished.

Sooner as the result of inspiration rather than carefully considered planning, Drossel had purchased tickets to Hanover the day before with his Reichsmarks. Since then, the old money had become worthless in the western sectors. However, that afternoon the Drossels were able to travel to Hanover in the hope that in the big city they might be able to find assistance sooner than they could in small Helmstadt.

In Hanover, an employee at the welfare office gave them several street car tickets, directing them to a refugee camp. The Drossels were provided places to sleep in a room with seven bunk beds. All of the beds were already taken. The space was stuffy, and the atmosphere was desperate. No one knew how to escape the situation. The Drossels spent two or three nights in the camp. On the second day, they encountered a chaplain who went up and down the rows, offering comfort to those there. One woman dropped down on her knees in front of him, praying and loudly announcing that she was a Catholic.

This behavior made an impression. Within a few hours, the woman was given a care packet. She was the only one in the room to receive one. The Drossels were repulsed by the woman's behavior and the chaplain's reaction. Marianne and Heinz decided to take their fate into their own hands. Marianne was able to locate the headquarters for the Jewish congregation in Hanover. The next day, the family made its way there.

The Nazis had almost completely destroyed the Jewish congregation in Hanover. In 1938, there were approximately 4,800

Jews living in the city set on the Leine River. By the time the city was liberated by American troops in April 1945, no more than 100 Jews remained in the city. On August 10, 1945, the English occupation authorities granted permission for the establishment of a new Jewish congregation.[120]

The Drossels were given accommodation in the interior courtyard of a half-collapsed former hotel. The building's facade was riddled with bullet holes. A congregational staff member welcomed the three homeless Berliners, listened to their story, and asked Marianne Drossel if she could prove that she was Jewish. Marianne was speechless. She did not have any documents with her that could prove her religious membership. Then the Hanoverian turned to the 12-year-old Billy: "Are you Jewish?" When he said that he was, the man asked: "Do you know the Broche?" Billy mumbled through the traditional Jewish prayer. Nonetheless, this rendering was enough for the Jewish congregational representative, and the Drossels were warmly taken in.

All of the running around had exhausted the mother and son. The mental strain was the hardest on Marianne. The uncertainty and helplessness, especially the situation in the detention camp in Hanover, must have awakened some terrible memories. She was very depressed. The family was given their own room, which must have seemed a great luxury to them. They also received supper and the promise of additional assistance. For the first time in four days, the three of them could have a quiet night's sleep.

Billy was very proud of his significant contribution to their improved status. His recitation was so good because he had attended a religious school. His mother had sent him there so that he could become a registered member of the Berlin congregation—and could then have access to support offered through the religious entity. The care packages that Billy received were essential for the family's well-being. Billy celebrated his Bar Mitzvah on February 12, 1949, seemingly as the only boy on that day. Thanks to one of the numerous packages from Günter Fontheim, the family celebrated the special day with chocolate and coffee.

Life must have been confusing for the boy. Under Hitler, he was classified as a "non-Jew," which helped him, even if it would not have ensured his survival. After 1945, being Jewish was advantageous. During the Nazi dictatorship, Billy was not considered a "true" Jew. He bore the name of his "Aryan" father, whom he may not have ever even met. Billy had been baptized in the Lutheran church at the age of four, and he most likely spent some time in a Christian children's home. Billy surely knew that it was dangerous to be a Jew. He must have seen how his mother and other Jews were despised and persecuted.

After a recuperative night in the accommodations operated by the Hanover Jewish congregation, the Drossels set out for Hamburg on June 24, 1948. Here they received additional support from the congregation in the bigger city. This was the day that the currency reform was implemented in West Berlin—and the blockade of Berlin began.

The SOZ blocked all land and water access points for people and goods into West Berlin. Although there had previously been obstacles to transit through the SOZ, this measure was a drastic expression of the conflicts between the Allies—and the first high point in the Cold War. The Soviet authorities attempted to apply pressure on the western Allies to prevent the formation of a divided state. This option, favored by the western side, had further divided the former anti-Hitler coalition since the failed foreign minister conference in London in December 1947.

After arriving at the Hamburg train station, Heinz Drossel asked a policeman for directions to the Jewish congregation. The policeman was quite helpful and offered to take Drossel there in the sidecar of his motorcycle. Drossel pointed to his wife and child, and gratefully declined the offer. He long recalled that kind gesture in those days of uncertainty.

On September 18, 1945, the Hamburg Jewish congregation had received its new home at Rothenbaumchaussee 38. As in many other places in Germany, the congregation had been dissolved in 1942. At the beginning of the war, Hamburg's Jewish congregation numbered 19,904.[121] By April 30, 1945, only 647 individuals in Hamburg met the Nazi definition of "Jew."[122] In October 1947, the number of "practicing Jews" in Hamburg was approximately 1,400.[123]

This time the acceptance took place without an oral examination. The reference letter from Hanover was sufficient for the congregational staff member who provided the three homeless Berliners with food and lodging. The Drossels ate their meals in the Jewish nursing home at Sedan Street 23, which had been returned to the Hamburg Jewish congregation on December 31, 1945. From where they were staying, the nursing home was only 15 minutes away by foot. This would not have been worth talking about if it had not rained constantly at this time. This was why Heinz Drossel remembered so precisely how he had invested the majority of his first new money: in an umbrella.

Despite the Drossels' special status as Berliners, because of the support of the Hamburg Jewish congregation, they were able to claim their share of the new currency "head money." At one of the social welfare offices, they received their "West Marks."

On the second day of their stay, the Drossels were advised to let their son be sent to stay at the Jewish children's home in Blankenese. This seemed like the most reasonable and comfortable choice available to them. The lodgings at Rothenbaum were cramped, but in Blankenese Billy would meet other children his own age with whom he could play and run around. Billy was taken to the Warburg Villa on Kösterberg Hill by a group of British soldiers in a military jeep. His arrival must have made a considerable impression at the children's home. The other children immediately gave the new boy the nickname "Jeep."

Heinz Drossel told the following story: "We hardly saw him when we were there. The home had a really nice garden where the children ran around. Billy was always being called by someone: 'Jeep, Jeep, come here!' He would always run off and leave us standing around." Every two or three days, a British soldier drove Heinz and Marianne Drossel to Blankenese to visit their son. They soon saw for themselves that Billy was very happy there and that he had immediately been accepted by the other children.

The Warburg Children's Health Home was operated by the American Joint Distribution Committee (AJDC), a Jewish charity organization, between 1946 and 1948. The initiative was spearheaded by Eric Warburg, who had fled Nazi Germany and then become an American citizen. As an officer in the US Army, he had visited the former Bergen-Belsen Concentration Camp in August 1945. At that time, the camp functioned as a Displaced Persons Camp (DP Camp) for refugees and Holocaust survivors. The conditions there were catastrophic. Warburg decided to give the AJDC use of his family property in Blankenese, which had previously been confiscated by the Nazis. During the course of the discussions of how to utilize the property, which involved among others the Jewish Committee at the DP Camp in Bergen-Belsen, they decided to open on the site a place that would provide care and enjoyment to Jewish children. The AJDC financed most of the renovation and furnishing of the property. Additional monies were collected from the British Red Cross, other Jewish charity organizations, and the Central Jewish Committee of the former Bergen-Belsen Concentration Camp.

The Warburg Children's Health Home operated its own hospital and school. The children received both schooling and religious instruction, and they were introduced to Jewish cultural life. The goal was to take these orphaned children as quickly as possible to Erez Israel. Jewish festivals were celebrated, and Jewish films and plays were shown.[124] The first registered group of Jewish boys and girls from Bergen-Belsen met in the Warburg home in January 1946.[125]

Children who had either managed to stay hidden or who had survived their imprisonment felt especially good among others like themselves. After years of isolation, they were finally offered the possibility to communicate with each other: with peers who really understood their personal experiences, with others who never told them to keep quiet because they no longer wanted to hear about suffering, fear, or the unimaginable. One such child described the post-war experience of being told to remain silent as "pure insanity": "When we were together, we discussed everything. The children were not afraid to call things by their rightful names . . . If any adult . . . claims that children have nothing to say about the past or do not wish to talk about it, then this person is a living example of someone who was neither in a position or willing to listen to us."[126] The adults were the ones who did not want to hear about the past, thus the children stayed silent. And many of them suffered under this enforced silence their entire lives.

Years of hiding, silence, and lies left wounds. Later in life, many children who had survived the Shoah in hiding battled identity problems. Some of them came to view the traumatic situation as a punishment for something they could not comprehend: "I did not understand why one had to be ashamed of being Jewish. Nonetheless, I knew undoubtedly that I had to somehow be repulsive because I was Jewish. Since I did not know the reason why, it felt like the best course was to conceal my true self . . . If someone had at least told me that I had done something wrong, I could have at least felt guilty. But the issue had nothing to do with something I had done; it was tied to my mere existence. How can you live with that?"[127]

Living in hiding was often bad enough. Not all helpers were compassionate individuals. However, for the children, the worst aspect of the situation was the separation from their parents. The hidden children were plagued with the sense of being abandoned for reasons they could not grasp. They dwelt on this problem and tried to explain to themselves the very thing that the adults could not express in words: "Many of the underground children . . . came to the same conclusion: Their lives were of little value because they were seemingly unworthy of attention and affection. The children who came from the assimilated families, those in which their Jewish identity was only mentioned occasionally, saw in their ethnicity nothing more than the direct cause for their unfortunate condition. Once they had come to this conclusion, shame in their Jewishness grew unhindered, like a poisonous weed."

Many needed decades before they could acknowledge their roots and find peace. Some of them completely turned their backs on their Jewish identities: "Being Jewish remained for them a reason to be ashamed. They changed their names, married Christians. Some of them even spouted anti-Semitic sentiments in an attempt to be accepted by a world that had cared so very little about their ethnic and religious heritage."[128]

In June 1948, as Billy arrived at the Kösterberg children's home, the AJDC had already ceased its involvement in the endeavor. In April, the final group of children had been sent to Palestine. At this point, the house in Blankenese functioned as a recuperative home for handicapped Jewish children from the British and American occupation zones. In 1949, the Jewish children and youth work at Kösterberg was discontinued.

In mid-July, the congregational representative informed the Drossels that the Soviets had given permission for a bus to travel to Berlin. Billy was not very enthusiastic at the prospect of returning home. On July 17, they arrived in the blockaded city.

Drossel did not miss the portfolio that he had forgotten in Helmstedt in the midst of their flight. As expected, his contract with Büttner & Co. was not extended, and it officially ended on July 23, 1948. Under the current conditions, his work for the company could not continue: No person was allowed to travel out of Berlin.

"We Have to Get Out"

Berlin, October 20, 1949

Immediately after their return, Heinz and Marianne renewed their efforts to leave Germany. Their attempts to emigrate were revealed in a letter from January 1948: "Despite our best efforts over the second half of last year, we were not successful in finding a way to get out. And since it seems as if absolutely nothing is going to

Heinz and Marianne at the Tempelhof Airport during the Berlin Air Lift (June 1948–May 1949)

change any time soon, we will have to slowly give up our hopes and accept our fate.

I know that I do not need to explain that we cannot be happy here."[129]

One promising opportunity to emigrate to South America failed for financial reasons. The charity organization Joint would have paid the transatlantic passage for Marianne and her son, but not for Heinz. Neither of them was open to the possibility of separation.

Of course, during the Berlin blockade, the already-poor food situation did not improve. Officially, the calorie ration remained the same, but there were no vegetables or fruit to be had. Potatoes were replaced with powdered imitations, and there was no possibility whatsoever to scavenge for food outside of Berlin. "The 'black market' was broken by the extremely brutal measures to cordon off the sector. For example, on the other side of Lichtenrade, which lay on the border, ditches had been dug on the Soviet side, and the roads were barricaded off. These streets were heavily patrolled. For those who were caught, every bit of food was confiscated, and they were put into forced labor units for up to three days."[130] During this period, the care packages from Günter Fontheim became especially critical, since they contained not only food but also items to trade.

At the beginning of the blockade, a kind of euphoria reigned in the western sectors. Many Berliners felt connected to one another, a sentiment that they had not experienced for a long time. The support by the western Allies was apparent everywhere. The blockade lasted until May 12, 1949, and during that time, Berlin's western sectors were exclusively supplied by air. Over those critical months, more than 250,000 British and American air missions were flown to Berlin, bringing over 2 million tons of supplies to the city.

When the Drossels arrived, Berlin was already being supplied by the Air Lift. In a letter to Günter Fontheim, Heinz described the feeling in the city: "Now the mood of the Berliners is exceedingly joyful. It is as if through their steadfastness against the threat of the totalitarian powers, they are, in part, making retribution for their nation's guilt . . . The Air Lift is incredible. The machines roll through the landing fields day and night . . . and bring valuable loads. The program, organized by the Allied forces, runs with precise punctuality—attention to everything! . . . The Berliners are glowing and proud of 'their' Allied air force."[131]

Drossel also did not conceal the negative aspects of this time from his friend in America. The constant drone of planes and the feeling of being imprisoned was nerve-wracking. The future did not seem all that rosy: "I seem to recognize everything that is going on now. Again we are sitting here and waiting for the thunder of machines. Again we are waiting on the end of the terror. And may it be an end with terror. Everything recalls the war, but this time, it is a war with despair. It cannot continue this way."[132]

The longer the blockade continued, the more tense the situation became. The Drossels and tens of thousands of other Berliners suffered under enormous material and psychological stress. They were depressed by their total dependence on the outside world, and the constant fear of another war overshadowed everything. In mid-August 1948, Heinz Drossel sent another letter to America. The request for additional support was more pointed than usual, but the description of their personal conditions was surprisingly simple, light, and conversational in tone.

Coping with daily life became increasingly difficult. Berlin's special status as a four-sector city complicated the implementation of the currency reforms. The Allies could not agree on a single course of action for Berlin. The western powers refused to recognize the currency reform spearheaded by the Soviet occupation authorities. On June 23, the Soviet Union introduced the East Mark to the

German zones it controlled. One day later, the D-Mark was introduced to Berlin's three western sectors. Thus, in the city at large, two different currencies were in circulation.

Drossel tried to explain the chaos that was rampant in the city: "The West Mark is forbidden in the East, and carrying it is a punishable offense. The East Mark is accepted everywhere. In the West, rents and harvested foods can be purchased with East Marks. Similarly, transportation, gas, and electricity can be paid for with East Marks. This is what it looks like: The light rail system only accepts East Marks, but the streetcars in the western sectors take whatever the ticket purchaser happens to have. The newspapers in the East only accept East Marks. The newspapers for the western readers near the Tempelhof train station [can be paid for] in West Marks (only), in the Tempelhof train station only in East Marks (since the Reich train system is administered by the Russian authorities), bread in East Marks, salt in West Marks . . . the black market exclusively takes West Marks . . . Now all of the salaries in the western sectors, at least those that are still being paid, are ¼ in West Marks and ¾ in East Marks. Perhaps you can imagine the run there has been on the West Marks. The landlords will (unjustly) send back the rents paid in East Marks. Depending on their mood, they then demand 5–55 percent to be paid in West Marks . . . Result: there is chaos from morning to evening . . . The old people have no idea what is going on. A total madhouse!!"[133]

Identification papers were examined at the sector boundaries. The Soviets were the harshest of the controllers, but the French, British, and American forces also asked to be shown the papers. In Summer 1948, the final division of the city took place.

According to Drossel's letter: "Inter-sector travel. The identification papers of the westerners (Berliners) are marked with a big 'B.' If someone in the Russian sector is caught in a raid or at a control point with a B in his or her papers, the authorities are particularly tender. It is not uncommon for you to get your papers 'laid' at your feet in pieces. Then you are out of luck. If you are further out, for example along the stretch between Grünau and

Königs Wusterhausen, you have to walk back into the city, or what is more likely is that you will be detained for 1-3 days of 'useful labor.' If you have D Marks (West) with you, they will be a) torn into pieces or b) collected while you sometimes (not always) will be stuck behind bars."

Drossel was proud of the Berliners' resolute attitude. They refused to be intimidated by the Soviets. At the same time, he was overwhelmed by the situation that existed in early August 1948: "The Berliners do <u>not</u> want to be guilty of a new dictator! Hopefully the world will not forget us!!! In any case, life here is no kind of life at all. And yet it is a health resort compared to the Soviet Zone 'paradise.'"

A kind word or a small anecdote from some other, free parts of the world was just as important as the material support that came in the care packages. Drossel wrote to his friend that his family was "immensely" delighted whenever they received mail. He even went so far as to beg for "a sign of life from out there," although not without ameliorating his request with a comment that he knew that his friend was busy these days. By the end of August 1948, Drossel had reached the end of his tether: "Gradually it is becoming unbearable here." And: "We have to get out."[134]

The process to obtain immigration papers for the United States was difficult and time-consuming. Countless papers, police statements, and health forms were required. Excepting the huge issue of travel finances, the biggest program was the affidavit, the paper in which a US citizen promised to provide financial support in case an immigrant was not able to support himself or herself. Naturally a verbal assurance was not sufficient in this case. The financial situations of the US citizens who filed affidavits were carefully examined. Each citizen had to be free of debt and had to have a job. Although he was a good friend, Ernest Günter Fontheim did not fulfill any of these criteria. He would have gladly done anything to help bring the Drossels to freedom, to true liberation. He tried his best to establish contacts for his Berlin friends. He corresponded with other emigrants; he sent care packages. Unfortunately he could not provide the desired papers.

In February 1949, the Drossels suffered a new disappointment related to their desired emigration. Marianne had discovered that she had relatives in California. After a long period of silence, they communicated with her that they would not be able to provide the affidavit. However, Marianne could put their names down as relatives on her emigration request. This was well-intentioned, but it did nothing to help the Drossels' cause. They were still stuck.

On March 20, the western Allies declared the D-Mark to be the solely valid currency in their Berlin sectors. Effective immediately, East Marks were no longer accepted. At an exchange rate of 1:1, each person was allowed to trade 15 East Marks for West Marks. Any sums greater than this had to be exchanged at the official rate of 5.6 to 1. For his position as assistant at the Free University, Heinz Drossel was paid an honorarium of 150 Marks that would be paid out at a fraction of that sum in West Marks. Marianne did not have paid employment, and they had no savings. The financial situation was strained.

In Summer 1949, Heinz's "honorarium" was reduced to 70 D-Marks. The Drossels' financial situation was then completely destroyed when he was informed in September that his position was being cut entirely. The attempts to emigrate had required much effort, and they had resulted in no progress. The fight for survival was closely linked to the fight to leave. Heinz and Marianne were fiercely devoted to their goal. Their energies were seriously overtaxed. However, as Heinz expressed in one of his letters, their "yearning for freedom," "for reasonably managed democracy," motivated them to not give up. He saw their "only chance" in "leaving the entire horrific episode behind them."[135]

The hope that through the Jewish charity organization, Joint, Marianne and Billy could find a way to reach America and only Heinz would need the supporting affidavit vanished in July. All three of them would need separate affidavits from three different citizens. No one knew how these were to be arranged. The family was now directed to the welfare office, but there was no hope for employment. Berlin's economic collapse seemed imminent, and in addition, there were "political folly, anti-Semitism, and similar things. All you can do is despair."[136]

The circle of acquaintances had grown appreciably smaller. Everyone who could gather the required papers emigrated. Those who remained fought to survive. The Drossels withdrew from social life. And although Heinz never accused "his" Berliners of wrongdoing, sixty years later he did complain about varying degrees of subtle anti-Semitism that the family continued to experience long after the war years. No new close friendships were formed. Heinz confessed, "We were distrustful. But the others were also distrustful."

One small beam of light came from a neighbor by the name of Karl Kmoth.

During the Nazi period, Kmoth had not stood up against the Nazis. Rather, he was one of the countless followers who suspected the worst but chose not to get involved in fighting it. After the war, he treated the Drossel family very kindly, Heinz recalled later. Kmoth was not pushy, but he did talk about the past. His behavior, especially in connection with Marianne, showed his sensitivity and sympathy. From this, they developed a pleasant acquaintance. Late in life, Heinz admitted that he had hoped for just this kind of behavior from many Germans: "From the very start, they should have said that they thought what had happened had been terrible. Or something like that." Drossel believed that the period of silence stretched on much too long.

Against all expectations, in October 1949, three affidavits arrived from America. After so many disappointments in their attempts to emigrate, this was hard to believe: "Gradually we realized that our great wish and yearning was a reachable goal. We felt totally nuts for the first two days."[137] Today it is impossible to figure out who sent the long-desired documents. The Drossels submitted all the requisite papers and waited on an invitation from the American consul. Joint had already declared its willingness to finance the emigration costs for both Marianne and Billy. All that remained was for Heinz to collect the money that would cover his passage. Heinz and Marianne had never been so close to achieving their goal.

The preparations—and the attempts to find the last of the money—set the couple into a feverishly happy state of expectation. On December 13, they had one final appointment at the consulate. Before they could take this last step, though, everything collapsed. Heinz came down with yet another outbreak of tuberculosis. He almost died.

At this point, the emigration plans shattered. It took Heinz a long time to accept the ending of this dream.

In July 1950, he shared the details with his friend Fontheim: "Yes, my friend, it looks like this: it all hinges on a small, newly developed hole in the upper part of my right lung that, with the help of a tire (Zauberberg-Th. Mann), was pressed back together until it disappeared . . . They assured me that within the next 3–4 months . . . I would be able to go back to work. The doctors have seriously advised a change of air to help assure a full recovery." As Heinz continued, an emigration could only take place, "according to information from the U.S. consulate, after a stay of 2–3 months in Switzerland. From a health standpoint, Bavaria would also suffice. It is an issue of money . . . Thus, dear Günter—these words have become damned sour, but everything hinges on the primary question of health and, with it, the continuation of this miserable existence. It is clear that you alone are not in a position to support us financially, and I ask that you not make any attempts to help us this way."[138]

"Tabula rasa"

Bonn, December 31, 1949
"During the de-nazification process, much unhappiness and harm have been caused . . . The war and the confusion of the post-war period presented such hard trials and temptations for many people. Understanding needs to be shown for numerous failings and wrongdoings. Thus, the issue of an amnesty is being examined by the Federal Government."[139] This statement was given by

Chancellor Konrad Adenauer in his first government speech on September 20, 1949, in the Parliament in Bonn.

Trying to reach across party lines, Adenauer spoke to the people from his heart: "The years behind us were so confusing that it is advisable for us to create a general *tabula rasa*."[140] However, the "clean table" was not to be achieved through the confession of guilt, punishment, penance, and regret. No, the final blow was to be held back altogether. Instead, silence was to be held about the terror and crimes that had been allowed to reign for four years in the name of the German people, with the cooperation of countless German men and women. As one member of parliament stated in 1949, the silence was to help "forgetfulness cover the past."[141] The "Freedom from Punishment" Act was passed in record time and by a large majority of votes. The law was announced on December 31, 1949.

Superficially the law was touted as providing amnesty to those guilty of economic crimes, such as black market trade or property crimes. These had occurred frequently in the early years of the war: potatoes were taken out of their fields, coal was collected from along railroad tracks. Since these crimes only resulted in one-year imprisonments, those who truly profited from this law were the violent criminals, many of whom had managed to escape prosecution since the Night of the Broken Glass.

In addition, parliamentary representatives from all of the parties decided to offer amnesty to those individuals who, since May 10, 1945, had "vanished by concealing their true identities because of political reasons." "Only those delinquents whom the law classifies as 'criminals' (those whose actions would result in 'jail or confinement of more than five years') would not fall under this special provision."[142] This meant nothing more or less than the fact that the young democracy extended its hand to a large number of Nazi criminals who had, to date, managed to escape legal prosecution by the Allies.

Due to the "Freedom from Punishment" Act of 1949, by January 1951, "no fewer than 792,176 people had received what the jurists called 'relief.'"[143] Most of the relieved punishments related to waivers from imprisonments of up to six months and from financial penalties up to 5,000 D-Marks. This amnesty affected almost half a million convicts, and almost 250,000 legal cases that were presently in process were discontinued.[144]

According to the statistics, amnesty was offered to 3,000 individuals, "who had been convicted or accused of crimes or offenses 'against personal freedoms' . . . You can easily assume that the amnesties rarely impacted 'normal' kidnappers. Instead they were connected with SA, SS, and party functionaries who had hauled their victims to concentration camps and 'bunkers.'" In addition, 20,000 people, who had engaged in acts 'against life,' were freed from imprisonment, as well as 30,000 individuals who had been convicted for bodily harm. Furthermore, 5,200 others were granted amnesty, although they had been found responsible for "crimes and offenses in office."

The "Freedom from Punishment" Act had a grave side effect in that it resulted in the "first steps into a rapidly advancing delegitimization of persecutions of Nazi-era punishable acts— and in continually far-reaching demands for amnesty, until even outright calls were made for the most heinous war criminals to be included in the 'general amnesty.'"

Most Germans saw their need for penance, explanation, and punishment as covered by the war tribunals at Nuremberg. The guilty were named there and were harshly punished, right? Twenty-four defendants, twenty convictions. Twelve of these were given the death penalty in the first major set of trials against the most prominent war criminals in 1946.[145] Twelve other trials took place through 1949 in which 177 defendants had to give testimony to their actions.

Tens of thousands of others escaped retribution through lying and deception. For example, in the Allies' wide-scale surveys during the de-nazification period, people provided each other with 'de-nazification certificates,' absolving one another of responsibility. This was never discussed in the public forum. The numerous, formerly powerful Nazis living underground also received little attention. Some of them managed to remain hidden in the Federal

Republic, and they even received pensions, retirement payments, and public welfare monies. They were called "submarines" or "Silent Browns." On the other hand, those individuals condemned to lifelong imprisonment at Nuremberg soon enjoyed a rising tide of solidarity and support. In the end, it was the Lutheran Church that was responsible for the freeing of mass murderer Martin Sandberger only ten years after his trial.[146]

At the beginning, the German populace sympathized and agreed with the Nuremberg Trials. However, soon the talk turned to "the victors' justice." The people no longer wanted to be concerned about this subject. They did not want to see themselves or their acquaintances and relatives—fathers, brothers, as well as mothers or grandmothers, friends, and neighbors—scrutinized with suspicion. No one wanted to admit that they had collaborated in or been responsible for the horrific crimes. The strategy always remained the same: deny, forget, stay silent. The sentence, "We knew nothing about it," was both a self-justification and a defense; it hardly corresponded with the truth. Everyone "knew" something; one more, one less. In the early 1950s, the following statement by Adenauer expressed the general sentiment: "We need to stop hunting down Nazis."[147]

This was the atmosphere that surrounded Heinz and Marianne Drossel as they were forced to abandon their plans to emigrate to the United States. At first, it was possible that the efforts were mainly motivated by a desire to leave the place in which so many awful things had happened. As more time passed, it became clearer how the Germans were going to deal with the past and the crimes. It also became apparent to Heinz and Marianne that the future here promised nothing good. How could they continue to live with people who seemed to have learned nothing and who simply denied the crimes? Marianne especially must have been moved by this question.

Hardly anyone showed any interest in the victims. To the contrary, a public discussion with the survivors about the Holocaust would have hindered the achievement of most Germans' primary goal: forgetting. In their insightful and unsparing analysis *The Inability to Mourn*, renown German psychoanalysts Alexander and Margarete Mitscherlich described the situation as follows: "What was the collective to do when it was bluntly informed that in its name six million people had been killed for no other reason than their own aggressive wants? There was no other course than a concealment of motives or a withdrawal into depression."[148]

However, according to the Mitscherlichs, it rarely came to the latter. Not every person had to "feel directly responsible. Through denial and downplaying, various ways out of the calamity were sought. Depressive reactions, self-recrimination, or despair over the extent of the guilt that one had brought on oneself were quite seldom." From a psychoanalytical perspective, the suppression functioned as a kind of self-defense, and the opportunity for remorse never had to be recognized.

An Israeli psychoanalyst is said to have formulated the following theory: "The Germans will never forgive the Jews for Auschwitz." Over time, a grotesque reversal of perceptions occurred. With or without Hitler, "the Jews were guilty." Although Marianne Drossel had been persecuted and her life had been threatened during the Third Reich, after the collapse of the regime, she—and so many other Holocaust survivors—were seen as the threat.

The anti-Semitism that had been promoted and demanded for over twelve years (and which had struck a chord of understanding and acceptance among many Germans) did not vanish overnight. It was noticeable in the details of Heinz and Marianne Drossels' daily lives. Later in life, Heinz did not know what to call it. Sometimes what he sensed was not so much an open rejection as it was a subtle resentment.

A co-worker once commented: "You have a Jewish wife. It must not have been easy for her." At that time, Heinz thought this comment was both tactless and unfeeling.

He also told a story about a supervisor who regularly invited the Drossels and another co-worker and his wife to supper at his home: "He always formally escorted my wife to the table and did not betray his feelings." It was noticeable that the supervisor did not betray his feelings. In looking back, Heinz thought the oft-repeated gesture by the other man was meant to express respect toward his wife.

On the one hand, there was a subtle anti-Semitism in the eager efforts to rehabilitate many former Nazis. At the same time, the Federal Republic was trying to grow closer to Israel for foreign policy reasons. Despite resistance within his own cabinet, in 1952 Chancellor Adenauer with the support of the SPD authorized the sending of reparation payments to the Jewish state. Reconciliation and rapprochement were the goals, but they found little sympathy among the German citizenry. A representational survey from that time revealed that most Germans did not support these payments.

Other questionnaires revealed "regularly . . . a gloomy picture of ongoing anti-Semitic stereotypes. When viewed collectively, they showed that a relative majority of Germans thought it would be best if there were 'no Jews in the country.' Later this was conceptualized as 'anti-Semitism without Jews,' since during the 1950s only a few tens of thousands of Jews still remained in the Federal Republic."[149]

Nothing ever materialized in terms of public interest in confronting the Nazi past or in a concrete naming and penalizing of the perpetrators. Already as early as 1951, the re-employment of numerous former prominent individuals in the Nazi state had begun—academics, doctors, lawyers, and other officials. Most of these individuals had lost their jobs in 1945. In 1952, Adenauer publicly admitted that two-thirds of the higher-ranked officials in the foreign office and approximately four-fifths of the political division chiefs were former Nazi members. Not even Joachim von Ribbentrop, the Nazi Foreign Minister, had reached such high percentages.[150]

It was Article 131 that made this scandal possible, as well as the silent re-employment of prominent former Nazis in numerous other positions. The statute conceived by Adenauer's government in 1952 was passed with broad support from the other political parties. Public officials who had lost their jobs due to the de-Nazification that occurred in 1945 were obligated to be rehired: "All public service offices were required to favor members of this privileged cadre for open positions until a quota of 20 percent was reached."[151] This class of newly re-employed individuals included not only passive Nazi members but actual functionaries.

Few people seem to have been troubled by concerns about the motives of "the Germans who had let themselves become the followers of the Führer, who had led us into the greatest material and moral catastrophe in our history," the Mitscherlichs observed. "Instead, driven by an entrepreneurial spirit shaped by admiration and envy, we concentrated our energies much more on restoring what had been destroyed, on the reconstruction and modernization of our industrial potential, even down to kitchen furnishings."[152]

The general interest in politics was underdeveloped at this time. During the early years of the decade, only about one-tenth of all Germans understood how the Parliament actually functioned.[153] The majority of West Germans were skeptical of the new democratic system. They fed their distrust with various negative memories of the Weimar Republic or with the fact that their dependence on and control by the western Allies would not end in the foreseeable future.

Above all, the citizens in the new Federal Republic strove to improve their personal life conditions. And the people truly did develop Herculean strengths. The "Economic Miracle" began its unstoppable course. By the early 1950s, the Federal Republic's gross national product exceeded that of Great Britain, one of the Allied victors.

After World War II, the Germans manically filled their days with varied activities. The great achievements helped them to forget. If you worked a lot, you had little time left for contemplation: "Instead of working through the past in a political sense, as at least an attempt to redress what had happened, what happened was the explosive development of German industry. Soon industriousness and success covered the open wounds that still remained from the past."[154]

"I Could No Longer Endure It"

Berlin, Early 1954

The tuberculosis cost Heinz Drossel almost two years of his life. When he was finally recovered and was ready to resume his clerkship, he was informed that the decision had been made that the previous time reduction to 18 months was no longer valid. He had to fulfill the full three-year requirement. Drossel completed his second state exam in March 1954. He reported to the president of the Supreme Court with the firm expectation that he would be given a judge seat. However, he was mistaken. He was told that, at the moment, there were no available judge positions.

Drossel's personnel file contained the information that he had a Jewish wife. Was this the reason for him being passed over? Others who had also passed their second exams were immediately placed in office as "commissioned judges." After Drossel had overcome the initial shock, he went to the Supreme Court. After all, he had a family to feed. This time he was offered a position that he accepted. He would be employed as a law enforcement officer in the upper judicial service. He was told that he would receive the next judge position.

Several days later, Drossel ran into one of his old classmates on Ku'damm. They talked about this and that, and the classmate revealed that he worked as a judge in a district court. This former classmate had passed his state exam shortly after Drossel had passed his. Drossel was furious. He stormed over to the Supreme Court. This time he would not be appeased. It was not long until he was given a position as an associate judge in a regional court.

Drossel's first supervisor had not spent a single day as a law clerk. As a Nazi party member, he had been named an "Assessor K" during the war. An Assessor K was a clerk who did not have to serve a clerkship in the judicial context because he had fought as a soldier. He had been appointed as an "extraordinary" official, and he was not required to pass the major state exam. The appointment was automatic after the lapse of the three years it would have taken for the clerkship to have been completed.[155] Thus, this requisite training period was basically unnecessary, since the appointments granted by the Nazis were unhesitatingly accepted by the post-war justice system.

Because of his decision not to join any Nazi organizations, Drossel had been denied his clerkship. And he could not profit from this special regulation. By contrast, his new supervisor had been appointed a judge directly after his return from the war. This state of affairs was unbearable for Heinz. As he noted in looking back over his life, he had "considerable difficulties," and he was soon relocated to another court.

However, he did not feel well in his new workplace either. Too many lawyers, who had officially declared themselves to be "de-Nazified," made it clear to him that their perspectives and opinions had not changed in the least. One of the presiding judges even wore a uniform (without insignia) and boots under his robes. Drossel could not understand this. The others accepted it without protest. The old cliques continued to function. As Drossel found out, during the court proceedings, the defendants and prosecutors often faced intimidation. For example, the questioning lawyers were reprimanded in loud militant tones. Frequently Drossel intervened, reminding everyone that "we now live in a constitutional state and everyone has a right to be heard." He was depressed by the entire situation. He was always rubbing someone the wrong way and was constantly being reproved. Eventually he had to admit that his career prospects were poor.

Although later in life he could not remember the exact date, 1954 was also the year that Heinz's depressing professional situation was overshadowed by a conflict with his parents. Heinz would only discuss this in vague terms. He alluded to a crisis between his parents on the one side and he and his wife on the other. His parents were greatly disappointed that the existence of Marianne's daughter had been kept secret from them. Out of loyalty to his wife, Heinz had not shared this information with them.

He was tired—extraordinarily tired—after all the drudgery, the deprivations, the disappointments, the hopes, the perseverance. He had survived—but what for? He had worked so hard over the years to enter a profession whose leaders did not want him. He would never belong with them. He did not have the right pedigree. Many of his "dear" colleagues surely had much to fear insofar as Heinz Drossel represented a mirror of sorts. He reminded them on a daily basis that they had profited unjustly while others had been negatively impacted. As party members who had been granted the Assessor K title, as friends of the old judge who still wore jackboots under his gown.

Decades later, Drossel recalled this difficult time in his life: "I could no longer bear it." He did not want to live anymore. This was not an emotional reaction. He collected Veronal tablets, a powerful sedative. One afternoon, when Marianne was going to be gone for a few hours to run errands, he swallowed as many as he could. The drugs worked fast. He felt a little sick but primarily dizzy. He was on the point of unconsciousness when the door swung open.

Afterward Marianne told him that she had had to wait on the streetcar for a long time, and then suddenly she felt strange. She retraced her steps as quickly as she could to look in on him. In one glance, she took in all that had happened. She called for an ambulance on the neighbors' telephone. At the hospital, they pumped Heinz's stomach. The two of them never again discussed his suicide attempt.

" . . . And the Torture Goes On"

Berlin, April 1961

Marianne's health was so bad during the early post-war years that she could no longer work outside the home. She was plagued by an extreme loss in weight, heart and circulation problems, and horrible migraines. Between 1946 and 1948, she also had three miscarriages. The desire for a child must have been very strong. Then, despite the pronounced health problems and the economic hardships, she gave birth to her third child, a healthy daughter, on August 27, 1951, at the age of 38.

On May 22, 1951, Marianne Drossel, nee Hirschfeld, filed an application for reparation for "damages to freedom" and "damages to personal property" at the Berlin Reparation Office. The registration number 2040 was to accompany her for the next two decades. As a victim, she had to prove that she actually was what she claimed to be. An excerpt from the Jewish vital statistics index, proof of membership in the Jewish congregation, evidence that the lost property had actually been stolen by the Nazis, numerous notarized witness statements from the few, yet-living acquaintances were all required. The paper trail never seemed to end.

One year later, in May 1952, Marianne received a decision on her reparation application. For the 54 days she had been imprisoned, she was granted 270 D-Marks. However: "The other part of the application for compensation for the time lived illegally, from June 12, 1944, to May 8, 1945 . . . cannot be honored since the applicant, according to certificates provided by the BVG from March 13, 1952 . . . was engaged as a car washer between April 16, 1943, and April 30, 1945. Thus, she was not living illegally." In conclusion: "The decision is granted free of additional charges."

Marianne's attorney filed an appeal. The claims were strengthened, and new witness statements were filed. The office demanded additional documents, some of which, like "Identification Card J," had already been filed. Other documents verged on being absurd, such as "a written statement from the person who provided the illegality." This meant an explanation from someone who helped the victim by providing a place to stay one or more times. In Marianne's case, this would have been Oskar Drossel, Heinz's uncle, whose apartment she had listed as one of her hiding places during 1943. However, Oskar Drossel had been killed in late 1944 during one of the bombing attacks.

On April 27, 1954, Marianne Drossel wrote an angry and bitter complaint letter to the "Senator for Social Affairs" in Berlin-Wilmersdorf. Her application for compensation for the time she had lived illegally had been declined several times.

"When I claim to have lived illegally since 1944, this is based on the fact that at that time, and even yet today, I consider my day-to-day behavior during the time in question as illegal. This perspective does not exclude the fact that today there may be a different definition for this concept. However, I must assume that the current use of the concept can still be used in considering my actual circumstances during the Nazi period. If I was in danger then, I cannot imagine that this danger would not have existed if the concept had had a different definition, as it may today . . . During the Nazi period, the concept of 'illegality' was primarily connected with behaviors related to reporting regulations and locations of residence . . . I stayed in locations other than the one that I officially registered, starting after the time I reported, and thus, I violated these regulations. Naturally I did this to protect myself. I only mention as a side note the fact that because of my Jewish ethnicity, my behavior at this time would have been judged much more harshly than it would have been for others. It would have resulted in my immediate deportation . . . This behavior was not made any less illegal because there were times that I stayed in a known location. Viewed logically, I must view my actions at that time as illegal in nature. If one wants to turn things around today, I only wish that this perspective had existed 10-15 years ago. However, I am exercising my freedom to utilize basic concepts as continuous in nature, as opposed to relativizing them to the contingencies of changing times . . . In addition, my mental stability has been damaged by the stirring up of these awful memories, and my health has been negatively influenced. I have given up hope for a fair compensation and am convinced that the little money that will come from this effort will not be a blessing to the German people."[156]

In April 1961, almost exactly ten years after her first application, Marianne received 6,000 D-Marks "for wearing the star and living illegally from September 19, 1941, to January 31, 1943." The claims for financial loss and damages due to the inability to pursue professional goals were settled in 1962. The Reparation Office granted Applicant Number 2040 10,000 D-Marks in damages.

In August 1963, the Drossels' attorney, Dr. Karl Heinz Simon, pointed out that his client had not yet filed any claims for compensation for "persecution-related health damages." No rational individual could deny that the poor condition of her health was directly connected with the time of persecution. Nonetheless, how could one prove from a legal perspective that a shattered health twenty years later had been caused by the earlier persecution, hardships, and deprivation? Once again, Marianne had to gather together notarized statements. During one interrogation, a tooth had been broken. That was the easiest to prove. But what about the migraines, the constant exhaustion, the chronic state of being underweight (she only weighed about 90 pounds), and the hand tremors?

She often wanted to give up, but her husband Heinz encouraged her to hold out. He sometimes even pressed her about the fact that she had a right to the money and that the family could use it. It was a form of justice that had to be demanded. However, the cost was high. Time and time again, she had to face what had happened to her, things that she would have preferred to suppress. The torture began anew. New public health officers and former doctors had to be consulted. Witnesses had to be named. She had to bare herself to absolute strangers. Her dental status, as well as the findings of her gynecological exams, went on public record. She had to prove that others were guilty. It was as if, from the beginning, she was accused of lies and was the one who had to uncover the truth.

In the early 1970s, Heinz Drossel corresponded with a Berlin lawyer on the subject of Kurt Sigismund Hirschfeld's inheritance matters that were then closed with a settlement. In the end, all of Marianne Drossel's claims were recognized. Even her time living illegally was eventually acknowledged through reparation payments. It was only a hollow victory though. The strength it took to keep the process in motion over the years, as well as the humiliation that went along with it, had taken an immense toll. The money brought hardly any consolation.

VII. The End of a Dream

Yearning for Normalcy

Berlin, October 1962

Heinz Drossel could hardly believe his ears when he heard the news: a judge, who had been a Nazi party member prior to 1933, had been promoted to presiding judge of the Berlin Superior State Social Court. Drossel filed a complaint against this decision in October 1962. After various letters and personal conversations, the Senator for Labor and Social Services offered Heinz this very position as presiding judge—after the two years it would take for the colleague in question to be pensioned off. Drossel interrupted the conversation at this point: "Your Honor, you do not understand the point here!"

Drossel had finally reached his breaking point. Under these conditions, he neither could nor wanted to continue working. He had risen in recent times to a position in the Superior State Social Court. He decided to leave Berlin. In his attempt to find another position, he wrote that he was married to "a racially persecuted Jewish woman, whose family had been almost completely murdered by the Nazis." He wished to commit himself to representing the interests of "an array of Jewish victims." He could not stand the fact that old Nazis were allowed to pursue careers in post-war Germany: "Today I see myself under constant pressure to expose myself to an environment that primarily endorses the policies of the Nazi regime."[157]

Drossel never received a concrete reaction to his statement. The Senator simply let him know that he "had no qualms" about his application as a judge in the Federal Republic.

However, withdrawal from the Berlin jurisdiction was only possible "through resignation or re-assignment." A "transfer" was not viable. In other words, Drossel did not have the least hope for a recommendation from the Senator.

Furthermore, the supervising upper court councilor informed Drossel that the events leading up to his transfer could have a negative influence on his professional future. Would he agree for his personnel file to be "purged"? By this time, Drossel "did not really care." He "only wanted out," he recalled at the age of 87. He added with a wink: "Besides, I had copies of everything."

The councilor rang for a bailiff, who promptly appeared bearing a skillet. Drossel's correspondence and complaints about the old Nazis in the justice system were carefully burned. In good Prussian fashion, the two men took formal leave of each other. By late 1962, the Berlin justice system was made worse by one troublesome, yet fair, judge.

The episode with the former Nazi judge was the final catalyst for Heinz Drossel's decision to finally turn his back on Berlin. By Fall 1962, the city had already been divided by the Berlin Wall for about a year. This did not make life easy for its residents, who wished to feel well and secure. More than once, American and Soviet tanks stood confrontationally across from each other along the sector borders. Looking back over the dicey political situation that was evident to everyone in the city on the Spree River, Heinz Drossel recalled that "this often made us feel uneasy." The fear of a new war spread through all.

Thus, there were good reasons for the Drossel family to leave Berlin: the sense of being imprisoned in the DDR, the pervasive threat through the military presence of the Soviet army and Allied troops, and the negative prospects for Heinz in the justice profession. How did Marianne view the situation? What was her opinion of Berlin? She would have gladly left Germany forever ten years earlier. At least, she would have left the city in which she had experienced so much pain. The prospect of escaping the city must have seemed enticing. Of course, her Aunt Thea was still alive (she died in 1966). However, the connection between the two women does not seem to have been close enough for Marianne to have had any doubts about moving away. She basically had nothing to say against the relocation prospect. Her good friends had all emigrated long before; she had no position or good career to lose.

Professional development was not only impossible for Marianne because of her serious health problems. For the wife of a judge and the mother of a small child during the 1950s and later, it was inconceivable to work outside the home. The social conventions of the time worked against the professional engagement of women.

Even well into the 1960s, women in West Germany had only one purpose in life, one determined by nature: motherhood. Advertisements reflected the image and representation of women in German society. In these pictures, wives and mothers beamed at the viewers as they cleaned, cooked, or sewed. The men, in contrast, were depicted reading the newspaper or busying themselves happily with the food prepared by their wives. The woman's sphere of influence was limited to her own four walls, where she was expected to take care of domestic concerns. The advertisements suggested that whoever fulfilled these expectations would be rewarded with attention and satisfaction. Society ostracized single mothers. As the best of the lot, widowed working mothers were pitied.

Marianne and Heinz, early 1960s

The yearning for "normalcy" was great during these years of instability, and normalcy offered familiar roll models. The 1950s functioned as an era of restoration. As approximately 11 million prisoners of war returned home, women increasingly withdrew from the working world. With the establishment of the Federal Republic in 1949, the previously heightened divorce rate sank again, as the era of the housewife again gained general recognition and acceptance.

The development potential of women was not only limited by the societal climate and the corresponding social controls, but also through legal regulations. Initially, the gender equality clause in the Bonn Constitution was, in reality, only a nice but ineffective point in the lives of most women. The group of advisers for these paragraphs was composed of 61 men and 4 women. The formulation and inclusion of Paragraph 3, Section 2, set off a series of bitter arguments.

It was only thanks to the stubbornness of Social Democrat Elisabeth Selbert that the equality of men and women was firmly anchored as a fundamental right in the Constitution. Her proposal was defeated twice due to voting blocks from the CDU (Christian Democrats) and FDP (Liberal Party) parties. However, Selbert reached her goal in her third attempt.

Nonetheless, at first marriage and family law remained unchanged from the pre-war period. This cemented the traditional division of labor between men and women. He was the bread winner, and she was the homemaker. Between 1953 and 1961, Franz-Josef Wuermeling (CDU) was the Minister of Family Affairs, and he described the employment of women as "socially destructive in nature," since it overly emphasized individualism.[158] Born in 1900, Wuermeling defended the concept of the family as the "basic unit" and "point of order" for state and society. He passionately urged the members of Parliament to keep in mind "the unique cultural and ethnic task and significance of our families."[159]

The reality did not correspond with these notions. Between 1950 and 1960, the involvement of married women in the workforce increased at an above-average rate.[160] As "marginal wage earners," married women were often welcomed. In many cases, this was the only way that a family's increasing rates of consumption could be met. They contributed significantly to the gross national product, but their activities did not receive societal recognition. This type of employment was sooner viewed as a private affair that did not warrant any special attention.

Only gradually did the politically entrenched power of a husband over his wife vanish from the law books. Even in the introduction to the Equality Law of 1957, the following language appeared: "It belongs to the functions of a man that he is fundamentally the preserver and provider of the family, while the most noble duty of the woman is to care for the heart of her family."[161]

With the passage of the law on July 1, 1958, the masculine "right to final decision-making" in all marital matters was abolished. For example, until this time, husbands had the sole right to choose where to live. Furthermore, control over a woman's property no longer passed automatically to her husband at the time of her marriage. If a woman defied her husband's wishes and sought professional employment, her husband no longer had a legal claim to her earnings. She was now permitted to open a bank account without needing her husband's permission. Another right was also ended with this legislation; a man could no longer end his wife's work contract if, for example, he decided she was neglecting her marital duties because of her employment. Nevertheless, it was only first in 1977 that a married woman in the Federal Republic could work outside of the home without the expressed agreement of her spouse.

The women's rebuke to the masses came out of a phase of incredible achievement. It was the women who organized survival in the immediate post-war years. They cleaned up the rubble; they drove trucks and streetcars; they took care of the children and the elderly. The female citizenry behaved pragmatically. They did what had to be done. There was no one else there to do the work since so many men were either dead or in prison. At the end of World War II, there were seven million more women than men living in Germany.[162]

Cynical Whims of Fate

Stuttgart, May 23, 1978

Heinz surely talked to his wife when he was considering a move away from Berlin. Where should they go? Daughter Ruth Drossel recalled that he had two possible positions open to him: one in Frankfurt am Main and one in Stuttgart. Marianne wanted to move to Frankfurt, however Heinz "categorically" refused to move here, his then-11-year-old daughter remembered. Ruth stated that he preferred to work in a state ruled by the CDU, as opposed to the Social Democrats, as had been the case in Berlin. The two parents argued about this.

In the city on the Main River, Fritz Bauer worked as Hessen's District Attorney. He was primarily responsible for initiating the first of the so-called Frankfurt Auschwitz Trials in December 1963. The Jewish Social Democrat had fled from the Nazis to Denmark and then to Sweden. For many years after the war, he sought to find a way to prosecute the SS men who had worked in the Auschwitz Death Camp.

Heinz Drossel's aversion to the Social Democrats, as witnessed by his daughter, was rather irrational in nature. Heinz's bad personal experiences with the communist regime in the SOZ and the GDR, the one that imprisoned his father, shored up his convictions. For many West Germans, the SPD was a blot on the political landscape. Despite all of its efforts to distance itself from the policies of the SUP and its active resistance to the GDR, many Germans associated the party with Communism.

For many, this was an absolute taboo. In the 1950s, anti-Communism was a "pre-condition of the political culture," and the "accusation of being hand-in-hand with 'Bolshevism'" functioned "above all, as a moralistic cudgel against the Social Democrats, who did not benefit much from the fact that they opposed the SUP more than anyone else."[163]

In West Germany, the fear of Communism was fervently kept alive for well over a span of almost two decades. The entire political

174

endeavor, the "final stroke" strategy, the societal reintegration of former Nazi functionaries, the rapprochement with Israel, the close ties to the western powers—all of this took place "under the umbrella of an ever-present anti-Communism, which demanded a stark friend-enemy mode of thought characterized by strong speech and a bizarre anti-'Bolshevism' strategy related to the western world."[164]

As the prosecution of Nazi offenders came to a halt, 1954 witnessed a wider-reaching amnesty than had been in force in 1949.[165] At this time, tens of thousands of cases were opened against (suspected) Communists. Between 1951 and 1968, about 138,000 preliminary proceedings were in process, and approximately 7,000 convictions were made. Some Jewish victims were also caught up in these trials.[166] Comparatively banal activities, such as organizing field trips for children to the GDR, could result in prison sentences. On August 17, 1956, the KPD was banned.

The proposal to ban the KPD, which had already been filed in the Federal Constitutional Court in 1951, was supported by the majority of West Germans. In 1953, Communist resistance fighters were excluded from the reparation payment procedures, despite the fact that Communists "had shed the most blood in the fight against National Socialism."[167] The populace clearly had little trouble conceiving of "Bolshevism" as the enemy. Already under Hitler, the "Bolshevist masses" had been demonized as the archenemy to be battled.

Heinz had the final say in his and Marianne's conflict over whether to move to Frankfurt or Stuttgart. In January 1963, he started work for the Baden-Württemberg Ministry of Labor, where he was appointed a welfare councilor in Stuttgart.[168] This entailed a demotion for him, as well as a salary decrease.

In June 1963, shortly after their relocation, Marianne Drossel decided to have herself baptized into the Catholic Church. Heinz Drossel explained that she did this "because we wanted to belong to the community." Their daughter suspected a more pragmatic motive: her mother did not want to harm her husband's career prospects ever again through her Jewishness.

In 1957, Ruth was also baptized shortly before she started school.

It was Marianne's desire to broaden her daughter's perspectives. Only those who are acquainted with a religion can later decide if they truly believe anything; Ruth remembers today that this was her mother's argument. From Heinz's viewpoint, Marianne wanted to prevent her child from being viewed as an outsider. She also wished to feel that she belonged to something.

It was in vain. Throughout the 1970s, the entire family felt like outsiders. As Heinz explained decades later, they were never fully integrated into society. Marianne probably felt this way until her death. She once said, "In Germany, I am a damned Jewess, and abroad I am a damned German."

By the time the family moved to their new home, Kurt Georg Kiesinger was in his second legislative term as Minister President. Three years after the Drossels arrived in Baden-Württemberg, Kiesinger became the Chancellor of the first Great Coalition in the Federal Republic. Although his membership in the Nazi party had not gained much attention prior to this point, it now was the cause for loud protests. Yet it was to no avail—after the end of his chancellorship in 1969, Kiesinger remained CDU Party Chair for two additional years.

Hans Karl Filbinger, Kiesinger's successor as Minister President of Baden-Württemberg, was also plagued by his past in Nazi Germany. The "Filbinger Affair" has gone down in the history books.

Through a piece published by playwright Rolf Hochhuth in the weekly newspaper *Die Zeit* on February 17, 1978, the extent of naval judge Filbinger's connection with Hitler's regime became public. In a quotation taken from the final sentence in the short story "Eine Liebe in Deutschland" ("A Love in Germany"), Hochhuth called Filbinger a "dreadful judge," whom one had to assume was allowed "to go free thanks to the silence of those who knew him." Furthermore, Hochhuth claimed that the naval judge, "while in a British prison camp, had prosecuted a German sailor under Nazi regulations, even after Hitler's death."[169]

On May 29, 1945, Filbinger sentenced Lance Corporal Kurt Olaf Petzold to six months imprisonment for "exciting displeasure, insubordination, and defiance." In addition, the defendant "had shown an extreme loss of conviction."[170] According to the complaint, on May 10, 1945, Petzold had refused an order with the following words: "The time is passed. I am a free man. You are fucked up. You Nazi dogs. You are guilty of this war. I will tell the English what kind of Nazi dogs you are, and then it will be my time."[171] The "field tribunal" held court in a British prison camp. Everyone involved in this grotesque process, which took place three weeks after the unconditional surrender, were inmates in this camp.

Filbinger accused both Hochhuth and *Zeit* of omittance. During the course of the trial, it came out that Filbinger had been involved in four death sentences, two of which he personally handled. Further research by Hochhuth unearthed files that proved this connection. The public soon learned about the fate of the former naval officer Walter Gröger.

After a night of partying, Gröger did not return to his ship and had taken refuge with the Norwegian nurse Marie Severinsen Lindgren. He was captured by the Gestapo. Lindgren was also taken into custody and later given a prison sentence.

In Hitler's regime, desertion and attempted desertion often resulted in the death sentence. In the first trial against Gröger, the court made a clear distinction between "attempt" and "preparation," explaining that "an attempted escape abroad had not been made."[172] On March 14, 1944, Gröger was sentenced to eight years imprisonment. In June, the sentence was reversed. In the second trial on January 16, 1945, the prosecuting attorney Dr. Hans Filbinger demanded the death penalty. The military court sentenced Walter Gröger to death via firing squad.

Filbinger urged speed, and after naming himself the commanding officer of the execution process, he personally oversaw the shooting of the 24-year-old sailor on March 16, 1945.

As more and more details about Filbinger's actions in the Gröger case came to light and the Minister President of Baden-Württemberg seemed to show no signs of regret, guilt, or remorse, his party slowly began to turn its back on him. On August 7, 1978, Hans Kurt Filbinger resigned as Minister President.

The Filbinger Affair kept the Republic in an uproar for several months. For the post-war generation, he was "the symbolic political figure for the insufficiently addressed Nazi past." Even today, "he functions as a representative of the state of the judicial system, the spokesman for which, even after the end of World War II, justified or whitewashed the terror-based justice that had been practiced in the Nazi state."[173]

Filbinger revealed his true colors with the following statement: "What was legal then can not now be deemed illegal."[174] He possessed no sense of being wrong, and that is what ultimately sealed his political fate. Filbinger did not fail because of his actions during the Nazi period, but "due to his handling of historical facts in a politically sensitive public realm."[175] Filbinger's statement disclosed the fact that this CDU politician, one who held a high political office, continued to embrace "a legal continuity in the sense of an uncritical and unexamined adherence to Nazi laws and 'Führer directives.'" "Without a single hesitation, he glossed over the differences between the unconstitutional Nationalist Socialist state and the constitutional democratic state."[176]

In Filbinger's case, the question of personal guilt and involvement was not ignored. By arguing that the Hitler dictatorship came upon the German people like a natural disaster and that no one could have done anything to prevent it, the individual sought to escape his responsibility. This strategy fit perfectly with other efforts to forget and suppress. Anyone who had confessed the reality would have had to admit "that the murder of millions of defenseless victims had resulted from numerous culpable decisions and actions made by individuals, and that this could not be displaced onto the interpretation we have claimed of blaming everything on our superiors, ultimately the Führer. The fact that everything that happened did happen cannot be solely attributed to the Führer's miraculous abilities; instead it should be also blamed on an 'unbelievable sense of obedience.'"[177]

On May 23, 1978, the Stuttgart court forbade the spreading of the claim that Filbinger was able "to go free thanks to the silence of those who knew him." His freedom was also based on an obstruction of justice. This was not enough for Filbinger. However, in June, the State Court in Stuttgart ruled that all of the other statements ("terrible judge," "Hitler's naval judge," and "Filbinger even tried a German sailor according to Nazi laws in a British prison camp, after Hitler's death") were free expressions of opinion.

Until his death, Filbinger maintained that he had behaved rightly. As prosecuting attorney, he had acted justly in following directives and orders. His decisions were in accord with Nationalist Socialist laws, and he had no room to maneuver differently. Yet, there was room to maneuver otherwise. In Gröger's case, he could have argued against the judge's request for the death penalty without fearing that there would have been personal repercussions for him.[178] Filbinger did everything he could in the hopes of rehabilitating himself.

He even claimed to have been an anti-Nazi. He never did say how this perspective fit with his decision to join the Nazi party in 1937 and his sentencing of a man to prison time for "lapsed convictions" weeks after the capitulation.

Heinz Drossel had very little to say when asked his opinions about the affair. He had left Berlin because of the Nazis that were working in his professional sphere, and he landed in Baden-Württemberg where Hans Karl Filbinger was in control. An ironic, even cynical twist of fate, wasn't it? At this observation, Drossel looked a little surprised, then he said: "Yes, that is the way it was."

How did Marianne react to the events? Had she been upset or troubled by the Filbinger scandal? Was she furious, offended, sad? Or had she tried to ignore the coverage as much as she could, since she wanted to avoid strong emotional swings? Since she did not feel comfortable dealing with the controversy?

By reading the foreword to the second edition of Heinz Drossel's memoirs, you can get a glimpse of how Marianne dealt with the shadows of the past: "These most difficult minutes of her life [this is a reference to the situation on the Jungfern Bridge, when she wanted to kill herself and Heinz prevented her from doing so] were the catalyst for such a great shock that all subsequent mentions of this experience brought her to the verge of nervous collapse."[179]

Perhaps it would have helped her if the social climate had been other than it was, if the public had been willing to discuss the Nazi past more openly and honestly. She may have been strengthened through encouragement, sympathy, and sincere attempts to name and punish the guilty parties. However, it took a long time before German society was willing to adequately distance itself from the perpetrators from the past. May 8, 1985, witnessed the first time that anyone publicly spoke of the "Nazi tyranny." Then-Federal President Richard von Weizsäcker used this phrase in his official speech given on the 40th anniversary of the end of the war. With this, he clearly distinguished "the fundamental difference to a constitutional democratic nation that definitely affirms the inviolable and inalienable human rights."[180]

However, Marianne Drossel never experienced this new era. She died in Freiburg in 1981 at the age of 68.

From the very beginning, Heinz Drossel immersed himself in his new work in Baden-Württemberg. Finally, he wanted to make a career for himself. He wished to show what he had in him. He proved to be successful in his profession, and his activities brought him great satisfaction. He was promoted to State Social Court Councilor and then later to regulatory judge. He ultimately became the President of the Social Court I in Freiburg. Heinz enjoyed his place as a figure of authority. He gladly took on responsibility and liked being in charge. At times, Ruth found him to be "despotic." For example, her father always selected where they went on vacation. Her mother would have loved to visit the Mediterranean once, but they always went to the mountains during the vacations. Heinz liked to go hiking.

The couple grew closer together as they raised their daughter Ruth. Since Marianne was no longer employed outside the home, she spent more time with the child than Heinz did. She energetically and lovingly trained and took care of her daughter. She sent her into life with a sentence that Ruth has never forgotten: "Do not <u>ever</u> become financially dependent on a man."

Under dramatic circumstances, Heinz and Marianne learned to love each other. When they married, they hardly knew one another. They remained together for 35 years. They were both troubled by the past, but they supposedly never spoke about it. They tried to create a new life and to look forward. Sometimes they might have lost sight of one another.

"A Certain Inner Peace"

Waldkirch, April 28, 2008

After his wife's death, Heinz Drossel at first felt very lonely. He decided to retire several months after she had died. He spent most of his time with his dachshund Petra. Then he began to write his memoirs. He had long wanted to write a memory book together with his wife. The first sentence was supposed to read as follows: "Marianne, who now went by Sarah, stood before the city hall." However, nothing ever came of these plans. Marianne never found the strength to grapple with what had happened to her under the Nazi dictatorship.

Heinz Drossel could not find a publisher for *Die Zeit der Füchse*. He paid to have it self-published. At about the same time, he decided that he wanted to move. He relocated to Simonswald in the Black Forest, where he found a home with Renate Silabetschki and her children.

Renate Silabetschki had been a friend of Heinz's stepson Billy, who had died in 1988. Now she was Heinz's landlady and housekeeper, and he became a surrogate Grandpa for the small family. Heinz Drossel dressed up as St. Nicholas and visited the kindergarten. Later, he helped the children with their homework. All of this made him very happy. He led a modest, quiet life, the high points of which were spending time with the children and long walks out into the countryside.

Then a letter arrived from Jerusalem. Already back in 1991, his friend Ernest Günter Fontheim—Heinz stayed in touch with him and his family over the years—had tried to have Heinz Drossel and his parents (posthumously) honored by Yad Vashem as "Righteous among the Nations."

Heinz had ignored the first application. Then in 1999, another request for his comments arrived, and this time he responded. Everything happened very quickly. The ceremony took place on May 4, in Berlin. May 4 was Heinz Drossel's lucky day, as he sometimes said; it was the date on which he should have been executed and the day he married Marianne in 1946.

On the one hand, he was touched by the recognition. On the other hand, he had an uneasy feeling about this. He never saw himself as a hero, and he did not want to be viewed as such. In a comment from 2004, he explained: "I don't know—I was honored because others didn't do anything."

Heinz Drossel and Ernest Günter Fontheim in Berlin, 2000

He did not see himself as a "rescuer." He had acted according to his conscience and his feelings. "I cannot say that I 'rescued' my wife. But the fact that she and the others survived, and she then died a natural death, gives me a certain inner peace." He believed that his behavior was only a drop on a hot stone: "I could not do more. I simply did not have the contacts. You have to know someone who is being persecuted before you can help them." Everyone knew that they needed help: "Anyone who says that he did not know what was going on is a liar."

At first, Drossel's honoring as "Righteous among the Nations" attracted hardly any attention. The regional press did not cover the story, and only a couple of Berlin city newspapers provided detailed accounts. Later, it was primarily the Freiburg historian Wolfram Wette who wrote about Heinz Drossel and educated the public about what he had done.

Wette realized that as a witness to the past Drossel could offer valuable perspectives to young people. He invited Drossel to come to the Scholl Siblings High School in Waldkirch on the Auschwitz Memorial Day in January 2001. At first, Drossel hesitated, but Wette was able to convince him to come. Drossel visited the school and spent two hours telling stories from his life. Uli Weissberger, the history teacher, and his students were deeply moved by this meeting. Shortly thereafter, the teacher sent a letter to Drossel. He asked him if he would be interested in being involved in a history project. Drossel immediately agreed.

In November 2001, Heinz Drossel accompanied Uli Weissberger and a group of teenagers to Berlin, where the students made a documentary film about Drossel. The cooperative work was very productive and fulfilling for everyone involved. The teenagers valued Drossel's honesty, and he felt good to be among young people again. The sympathies that were shown to him were invigorating.

After Weissberger, Reinhard Egge came along next. As he did then, the former military officer still volunteers for youth-related endeavors today. Drossel let himself be roped in, and up to one year before his death, Drossel was still speaking to school groups about his experiences.

His work with young people became his personal elixir of life.

He was especially delighted when the former Seelbach Civil Service School, where he spent many hours with the civil service providers, was renamed in 2006 as the Heinz Drossel Training Center. For this reason, he was all the sadder when, due to financial reasons, the school was shut down two years later.

After his honoring as "righteous," other things started to happen in Heinz Drossel's life. The feeling that he was doing something worthwhile and useful through his life experience talks rejuvenated the old man. Initially, no one in Simonswald congratulated Drossel. Only first after then-Federal President Johannes Rau awarded Drossel the Federal Cross of Merit did things gradually change.

Shortly after this honor, Heinz Drossel celebrated his 85th birthday. When the Simonswald mayor learned that President Rau would visit the village on Heinz Drossel's special day, the mayor announced that he too wanted to offer his congratulations.

Heinz found the whole situation to be quite ironic. The man who had rarely expressed any interest in community member Drossel, even after he had received the highest honor that the State of Israel could give a foreigner, now came to his apartment. In Drossel's opinion, this change of heart happened because the mayor wanted to bask in the glow of the esteemed visitor.

Wette and an SPD Parliament member had arranged Rau's visit. The President and Drossel apparently got along very well. They drank coffee together and sat comfortably in Drossel's living room. The Social Democrat made it very clear what he saw as the significance of Drossel's actions during the war: "There are more quiet heroes than we know, and many fewer than we could have used."[181]

Germany's highest leader made a lasting impression in the community after his visit with Heinz, who clearly enjoyed the attention that came his way. After their chat, Rau was chauffeured to the sports field, where a giant helicopter waited for him. No one missed the dramatic departure of the distinguished visitor from Simonswald.

Federal President Johannes Rau visiting Heinz Drossel, September 2001

After this, Heinz was occasionally addressed in the village. Some simply congratulated him, while others thanked him for his brave deeds. The number who expressed their gratitude was few, but Heinz had long given up hoping for a positive reaction. He was happy. He was less delighted by a couple of old men who had also participated in the war. Despite their attempts, they found little sympathy for their nostalgic statements: "Those were wild times. However, everything wasn't all that bad then." As always, Heinz Drossel had little patience for war-time romanticism: "I never would engage in such conversations. They had never understood any of it."

Beyond the boundaries of the Black Forest, Drossel had become a minor celebrity. In October 2004, he received the Raoul Wallenberg Medal from the University of Michigan. He was invited to be on television talk shows, which he refused, but he did give a few interviews. In 2005, at almost 89 years of age, he agreed to take part in the filming of a television documentary about the Yad Vashem memorial site in Jerusalem. He spent a week in Israel with an RTL team led by Peter Kloeppel.

Heinz Drossel in Yad Vashem, 2005

Heinz Drossel located the names of his parents and himself engraved in stone on the Allee of the Righteous. The trip moved him deeply. In the 1970s and 1980s, he had repeatedly turned down his sister-in-law's invitations to visit Tel Aviv. But now he discovered that he "somehow felt at home" in the streets of the historic Jerusalem city center. According to the Jewish faith, the souls of those who have visited the Holy City reach God faster after their deaths than those of others.

Drossel had been raised Catholic, but he was not dogmatic. Instead of speaking of God, he talked about the "incredible power that I trust." He had discovered his faith as a boy, finding strength and comfort in the spiritual dimension, even during the most challenging hours of the war. In middle age, he occasionally would retreat to a Buddhist cloister for several days in search of meditative silence and peace of mind.

On April 28, 2008, Heinz Drossel died in Waldkirch in the Black Forest. It is to be hoped that he was able to fulfill his greatest wish, which he had expressed at the age of 87: "to pass on in quiet and peace." During his final years, he spent much time thinking about life and death. He was not self-pitying in this. Instead, he was accepting of the course of things. He once said that he was not afraid. Death was, after all, part of life.

He must have felt some satisfaction in the fact that, at the end, he had experienced public recognition. He himself would probably never have thought of it this way. Nonetheless, after all of the injustice that he had lived through, he did express the great value and inner peace he took from the respect that was shown to him late in life. There was an element of reconciliation in the developments that occurred after the Yad Vashem honor. He was less withdrawn. It was easier for him to talk to people, and he felt a greater joy in life.

He knew that he was lucky to have reached such an advanced age in relative health. But what had he actually done? Could he have done anything better? These questions dogged his steps. He fought for serenity, which he was not always able to achieve. The terrible images from the war followed him at all times. He explained that he felt fortunate that, despite these memories, he had found a "certain inner peace." However, he was also haunted by awful nightmares during

his final years. In these, he imagined himself back in the Russian trenches, full of fear.

The night before his 90th birthday, he had another dream. This time, though, it was a beautiful one. He dreamed that he was with his wife Marianne at the renowned Vienna Opera Ball. He was in a tuxedo, and she was in an elegant gown. They dance harmoniously. In reality, he confessed, he had been a lousy dancer his entire life.

Marianne, ca. 1946

Afterword

William Albinus, Marianne's son, received training as a public service administrative assistant, and he worked in the Freiburg military archives. Billy got married, had a son, and was divorced shortly thereafter. He increasingly distanced himself from his family. Over time, his connection with Heinz Drossel was completely broken. He died in 1988 at the age of 53 in a hospital in Freiburg, shortly after an acquaintance had found him unconscious in his apartment.

Marianne's older daughter Judis spent her childhood in Israel until the age of 15. In 1956, Marianne and Heinz brought her to Germany. She became a pastry baker and got married in 1972. She had always wished to have children, and she had two sons. Today she lives under another name in Hessen and stays busy with two grandchildren.

Ruth Drossel's resemblance to her mother is not just limited to her appearance. Her dancing talent and her mathematical and scientific skills link her to her mother's family. She studied mathematics in college and became a teacher. Today she works an an independent financial adviser. She has long been interested in genealogy. As a young woman, Ruth traveled to Israel, where she met her uncle and cousins. She asked numerous questions and learned much about her mother, things that no one else knew. However, many things remained hidden to her as well. As an adult, she has repeatedly called for attention to be given to political developments in Germany.

She often worries about right-wing tendencies in the country.

The views of Heinz Drossel seem to her too one-dimensional. For her, her father was "a totally normal person, with the emphasis on normal." She expressed this in a talk she gave on the occasion of a memorial celebration for him at the Scholl Sibling High School on June 27, 2008. She wanted to "help curb the development of hero worship," which she thought she had observed in the way the public viewed her father in recent years. Ruth Drossel wanted to emphasize to the young people that, in principle, decent behavior was achievable by every person.

"'Heroes,' in both a human and in a military sense, receive a kind of adulation for their actions. This makes those actions 'inimitable,' in the truest sense of the word. I view both of these things as fatal for varying reasons . . . The values that we embrace in our lives are usually shaped by our parents, our schools, and our social and political frameworks. For Heinz Drossel, the most influential person was his father, who generated and lived his values in an authentic manner . . . It was, therefore, not unusual that the son adapted and lived according to the expectations of his parents. Thus, during the Nazi period, it was logical and 'normal' for Heinz Drossel to handle certain circumstances in a way that reflected his paternal shaping. ("Always stay human, my boy, even when it requires sacrifice."[182]) At this time, this undoubtedly required courage, intelligence, and a sense of what was possible, as well as knowledge of the structures whose mechanisms could allow one to recognize what could done. Otherwise, his humane actions could have easily cost him his life."[183]

Documents

Sworn Affidavit

As a justification for the current reparation request, I provide the following statement under oath:

In 1938, I lived in an apartment at Bambergerstr. 4. Because of the impossibility of gaining legal employment as a Jewess and because of the increasing difficulties caused by the Nazi regulations, I found myself in extreme financial difficulties and was behind on my rent by 3–4 months. As a result of the so-called Night of the Broken Glass and the violent death of my father, I had to leave the apartment in December 1938. I was then forced to sell the rest of my furniture to the people who moved into the apartment. They paid the back rent in the amount of 240.–and an additional 70.– The value of my furnishings was about 1,300.–and a loss of 990– incurred. After the birth of my child in 1942—because of the threat of a so-called Racial Defilement charge, I had to claim that the father was Jewish—I was arrested in late December 1942 and spent several weeks in the prison on Grosser Hamburgerstr. At this time, my fur coat and my jewelry were confiscated. After about 6 weeks, I and my son (a mixed blood) from my first marriage, divorced in 1936, were released under the stipulation from SS leader Duberkel that we had to wear the star in the future. The fur and the jewelry were never returned.

Tempelhof, 24 August 1949
Marianne Drossel, geb. Hirschfeld
Tempelhof, Friedrich-Franz-Str. 38

Dokumente

Eidesstattliche Erklärung.

Zur Begründung über den Grund des entstandenen Vermögensschadens erkläre ich das Folgende an Eidesstatt:

Ich bewohnte im Jahre 1938 eine Wohnung in der Bambergerstr.4. Infolge der Unmöglichkeit, als Jüdin geregelte Arbeit zu bekommen, und der wachsenden Schwierigkeiten durch die nationalsozialistischen Maßnahmen befand ich mich in starken finanziellen Schwierigkeiten und war 3–4 Monate die Mieten rückständig. Als Folgen der sog. Kristallnacht und des gewaltsamen Todes meines Vaters mußte ich im Dezember 1938 die Wohnung räumen und war dabei gezwungen, die Reste meiner Einrichtung den Leuten zu verkaufen, die die Wohnung übernahmen. Sie zahlten dafür die rückständigen Mieten in Höhe von 240.– und außerdem 70.– bar, sodaß mir bei einem Wert der Einrichtung von etwa 1300.– ein Schaden von 990.– entstand. Nach der Geburt eines Kindes im Jahre 1942, für das ich wegen der drohenden Gefahr eines sog. Rassenschandeprozesses einen jüdischen Vater angeben mußte, wurde ich Ende Dezember 1942 abgeholt und mehrere Wochen in der Großen Hamburgerstr. in Haft gehalten. Bei dieser Gelegenheit wurde mein Pelzmantel sowie mein Schmuck beschlagnahmt. Ich wurde dann nach ca 6 Wochen mit meinem Sohn (Mischling) aus erster Ehe, geschieden 1936, mit der Auflage durch den SS-Führer Duberkel entlassen, in Zukunft den Stern zu tragen. Der Pelz und der Schmuck wurden einbehalten.

Tempelhof, den 24. August 1949
Marianne Droßel geb. Hirschfeld
Tempelhof, Friedrich-Franz-Str. 38

Sworn Affidavit

After vacating the apartment at Bamberger Strasse 4, I sublet apartments from Jewish families; first in 1942 from the Fleischers, Knesebeckstrasse 76. Here I had a room that contained the items entered on Form D and jewelry that is described in the Immediate Aid application.

I knew that the Fleischers wanted to "go underground," and they left the apartment in late 1942 under the cover of night and fog. Beforehand, they had asked me to first report their disappearance several days later, so they could have a head start. I waited one week after they left the apartment to report the disappearance to the relevant police station. Nothing came of it.

On 27 December 1942, together with my son, I was picked up and taken to the prison on the Grosser Hamburgerstr. The arresting parties left together with me, and they did not seal the apartment. I was told that I could leave everything there, including the valuables that were packed in suitcases. The packed items would be fetched later. I only took one small suitcase with the minimum of necessities. Upon my return on 17 February 1943, the apartment was sealed. As I learned from the statements at the police station, the sealing was done shortly before my return because of the disappearance of the Fleischers.

I was then able to get the rest of my things from the apartment; this included the remainder of my clothes and linens. The suitcases with the valuables were gone. For obvious reasons, I did not inquire about them at the time.

I only assumed that these things were confiscated. I do not know where these things went. I can only say that they vanished after my return. I immediately moved to another room (Lietzenbuergstr. 8 at the baker's). Ten days later, I was arrested again.

Eidesstattliche Erklärung

Nach Aufgabe der Wohnung Bamberger Straße 4 lebte ich bei jüdischen Familien in Untermiete; zuletzt im Jahre 1942 bei dem Ehepaar F l e i s c h e r , Knesebeckstraße 76. Dort hatte ich ein Zimmer, in dem sich die im Antragsformular D aufgeführten Gegenstände und der im Soforthilfe-Antrag vorab bezeichnete Schmuck befand.

Das Ehepaar Fleischer, von dem ich wußte, daß es »untertauchen« wollte, verließ Ende 1942 bei Nacht und Nebel die Wohnung. Sie hatten mich vorher gebeten, ihr Verschwinden erst nach einigen Tagen zu melden, damit sie einen Vorsprung hätten. Ich meldete das Verschwinden etwa eine Woche, nachdem Fleischers die Wohnung verlassen hatten auf dem zuständigen Polizei-Revier. Darauf erfolgte nichts.

Am 27. 12. 1942 wurde ich zusammen mit meinem Sohn abgeholt und in das Lager Große Hamburgerstr. gebracht. Die Abholer verließen mit mir zusammen die Wohnung, ohne diese zu versiegeln. Mir wurde gesagt, ich könnte alles stehen lassen, auch die in Koffern verpackten Wertsachen; die gepackten Sachen würden nachgeholt. Ich nahm nur ein Köfferchen mit notwendigstem mit. Bei meiner Rückkehr am 17. 2. 1943 war die Wohnung dann versiegelt. Wie ich aus Bemerkungen auf dem Polizei-Revier entnahm, war die Versiegelung wegen des Verschwindens des Ehepaares Fleischer erst kurz vor meiner Rückkehr erfolgt.

Ich konnte dann meine restlichen Sachen aus der Wohnung holen; es handelte sich um meine restliche Kleidung und Wäsche. Die Koffer mit den Wertsachen waren verschwunden. Ich habe aus naheliegenden Gründen damals keine Nachforschungen angestellt.

Daß diese Sachen beschlagnahmt worden sind, war lediglich eine Vermutung; wo die Sachen geblieben sind, weiß ich nicht. Ich kann nur sagen, daß sie nach meiner Rückkehr verschwunden waren. Ich habe dann sofort ein anderes Zimmer bezogen (Lietzenburgerstr. 8 bei Bäcker). Zehn Tage später wurde ich erneut verhaftet.

Copy

Marianne Drossel, nee Hirschfeld, div. Albinus
Berlin-Tempelhof, Friedrich-Franz-Str. 38

Tempelhof, 14 January 1952

> To the
> > Jewish Synagogue
> > > Berlin
> > > Oranienburgerstr. 28

In aid of my reparation request, I am requesting from you a certificate that I am ethnically Jewish and that I was a member of the Jewish synagogue. Please note that I have remarried, and at that time, I was either using my maiden name (Hirschfeld) or the last name of my first husband (Albinus).

> I would be grateful for a quick response to this request.
> > With high regards

Copy

Marianne Drossel, nee Hirschfeld
Berlin-Tempelhof
Friedrich-Franz-Str. 38
> Appendix to Form E

After attending Dr. Richter's Lyceum in Berlin, Grossbeerenstr., which I left after upper secondary levels, I successfully completed a two-year higher commercial study course at the Lettehaus in Berlin. Among other things, courses were offered in business calculations, book keeping, stenography, and typing in German, English, and French. After concluding my studies at the business school in 1931, I accepted a position as a correspondent with the South German Textile Company, Inc., Berlin Poststr. My monthly salary was 200.– M. After about a year, I was employed in the newly founded Hirschfeld & Co. as head clerk with the goal of eventually being hired as a manager. In my new position, I was

Abschrift

Marianne D r o ß e l geb. Hirschfeld gesch. A l b i n u s
Berlin-Tempelhof, Friedrich-Franzstr. 38

Tempelhof, den 14.1.1952

    An die
        Jüdische Gemeinde
            Berlin
        Oranienburgerstr. 28

Zum Zwecke meiner Entschädigungsansprüche benötige ich von
Ihnen eine Bescheinigung darüber, daß ich in der Sippenkartei geführt
worden bin und der Jüdischen Gemeinde angehöre. Ich bitte dabei zu
berücksichtigen, daß ich in zweiter Ehe verheiratet bin und seinerzeit
entweder unter meinem Mädchennamen Hirschfeld oder dem Namen
meines ersten Mannes A l b i n u s geführt wurde.

Für baldige Erledigung wäre ich dankbar.

        Mit vorzüglicher Hochachtung

Abschrift

Marianne Droßel geb. Hirschfeld
Berlin-Tempelhof,
Friedrich-Franz-Str. 38

        Anlage zu Einlageformular E
        =========================

Nach dem Besuch des Dr. Richter'schen Lyceums in Berlin, Großbee-
renstr., das ich mit der Obersekundareife verließ, absolvierte ich eine
zweijährige höhere Handelsschule am Lettehaus in Berlin mit Erfolg.
Gelehrt wurde u.a. kaufmännisches Rechnen, Buchführung, Stenogra-
fie und Schreibmaschine in Deutsch, Englisch und Französisch. Nach
dem Abschluß dieser Handelsschule im Jahre 1931 nahm ich eine Stel-

responsible for the supervision of the registrations and book keeping, as well as the handling of complicated, especially foreign-language, correspondence. My initial monthly salary with Hirschfeld & Co. was 250.– M. An intended raise of this salary was never possible because of the Jewish boycott on 1 April 1933. The fact that the business could never recover from the effect of this and subsequent anti-Semitic actions resulted in the collapse of the company and my unemployment in 1935. I was unemployed from this point until the time of my divorce in 1936. Because I was Jewish, I could no longer get a job due to the legislation passed by the Hitler regime. Even after my divorce, I could not find a position because of the anti-Semitic regulations. Although theoretically there were still a few possibilities, it was practically impossible to find a position in my career. It would have only been possible to pursue my career in a Jewish company, but because of the Nuremburg Laws, these companies were basically forced to be liquidated or to eventually be expropriated. This is why I stayed in my father's household through 1938. After the murder of my father, I moved into the home of my aunt, Ms. Dorothea Hirschfeld, until 1939, when I was required to enter the forced labor force. I had to take part in this work until 1945. Between late 1939 and my imprisonment on 27 February 1943, I was with the Mark Cable Works, Keplerstrasse. Here I earned a net monthly income of about 140.– M. After my release from police custody on Levetzowstr., I worked nights (according to the statement by the BVG), under very difficult circumstances, for the BVG as a vehicle washer. My net salary here was about 175.– M per month. Between 1 January 1945 and 21 April 1945, I was not paid any salary.

Also, after the war, I received a salary of 250.– M or 225.– M from the American Joint through the Weintraub Bakery. However, it should be noted that even this final position was only a stop-gap solution, and with my training, I should have earned a minimum of 250.– M. I base my claims for reparation on the base salary of 250.– M, although under normal progressive circumstances, I should have been earning a much higher salary after the passage of a few years. According to my reparation calculations, I position my claim in Group VII of the TOA.

Here is the calculated basis for this claim:

lung als Korrespondentin bei der Süddeutschen Webstoffgesellschaft m. b. H., Berlin Poststr., an. Mein Gehalt betrug 2oo.– M. Nach etwa einem Jahr wurde ich bei der neu gegründeten Firma Hirschfeld & Co als Bürovorsteherin eingestellt mit dem Ziel, später als Geschäftsführerin übernommen zu werden. Meine Aufgaben nach Antritt der Stellung bestanden in der Führung der Registratur und Buchführung sowie der Erledigung der schwierigen insbesondere fremdsprachlichen Korrespondenz. Mein Anfangsgehalt betrug bei der Firma Hirschfeld & Co 25o.– M. Eine vorgesehene baldige Erhöhung dieses Gehalts war infolge der Auswirkungen des Judenboykotts vom 1. 4. 1933 nicht möglich. Da das Geschäft sich von den Folgen dieses und der folgenden antisemitischen Aktionen nicht erholen konnte, erfolgte mit dem Zusammenbruch des Unternehmens 1935 mein Ausscheiden. Bis zu meiner Ehescheidung im Jahre 1936 war ich dann ohne Beruf, da ich als Jüdin keine Anstellung mehr auf Grund der Gesetzgebung des Hitlerregimes bekam. Auch nach meiner Ehescheidung gelang es mir infolge der antisemitischen Maßnahmen nicht mehr, eine Stellung zu erhalten. Obwohl theoretisch noch einige Möglichkeiten bestanden hätten, war es praktisch nicht mehr möglich, Stellung in meinem Beruf zu finden, da dies nur in einem jüdischen Unternehmen möglich gewesen wäre, diese Firmen aber nach der Nürnberger »Gesetzgebung« gezwungen waren, mehr oder weniger schnell zu liquidieren oder sich einem Zwangsverkauf zu unterwerfen. Ich führte deshalb bis zum Jahre 1938 bei meinem Vater den Haushalt. Nach der Ermordung meines Vaters führte ich meiner Tante, Frau Dorothea Hirschfeld, den Haushalt, bis ich Ende 1939 zur Zwangsarbeit verpflichtet wurde und diese Tätigkeit bis zum Jahre 1945 ausüben mußte. Von Ende 1939 bis zu meiner Verhaftung am 27. Februar 1943 war ich bei den Märkischen Kabelwerken, Keplerstraße bei einem Bruttolohn von monatlich etwa 14o.– M tätig. Nach meiner Entlassung aus der Polizeihaft Levetzowstr. war ich vom 16. 4. 1943 bis zum 21. 4. 1945 (nach Angabe der BVG) bei der BVG unter besonders erschwerten Verhältnissen als Wagenwäscherin bei Nachtarbeit tätig. Mein Lohn betrug hier ca 175.– M brutto pro Monat. Für die Zeit vom 1. 1. 45 bis zum 21. 4. 1945 habe ich keinerlei Lohn oder Gehalt bekommen.

Auch nach dem Krieg habe ich dann sofort ein Gehalt von 25o.– M bzw. 225.– M bei dem American Joint bzw. der Bäckerei Weintraub erhalten, wobei zu berücksichtigen wäre, daß auch diese letztere Stel-

According to § 32 of the Reparations Act, a monthly adjustment of 100.–
DM West is to be used, and the received salary is to be taken from this
base. Based on the law, 10.– M is to be converted to 2.– DMW.

1.) January 1940 to March 1943 = 39 Months = 3,900.– DMW Conversion
Minus 28.– DMW (140.– M) for 39 Months 1,092.– DMW
Paid to me   2,808.– DMW
April 1943 to December 1944 = 21 Months = 2,100.– DMW
2.) Minus 35.– DMW (175.– M) for 21 Months 735.– DMW
Paid to me   1,365.– DMW
3.) January 1945 to April 1945 = 4 Months   400.– DMW
No deduction   ……………....
Paid to me   400.– DMW

Thus: 2,808.– DMW
         1,365.– DMW
           400.– DMW
         4,573.– DMW

Therefore, according to § 32 of the Reparations Act, I request damages for
        4,573 DM

Berlin-Tempelhof, 25 October 1952
                          Marianne Drossel, nee Hirschfeld

lung nur eine Gelegenheitslösung war und mir nach meiner Ausbildung ein Gehalt von mindestens 25o.– M zugestanden hat. Ich setze bei der Geltendmachung meines Schadens ein mir zukommendes Gehalt von 25o.– an, obwohl bei einer normalen Entwicklung ich nach wenigen Jahren ein wesentlich höheres Einkommen bezogen haben würde. Bei meiner Schadensberechnung lege ich daher eine Stellung nach Gruppe VII der TOA zugrunde.

Mithin ergibt sich folgende Berechnungsgrundlage:

Nach § 32 Entscheidungsgesetz ist pro Monat ein Ausgleich von 1oo.– DM West anzusetzen, von dem der erhaltene Lohn abzuziehen ist, und zwar für je 1o.– M nach dem Gesetz 2.– DMW.

1.) Januar 1940 bis März 1943 = 39 Monate =   3.9oo.– DMW Ausgleich
Abzüglich 39 Monate je 28.– DMW (140.– M) <u>1.o92.– DMW</u>
Zu meinen Gunsten   2.8o8.– DMW
April 1943 bis Dezember 1944 = 21 Monate = 2.1oo.– DMW
2.) Abzüglich 21 Monate je 35.– DMW (175.– M) <u>735.– DMW</u>
Zu meinen Gunsten   1.365.– DMW
3.) Januar 1945 bis April 1945 = 4 Monate   4oo.– DMW
kein Abzug   ....
3.) Zu meinen Gunsten   4oo.– DMW

Also: 2.8o8.– DMW
         1.365.– DMW
          <u>4oo.– DMW</u>
         4.573.– DMW
         ===========

Ich mache daher gem. § 32 Entschädigungsgesetz einen Schaden von
     4.573 DM d.B.d.L.
                              geltend.

Berlin-Tempelhof, den 25. 1o. 1952
                     Marianne Droßel, geb. Hirschfeld

Copy

Marianne Drossel   Tempelhof, 27 April 1954
Berlin-Tempelhof, Alarichstr. 6
PRV-6ache Soz. II H ??
        To the
                Senator for Social Services
                Berlin-Wilmersdorf
                Fehrbelliner Platz 4

In reference to the issues surrounding my illegality, I want to note the following: when I claim to have lived illegally since 1944, this is based on the fact that at that time, and even yet today, I consider my day-to-day behavior during the time in question as illegal. This perspective does not exclude the fact that today there may be a different definition for this concept. However, I must assume that the current use of the concept can still be used in considering my actual circumstances during the Nazi period. If I was in danger then, I cannot imagine that this danger would not have existed if the concept had had a different definition, as it may today.

One must assume that the application of this concept is based on the meaning of the word. The word "illegal" comes from the word lex, leges = the law, and the use of the prefex il- results in the converse of the concept, that is "non-legal" (similar to, illicitus = not allowed, illiteratus = not educated, illoyal = inequitable, illegitim = non-legal, also out of wedlock). Illegal behavior is, thus, behavior not sanctioned by the law. To act illegally entails behaviors that are contrary to legal restrictions.

During the Nazi period, the concept of illegality primarily pertained activities that related to reporting structures and residential locations. Even in considerations of this limitation, my behavior then was illegal.

According to the regulations on reporting notification (Reichsmeldeordnung) from 6 January 1938 RGes.Bl. I page 13, amended version page 204 from 1938, everyone who resided in the area of the German Reich had to register his/her address according to the stipulations of this law. According to § 3 of this art, every person was obligated to report his/her new address within 1 week of moving out of the registered residential address. Violations of this regulations were punishable according to § 26 of the act.

Abschrift

Marianne Droßel   Tempelhof, den 27. 4. 1954
Berlin – Tempelhof, Alarichstr. 6
PRV-6ache Soz.II H ??

     An den
         Senator für Sozialwesen
            Berlin – Wilmersdorf
            =================
          Fehrbelliner Platz 4

Zu den Angaben über meine Illegalität bemerke ich folgendes:
Wenn ich angegeben habe, seit 1944 illegal gelebt zu haben, so ist dies
darauf zurückzuführen, daß ich das von mir in der fraglichen Zeit an
den Tag gelegte Verhalten als illegales Leben aufgefaßt habe und auch
heute noch auffasse. Angesichts einer bis heute auch noch nicht vorlie-
genden eindeutigen Definition dieses Begriffs sind zwar verschiedene
Auffassungen darüber nicht ausgeschlossen. Ich muß allerdings auch bei
der heutigen Anwendung dieses Begriffs von meinen tatsächlichen Verhältnissen in der Nazizeit ausgehen. Wenn ich damals eine Gefahr ge-
tragen habe, so kann ich nicht heute feststellen, es wäre gar keine gewesen, weil ein Denkbegriff heute eine andere Auffassung findet als damals.
M. E. muß man bei der Anwendung dieses Begriffes von der Bedeu-
tung des Wortes ausgehen. Illegal ist abzuleiten von lex, leges = das Gesetz und bedeutet unter Voransetzung der Silbe il etwa das Gegenteil,
nämlich ungesetzlich (so z. B. illicitus = unerlaubt, illiteratus = ungelehrt,
illoyal = unbillig, illegitim = ebf. ungesetzlich, auch unehelich). Ein illegales Verhalten ist demnach ein ungesetzliches. Ungesetzlich ist aber ein
Verhalten dann, wenn gegen eine gesetzliche Bestimmung verstoßen wird.
Der Begriff der Illegalität während der Nazizeit bezieht sich nun
allerdings im wesentlichen auf das Verhalten hinsichtlich der Melde-
bestimmungen und des Aufenthaltsortes. Unter Berücksichtigung dieser Einschränkung ist aber mein Verhalten illegal gewesen.
Nach der Verordnung über das Meldewesen (Reichsmeldeordnung)
vom 6. Januar 1938 RGes.Bl. I Seite 13, Berichtigte Fassung Seite 2o4
von 1938 war jeder, der sich im Gebiet des deutschen Reiches aufhielt,
nach den Vorschriften dieses Gesetzes meldepflichtig. Nach dem § 3
dieser Rechtsverordnung war jeder verpflichtet, beim Auszug aus der

Insofar as I lived in various locations, besides the one I had registered, during the times in question means that I violated these regulations. Naturally I did this then to increase my safety. As a side note, this behavior would have been more harshly punished because of my Jewish ethnicity than it would have been by other violators. It would have resulted in my immediate deportation.

The repercussions of violating the legitimate policies at this time did not change the fact that I searched for temporary places to stay that were known to me. In reference to this behavior, specifically the continuation of my forced labor, I was compelled to keep working because I had no other options in order to secure even the bare essentials for my existence. Thus, I was forced to rely on the handouts that the proud German Reich made available for the most strenuous slave labor. This was also the reason that I had to risk being arrested on the work site in a so-called "Jewish Action." However, my unreported behavior outside of the work times alone counted as a violation of the restrictions. This reality was not negated by the fact that occasionally I stayed in a location that was known to me.

Logically, I must view my behavior at this time as having been illegal in nature. If people want to turn things around today, I only wish that this perspective had existed 10–15 years ago. In any case, I exercise my freedom to apply the basic terms equivocally across the board, instead of applying the assumption that the concepts only fit the circumstances of the times.

If I have not presented legal evidence for the assessment of the damages to freedom before the reparations office against the assessment of the 54 days of damages caused by imprisonment, this was only done because my husband was told during the process that the filing of a claim would delay the processing of the other reparation groups. On another occasion, the representative of the reparations office promised to immediately authorize the processing of the other damage claims. If I had known that this "immediately" did not reference a span of days, but decades, then I would have acted differently. In addition, my nerves have been and are harmed by the ongoing need to recall these dreadful memories. My health has been damaged. I already have given up hope for a just and actual reparation, and I am convinced that the little money that will come out of this will not serve to bless the German people in any way.

gemeldeten Wohnung binnen 1 Woche sich unter Angabe seines Verbleibs abzumelden. Zuwiderhandlungen hiergegen waren gemäß § 26 der VO unter Strafe gestellt.

Indem ich dadurch, daß ich mich seit der angegebenen Zeit an anderen Orten aufgehalten habe als dort, wo ich gemeldet war, habe ich gegen diese Bestimmungen fortgesetzt verstoßen. Ich habe dies zwar damals zu meiner größeren Sicherheit getan. Daß dieses Verhalten durch meine Zugehörigkeit zum Judentum zur damaligen Zeit wesentlich schärfer beurteilt worden wäre als bei anderen Personen und unweigerlich meine Deportation zur Folge gehabt hätte, sei nur am Rande vermerkt.

An der Tatsache dieses Verstoßes gegen damals geltende Bestimmungen ändert nichts, daß ich vorübergehend Orte aufgesucht habe, an denen ich bekannt war. Zu diesem Verhalten, nämlich der Fortsetzung meiner Zwangsarbeit, war ich gezwungen, weil ich keinerlei andere Möglichkeiten mehr hatte, um meinen allernotwendigsten Lebensbedarf in anderer Form zu sichern. Ich war also unbedingt auf die Almosen angewiesen, die mir von Seiten des stolzen deutschen Reiches für schwerste Sklavenarbeit zugebilligt wurde. Ich mußte auch aus diesem Grunde während der Arbeitszeit die Gefahr einer Festnahme an der Arbeitsstelle im Rahmen einer sogenannten »Judenaktion« auf mich nehmen. Allein mein unangemeldetes Verhalten außerhalb der Arbeitszeit stellt jedoch somit das Vergehen gegen gesetzliche Bestimmungen dar. Dies Vergehen wurde nicht dadurch ungeschehen gemacht, daß es Zeitpunkte gab, in denen ich mich an einem bekannten Aufenthaltsort aufhielt.

Logisch betrachtet muß ich somit mein damaliges Verhalten als illegal betrachten. Wenn man heute die Dinge umdrehen will, könnte ich nur wünschen, man hätte diese Auffassungen bereits vor lo –15 Jahren vertreten. Ich nehme mir jedenfalls die Freiheit, grundsätzliche Begriffe gleichmäßig auszulegen, statt die Auslegung so zu handhaben, daß sie den Bedürfnissen der Zeit entspricht.

Wenn ich bei der Festsetzung des Freiheitsschadens im Verfahren vor dem Entschädigungsamt gegen die Festsetzung von nur 54 Tagen Haftentschädigung keine Rechtsmittel eingelegt habe, dann nur aus dem Grunde, weil meinem Ehemann bei der Verhandlung erklärt wurde, daß bei Einlegung eines Einspruches die Bearbeitung der anderen Schadensgruppen verzögert werden würde. Andernfalls versprach der Vertreter des Entschädigungsamtes, die Bearbeitung des anderen Schadens sofort zu veranlassen. Hätte ich gewußt, daß dieses »sofort«

In terms of the question about wearing the star:

Until August 1942, I had a privileged status. I lost this status through the birth of my daughter J-, for whom I had to list a Jewish father in order to not risk being punished for "Racial Defilement." Based on the then valid legal regulations, I lost the protection of this status the moment I brought a full-Jewish child into the world.

In my case, I was only released from imprisonment in the Grosse Hamburger Str. Camp by SS leader Duberkel (or Doberkel) under orders to wear the star in the future. Since the birth of the child in August 1942, I was a star wearer.

Jewish Synagogue of Greater Berlin

Berlin, 6 February 1961

Ms.

Marianne Drossel

Berlin-Tempelhof

Alarichstrasse 6

In reference to your letter from the 29, we respectfully ask for a payment of DM 3.– (West) for the processing of your request. Please authorize the transfer to the Bekomark Konto 1100 of the German Notenmark, Berlin, at the Berliner Bank AG, Berlin-Charlottenburg.

Kind regards,

Jewish Synagogue of Greater Berlin

[Signature], Secretary

nicht einen Zeitraum von Tagen, sondern von Jahrzehnten umfaßt, hätte ich mich bereits damals entsprechend verhalten. Nebenbei bemerkt waren und sind mir auch meine Nerven zu schade, um mich fortgesetzt durch Aufrührung von diesen unerfreulichen Erinnerungen an meiner Gesundheit zu schädigen. Ich habe die Hoffnung auf eine aufrichtige Entschädigung in der Praxis auch bereits aufgegeben und bin überzeugt, daß die wenigen Gelder, die dabei herausspringen, dem deutschen Volke keinen Segen bringen werden.

Zur Frage des Sterntragens bemerke ich folgendes:

Ich war bis zum August 1942 privilegiert. Durch die Geburt meiner Tochter J███, für die ich einen jüdischen Vater angeben mußte, um nicht Gefahr zu laufen wegen »Rassenschande« verurteilt zu werden, entfiel die Privilegation. Schon auf Grund damals geltender gesetzlicher Bestimmungen entfiel die Begünstigung des Privilegs in dem Augenblick, in dem ich ein volljüdisches Kind zur Welt brachte.

Im meinem Fall wurde ich darüber hinaus aus der Inhaftierung in der großen Hamburger Str. seitens des SS-Führers Duberkel (oder Doberkel) nur unter der Auflage entlassen, in Zukunft den Stern zu tragen. Ich war mithin seit der Geburt des Kindes im August 1942 Sternträgerin.

JÜDISCHE GEMEINDE VON GROSS-BERLIN

BERLIN N 4, ORANIENBURGER STRASSE 28 / FERNSPRECHER 42 33 27 u. 42 33 28

Postscheckkonto: Berlin Nr. 215 02
Bank: Berliner Stadtkontor, Filiale 14
Berlin C 2, Rosenthaler Straße 40/41
Konto Nr. 1/8335

BERLIN N 4, den 6.Februar 1961

Frau
Marianne Drossel,
Berlin-Tempelhof
Alarichstrasse 6

Wir nehmen Bezug auf Ihr Schreiben vom 29.v.Mts.und bitten Sie höfl., für die durch Bearbeitung Ihrer Anfrage entstehenden Kosten um Einzahlung von DM 3.-(West) auf das Konto Bekomark 1loo der Deutschen Notenbank, Berlin, bei der Berliner Bank AG Berlin-Charlottenburg.

Hochachtungsvoll!

Jüdische Gemeinde von Gross-Berlin
i.A. Sekretär

205

Copy

Heinz Drossel
Landessozialgerichtsrat
Berlin-Tempelhof
Tempelhofer Damm 6
Tel. 66 21 81   13 June 1962

To the
Senator for Labor
via the
President of the State Social Court Berlin

Dear Honorable Senator!

I request your understanding for this letter that I am sending you today.

First of all, a few words of explanation about my personal situation. As I already shared with you in 1960 through the submission of pertinent documents, during the Nazi period, I risked my life to intervene for various Jewish victims. Almost the entire family of my racially persecuted Jewish wife was murdered during the Hitler period. The only yet-living relative in Germany is her 85-year-old aunt, Ms. Dorothea Hirschfeld. She was a leading figure from the founding of the labor charity movement, and was Ministerial Adviser in the former Prussian Labor Ministry and recipient of the golden Honor Pin from the SPD.

Soon after the end of the Second World War, I received an emigration visa for the USA from the American general consul in Berlin. After long consideration, we chose not to make use of this visa because we believed that democratically minded, politically untarnished individuals would be needed in Germany.

This assumption has proven to be false.

206

Abschrift

Heinz Droßel
Landessozialgerichtsrat
Berlin–Tempelhof
Tempelhofer Damm 6
Tel. 66 21 81   13. 6. 1962

<u>VERTRAULICH!</u>

An den
Herrn Senator für Arbeit
über den
Herrn Präsidenten des Landessozialgerichts Berlin

Sehr geehrter Herr Senator!

Ich bitte um Verständnis für das Anliegen, mit dem ich mich heute an
Sie wende.

Zur Erklärung zunächst einige Worts zu meiner persönlichen Lage. Wie
ich Ihnen bereits im Jahre 1960 unter Überreichung entsprechender
Unterlagen mitgeteilt habe, bin ich in der nationalsozialistischen Zeit
unter Einsatz meines Lebens für eine Reihe jüdischer Verfolgter einge-
treten. Fast die ganze Familie meiner als rassisch verfolgten anerkann-
ten jüdischen Frau ist in der Hitlerzeit ermordet worden. Die einzige in
Deutschland noch lebende Verwandte ist ihre 85-jährige Tante, die seit
der Gründung der Arbeiter-Wohlfahrt dort führend tätig gewesene Ministerialrätin i. R. im ehemaligen preußischen Arbeitsministerium Frau
Dorothea H i r s c h f e l d , Trägerin der goldenen Ehrennadel der SPD.

Bald nach dem Ende des zweiten Weltkrieges haben wir vom amerikanischen General-Konsulat in Berlin ein Einwanderungsvisum für die
USA erhalten. Nach langer Überlegung haben wir davon keinen Ge-
brauch gemacht, weil wir glaubten, in Deutschland würden demokratisch denkende, politisch unbelastete Menschen gebraucht werden.

Diese Annahme hat sich als falsch erwiesen.

Ich sehe mich heute einem ständigen Zwang zur Selbstbehauptung in
einer Umgebung ausgesetzt, die weitgehend die Politik des NS-Regimes

Today, I see myself under constant pressure to assert myself in an environment that is predominantly based on the policies set by the Nazi regime.

Mr. Senator, you can believe me when I say that it is not easy for me to hold out. I constantly sense certain opposition points, and I am the one who must defend his own skin. Admittedly, I am more strictly judged than is typical in the House, and I must constantly resist attempts to push me into the background. Until now, the Senate Administration has shown no interest in the difficulties that I have encountered.

In connection with this, the appointments of the senate presidents to the State Social Court Berlin have increasingly alienated me. Sadly, I was unable to determine the specific basis on which the last appointments were made. Collectively, as far as I could tell, the only general justification was previous political activity in the context of Nazism.

In terms of character—particularly in reference to activities during the Nazi regime—it seems that only very few colleagues in the court are comparable to me.

Considering the present situation, I do not see any significant structural changes in the staffing of the senate positions taking place any time soon. For me, this means the continuation of my activities in an increasingly tense relational field, which will already threaten to overwhelm my capabilities. I fear that my strength will only enable me to remain in my position for a limited period of time. I am sure you can understand that after so much sacrifice, I cannot risk my health and, by extension, the existence of my family.

After lengthy consideration, I have arrived at the conclusion that employment as an individual judge presents the lowest possible stress for me. In order to preserve my health, I need to avoid any work of a higher administrative level. For the same reasons, I will simply have to suffer the economic loss that a position as an individual judge will result in.

Since the work in social justice lies close to my heart, I would like to oversee a chamber of the social court. I have no doubt that you, Honorable

unterstützt hat. Sie können mir glauben, Herr Senator, daß es für mich nicht ganz leicht war, mich durchzusetzen. Ich spüre immer wieder gewisse Widerstände, ich bin es, der sieh seiner Haut wehren muß. Ich werde – zugegebenermaßen – strenger beurteilt, als es sonst im Hause Gepflogenheit ist und muß immer wieder Versuchen entgegentreten, mich in den Hintergrund zu spielen. Niemals bisher ist von der Senatsverwaltung dafür Interesse gezeigt worden, ob irgendwelche Schwierigkeiten für mich aufgetreten sind.

In diesem Zusammenhang haben mich auch die Ernennungen zu Senatspräsidenten am Landessozialgericht Berlin zunehmend befremdet. Es ist mir leider nicht gelungen, anhand der letzten Ernennungen bestimmte Grundsätze, nach denen diese Ernennungen erfolgten, herauszufinden. Gemeinsam war im allgemeinen – soweit ich dies beurteilen kann – nur eine frühere politische Betätigung im Sinne des Nationalsozialismus.

In leistungsmäßiger Hinsicht und in Bezug auf die Fähigkeit dürften an mich unbedenklich höhere Ansprüche gestellt werden, als offensichtlich in letzter Zeit bei Ernennungen verlangt worden ist. Altersmäßige Gründe können ebenfalls keine ausschlaggebende Rolle gespielt haben, da bereits jüngere Herren als ich zu Senatspräsidenten ernannt worden sind.

In charakterlicher Hinsicht schließlich dürften – wenn hierbei das Verhalten während dar Zeit der NS-Herrschaft berücksichtigt wird – nur sehr wenige Kollegen beim LSG einem Vergleich mit mir standhalten.

Angesichts der gegenwärtigen Lage ist mit einer wesentlichen strukturellen Änderung in der Besetzung der Senatsvorsitzenden auf längere Sicht nicht mehr zu rechnen. Das bedeutet für mich die Fortsetzung meiner Tätigkeit in einem ständig zunehmenden Spannungsverhältnis, das schon jetzt meine Kräfte zu überfordern droht. Ich muß befürchten, daß meine Kräfte meine jetzige Tätigkeit nur noch eine begrenzte Zeit zulassen. Sie werden Verständnis dafür haben, daß ich nach so vielen Opfern nicht noch meine Gesundheit und damit die Existenz meiner Familie aufs Spiel setzen kann.

Nach reiflicher Überlegung bin ich daher zu der Auffassung gelangt, daß eine Tätigkeit als Einzelrichter für mich nur noch die geringsten

Senator, understand well that a change to the Social Court Berlin does not come into question for me.

Thus, I ask for your written consent that you understand and agree with my attempt to change to another social court or to a court in another branch of the judicial system.

I eagerly await a positive response from you, Honorable Senator.

Copy

Dear Katharina Stegelmann,

On the occasion of this book and your request and in reference to my short talk at the honorary celebration on 27 June 2008 for Heinz Droßel*, here are a few of my basic thoughts from this talk—in a little more concrete detail.

"Norms" in the sense of values,
the turning point and lynchpin for actions driven by character?

In both a human sense and a military context, "heroes" experience a kind of glorification of their deeds, which makes their actions in the eyes of others somehow "inimitable." Both of these I view, for differing reasons as fatal.

* Due to Ruth Drossel's wish, the orthography of the name was not standardized.

I wanted to give a little restraint to this tendency toward heroification in my short honorary speech on 27 June 2008 when I stated: "Heinz Drossel was a totally normal person, with an emphasis on normal."

In my opinion, each of us is capable of doing something comparable. This capability is certainly strongly influenced by each individual's personal background. The childhood home, school, and the social and political environments normally shape the values that we honor as such in our lives.

Spannungsmomente enthalten dürfte. Auf eine Arbeit an verantwortlicherer Stelle muß ich im Interesse der Erhaltung meiner Gesundheit verzichten; den durch Verwendung als Einzelrichter entstehenden wirtschaftlichen Verlust muß ich – aus den gleichen Gründen – tragen.

Da mir die Arbeit in der Sozialgerichtsbarkeit ans Herz gewachsen ist, würde ich gerne den Vorsitz einer Kammer des Sozialgerichts übernehmen. Ich habe nicht den geringsten Zweifel daran, daß Sie, sehr geehrter Herr Senator, volles Verständnis dafür haben werden, daß ein Wechsel zum Sozialgericht Berlin für mich nicht in Betracht kommen kann.

Ich bitte Sie daher, schriftlich Ihr Einverständnis zu geben, daß ich mich um Veränderung an ein anderes Sozialgericht oder ein Gericht einer anderen Gerichtsbarkeit bemühen kann unter Hinweis darauf, daß Sie mit einer derartigen Veränderung einverstanden sind und ihr zustimmen werden.

Ich verbleibe in der festen Erwartung, von Ihnen, sehr geehrter Herr Senator, persönlich eine zustimmende Antwort zu erhalten.

Abschrift

Liebe Katharina Stegelmann,

anlässlich dieses Buches, deiner Bitte und in Anlehnung an meine kurze Rede zur Gedenkfeier am 27. 06. 2008 für Heinz Droßel* hier noch mal meine Grundgedanken zu dieser Rede – ein wenig dezidierter und ausführlicher.

»Normen« im Sinne von Werten,
   der Dreh-und Angelpunkt charaktervollen Handelns?

»Helden« im menschlichen ebenso wie im militärischen Sinn erleben gerne eine Art Verherrlichung ihrer Taten, die sie in den Augen anderer im wahrsten Sinne des Wortes »unnachahmlich« machen. Beides halte ich, wenn auch aus unterschiedlichen Gründen für fatal.

* Die Schreibweise des Namens wurde auf Wunsch von Ruth Drossel nicht vereinheitlicht.

211

The decisive person in Heinz Drossel's life was his father, who formulated and lived out his values in an authentic manner. The value codex of my grandfather, Paul Drossel, strongly resembled that in which my mother Marianne was raised. For this reason, the two of them liked and respected each other greatly.

It is, thus, nothing remarkable that the son would adapt to the expectations of his parents' home and wanted to live up to them. It was simply logical and "normal" that during the Nazi period Heinz Drossel responded to certain situations in accord with his paternal upbringing. (*"Always stay human, my boy, even when it requires a sacrifice."*) During the Nazi period, without a doubt, this required courage, intelligence, and a sense of what was attainable, as well as a knowledge of structures whose mechanisms could be manipulated. Without this, he very well could have paid for his humane actions with his death.

It was just this and contemporary analogies that I wanted to help the students at the Scholl Sibling Gymnasium in Waldkirch understand on the occasion of this honorary celebration.

I wanted to give the adults in attendance more information about my mother. I am afraid that in that short span of time, I was not successful in this, and so I would like to try again now in this context.

In 1945, my mother Marianne stayed in Germany and married, on 4 May 1946, the man who saved her life at a certain point during the Nazi period. She knew very well that, even with the ending of the war, the Nazis in Germany could not be converted to Democrats from one day to another.

We experienced something similar with the collapse of the Soviet Union and the GDR. Even yet today, you can recognize at multiple points, in our integrating society, structures and relationships that certainly do not have their roots in the former Federal Republic.

At that time, the mid-1940s, my parents did not succeed in following Günther and Margot Fontheim to the United States of America. The first time, this failed because of Hepatitis, and the second time, this was caused

Dieser Entwicklung zum Heldenhaften wollte ich in meiner kleinen Gedenkrede am 27. 06. 2008 ein wenig Einhalt gebieten, als ich sagte: »Heinz Drossel war ein ganz normaler Mensch mit Betonung auf normal.«

Jeder von uns ist meines Erachtens in der Lage, Vergleichbares zu tun, was von seinen persönlichen Prägungen sicherlich stark beeinflusst wird. Die Werte, die wir in unserem Leben als solche respektieren, werden für gewöhnlich durch das Elternhaus, die Schule und durch das soziale ebenso wie das politische Umfeld geprägt.

Bei Heinz Drossel war die entscheidende Person sein Vater, der in authentischer Weise seine Werte formulierte und lebte. Der Wertekodex meines Großvaters, Paul Drossel, entsprach sehr stark demjenigen, in dem meine Mutter Marianne groß geworden war. Daher mochten und respektierten beide einander sehr.

Nichts Ungewöhnliches also, daß der Sohn die Erwartungshaltung seines Elternhauses adaptierte und ihr entsprechen wollte. Es ist also nur folgerichtig und »normal«, daß Heinz Drossel während der Nazi-Zeit in entsprechenden Situationen im Sinne seiner väterlichen Prägung handelte. (*»Bleib immer ein Mensch, mein Junge, auch dann, wenn es Opfer kostet.«)* Das erforderte während der Nazi-Zeit ohne Frage Mut, Intelligenz und ein Gespür für das Machbare ebenso wie das Wissen um Strukturen, deren Mechanismen es zu durchschauen galt. Ansonsten hätte er sein menschliches Handeln leicht mit dem Tod bezahlen können.

Genau dies und deren heutige Analoga wollte ich den Gymnasiasten des Geschwister-Scholl in Waldkirch bei der Gedenkfeier zu verstehen geben.

Den anwesenden Erwachsenen wollte ich ein wenig mehr auf den Weg geben, indem ich von meiner Mutter sprach. Ich fürchte, es ist mir in der Kürze der Zeit nicht gelungen, und so versuche ich es an dieser Stelle hier und jetzt erneut.

Meine Mutter, Marianne, blieb 1945 in Deutschland und heiratete am 04. Mai 1946 den Mann, der auch sie zu einem bestimmten Zeitpunkt während der Nazi-Zeit vor dem Tod bewahrt hatte. Es war ihr bewusst, daß mit Kriegsende die Nazis in Deutschland nicht von einem Tag auf by my late father Heinz Drossel's open TBC. You must pardon my amazement, even today, about these two massive illnesses, as well as the repeated recurrences of the Hepatitis in later years. My mother prepared food accordingly. As far as I know, my father's last case of jaundice took place six months after the death of my mother in 1981.

In 1954, my grandfather Paul Drossel died as the result of his imprisonment in the Soviet Occupation Zone—this was one result of his authentic, democratic engagement during the 1st Free German Elections of 1949.

My mother, Marianne, was the one who had to experience how the values of one man, her husband, at first gradually and then more quickly changed. The paternal expectations of Paul D. were no longer in place.

On 31 January 1963, together with me, Heinz Droßel left Berlin (West) by airplane. The destination was Stuttgart where his new position in a social court was located. Marianne, his very delicate wife, accompanied the transport of the furnishings through the former Soviet Zone.

Elfriede Drossel, his mother, remained in Berlin, until her son fetched her to Konstanz on Lake Constance, where starting in 1972, he supervised a social court for three years. She died in Konstanz.

Looking back today, I believe that the relatively early death of my mother Marianne was connected with the change in the values and norms in the life of Heinz Droßel, and with the fact that, outside of my upbringing, she had no chance to escape or halt this change. Within our family, my father lived and cultivated other values than he did professionally.

The last time that my mother was able to set the course in her life was when the values and norms of Paul Drossel still held sway in the Drossel family.

She repeatedly and incessantly gave me the quintessence of her life with a single sentence that I did not really understand at that time:

"Never let yourself be economically dependent on a man."

I never did this! Instead, the men came to rely on me, which was not necessarily the better course in the context of my acquired and internalized values.

The Nazi period had prevented my mother from being able to take over the mid-sized company of her father, my grandfather.

den anderen zu Demokraten mutiert waren. Entsprechendes haben wir mit dem Zusammenbruch des Sowjetreiches und der DDR erlebt. Man kann heute noch und aktuell vermehrt an etlichen Stellen unserer zusammenwachsenden Gesellschaft Strukturen und Verhaltensweisen erkennen, die mit Sicherheit nicht aus der ehemaligen Bundesrepublik erwachsen sind.

Es galt damals, Mitte der 40iger Jahre, zwischen meinen Eltern als ausgemachte Sache, Günter und Margot Fontheim in die Vereinigten Staaten von Amerika zu folgen. Dies scheiterte das 1. Mal an einer Hepatitis und das 2. Mal an einer offenen TBC meines späteren Vaters Heinz Drossel endgültig. Man mag mir meine heutige Verwunderung nicht nur über die zwei massiven Erkrankungen, sondern auch über das wiederholte Auftreten der Hepatitis in späteren Jahren verzeihen. Meine Mutter kochte entsprechende Diät. Die letzte Gelbsucht hatte mein Vater ein halbes Jahr nach dem Tod meiner Mutter 1981, danach meines Wissens nie mehr.

1954 starb mein Großvater Paul Drossel an den Folgen eines Zuchthausaufenthaltes in der damals sowjetisch besetzten Zone – eine Folge seines demokratisch authentischen Engagements bei den 1. Freien deutschen Wahlen 1949.

Meine Mutter, Marianne, war nun diejenige, die erleben musste, wie sich Werte eines Mannes, ihres Mannes, anfangs schleichend, zunehmend veränderten. Die väterlichen Erwartungen des Paul D. waren weggefallen.

Heinz Droßel verließ zusammen mit mir am 31.01.1963 per Flugzeug Berlin(West) Richtung Stuttgart zu seiner neuen Dienststelle im Sozialgericht. Marianne, seine sehr zierliche Frau, begleitete den Umzug durch die ehemalige sowjetische Zone.

Elfriede Drossel, seine Mutter, blieb in Berlin, bis sie ihr Sohn nach Konstanz am Bodensee holte, wo er ab 1972 drei Jahre lang das Sozialgericht leitete. Sie starb in Konstanz.

Wie ich heute rückblickend glaube, hat der vergleichsweise frühe Tod meiner Mutter Marianne mit der Veränderung von Werten und Normen im Leben von Heinz Droßel zu tun und damit, daß sie außer in

Heinz Droßel was not only a good "actor," but he was also a master at being able to see through structures. During the Nazi period, he strived against them. In the later Federal Republic, he used them to his advantage. He understood brilliantly how to move between two parties, and as the youngest of the older generation in his field (Hitler's war had decimated many years of men), he was always a welcome joker.

In the Nazi years, an Anti-Fascist. A leading officer as court president. Politically a straight-line CDU voter. As family man and father, distant and despotic, at least as long as no one else was present. He characterized the Federal Republic justice system as "brown," and he socially isolated his very socially-inclined wife. The ability to play on fears of encountering covert Nazis in the Federal Republic was a wonderful manipulation tool, which even with me, his daughter, functioned very well for a long time. The societal norms changed, and he changed with them. During the last 10 years of his life, he increasingly socialized with Social Democrats, perhaps because these offered a better political platform for his performance as an eyewitness of the times?
— As before, he voted CDU!

Heinz Droßel saw through things, adapted, and then pulled the strings.

In later years, when he described my straight-forward actions in professional circumstances as courageous, I found myself reacting in stubbornness, as I had when young.

Were these not the values that I had learned? What all can happen when you live by ethics, morals, a sense of justice, human kindness, etc.?

In a moment, I realized that these no longer really had a place in our society. The "young norms" trumpet money, power, sex, and self-indulgence. I even think that this shift in values has contributed to the actual causes behind our social crisis and political bankruptcy in the so-called Old World. Strength of character, in the sense of "old values" require models, which no longer seem to be around.

Contrarily, I see the reason for this in the fact that the conflict between opposing ethical values never occurred in our society, as it did in the life of Heinz Drossel. Only such a collision can transform normal people

meiner Erziehung keine Chance hatte, diesem Einhalt zu gebieten oder zu entgehen. Mein Vater lebte und forderte innerfamiliär andere Werte als z. B. beruflich.

Meine Mutter hatte die Weichen in ihrem Leben ein letztes Mal zu einem Zeitpunkt gestellt, als Werte und Normen von Paul Drossel in der Familie Drossel noch galten.

Die Quintessenz gab sie mir wiederholt und nachhaltig mit einem Satz auf den Weg, den ich damals noch nicht wirklich verstand:
»Mach' dich wirtschaftlich <u>nie</u> von einem Mann abhängig.«

Ich war es <u>nie</u>! Stattdessen machten sich die Männer von mir abhängig, was bei meinen erlernten und verinnerlichten Werten nicht unbedingt die bessere Wahl war.

Die Nazi-Zeit hatte verhindert, daß meine Mutter den mittelständischen Betrieb ihres Vaters, meines Großvaters, übernehmen konnte.

Heinz Droßel war nicht nur ein guter »Schauspieler«, sondern auch ein Meister im Durchschauen von Strukturen. In der Nazi-Zeit lehnte er sich gegen diese auf, in der späteren Bundesrepublik machte er sie sich zu Nutze. Er verstand es brillant, sich zwischen den Parteien zu bewegen, und war beruflich als Jüngster der alten Generation (Hitlers Krieg hatte viele Jahrgänge ausgelöscht) immer ein willkommener Joker.

In der Nazi-Zeit der Anti-Faschist, als Gerichtspräsident der leitende Offizier, politisch ein kategorischer CDU-Wähler, als Familienvater irgendwie distanziert und despotisch, zumindest wenn es kein Dritter mitbekam. Die bundesrepublikanische Justiz charakterisierte er als »braun« und seine sehr kontaktfreudige Ehefrau isolierte er gesellschaftlich total. Das Spiel mit der Angst, in der Bundesrepublik Deutschland auf verkappte Nazis zu treffen, war ein wunderbares Steuerungsorgan, was selbst bei mir, der Tochter, lange ausgezeichnet funktionierte.
Die gesellschaftlichen Normen änderten sich und er sich mit ihnen. In den letzten 10 Jahren seines Lebens bewegte er sich gesellschaftlich zunehmend unter Sozialdemokraten, vielleicht weil es die bessere politische Plattform für seine Performance als Zeitzeuge bot?
– Gewählt hat er nach wie vor CDU !

Heinz Droßel durchschaute, adaptierte und zog dann die Strippen.

Erst als er in späteren Jahren mein geradliniges Verhalten in beruflichen Zusammenhängen als mutig bezeichnete, wurde ich, wie in jungen Jah-

into human heroes and role models. Just as in the war, without this, there would have been no military heroes.

If the behavior of the "Savior in Uniform" (Heinz Drossel) could serve as such a model, many people, not only the young, would be able to live with courage, ethics and morals, a sense of justice, and love for their fellow humans.

I wish this could be so!

Freinsheim, 30 July 2011
Yours, Ruth Drossel

P.S. There is no such thing as the right way for everyone. Also, except for in religions and/or dictatorships, there is no general, valid interpretation of the world under which everyone can be subjugated. A caring life in unity with basic moral and ethical principles can make one an important member of the reality of the entirety of this unfathomable world. It is always worth the effort. And in case there are any misunderstandings about this, I believe in a god, but in my own.

ren schon einmal, stutzig. Waren es denn nicht die erlernten Werte, die ich da gelebt hatte? Was kann schon passieren, wenn man Ethik, Moral, Gerechtigkeitssinn, Menschenliebe und dergleichen lebt?

Alles dies, so begriff ich schlagartig, hat in unserer Gesellschaft nicht wirklich mehr seinen Platz. Die »jungen Normen« künden von <u>Geld, Macht, Sex und Willkür</u>. Ich bin so frei zu behaupten, daß dieser Werte-Wandel mit zu den eigentlichen Ursachen unserer wirtschaftlichen Krisen und Staatspleiten in der sog. Alten Welt beiträgt. Charakterstärke im Sinn der »alten Werte« braucht Vorbilder, die abhanden gekommen sind.
Den Grund hierfür sehe ich perverser Weise darin, daß der Zusammenprall konträrer ethischer Werte wie im Leben des Heinz Drossel in unserer Gesellschaft nicht stattfindet. Nur ein solcher Zusammenprall macht Normalmenschen zu menschlichen Helden und Vorbilder. Ähnlich wie im Krieg gäbe es ohne diesen auch keinen militärischen Helden.

Wenn das Verhalten des »Retters in Uniform« (Heinz Drossel) ein solches Vorbild sein könnte, würden viele Menschen, nicht nur die jungen, den Mut haben, Ethik und Moral, Gerechtigkeitssinn und Menschenliebe gegen die heutigen gesellschaftlichen Normen zu leben.

Ich würde es mir wünschen!

Freinsheim, den 30. 07. 2011
Deine Ruth Drossel

P.S.: Den richtigen Weg, der für alle gangbar ist, gibt es nicht.
Es gibt auch keine allgemein gültige Weltdeutung, der man sich zu unterwerfen hätte, außer in Religionen und/oder Diktaturen. Ein liebevolles Leben im Einklang mit moralischen und ethischen Grundprinzipien macht einen zu einem wichtigen Glied der Wirklichkeit in der Gesamtheit dieser unfassbaren Welt. Es ist immer den Versuch wert. Und falls jetzt Missverständnisse entstehen. Ich glaube an einen Gott, aber an meinen.

About This Book

I gained information and inspiration for this book from numerous conversations, interviews, and correspondence with Heinz Drossel and his relatives and friends, primarily Ernest Günter Fontheim, who kindly made his personal papers available to me. I have made extensive use and quoted freely from Heinz Drossel's autobiography, *Die Zeit der Füchse*. Any derivations between this source and my representation result solely from oral information provided by Heinz Drossel.

After the war, Heinz Drossel changed the spelling of his name to "Droβel," because at his place of employment there was another person who had the same surname. This led to some confusion. Later, Heinz used both spellings of the name, and his book was printed under the name "Droβel." I decided to use the original spelling of the family name.

Letters were accurately transcribed. Obvious writing and syntax mistakes were corrected for improved understanding.

Literature

Adler, H.G. (1955): Theresienstadt 1941–1945. Das Antlitz einer Zwangsgemeinschaft. Tübingen

Leo Baeck Institute: Year Book 1993. XXXVIII. London

Beddies, Thomas/Andrea Dörries (Hg.) (2001): Die Patienten der Wittenauer Heilstätten in Berlin 1919–1960. Husum (Abhandlungen zur Geschichte der Medizin und der Naturwissenschaften 91)

Besymenski, Lew (2003): Bürger, Luftalarm–Über den deutschen Bombenangriff auf Stalingrad im August 1942. In: Burgdorff, Stephan/ Christian Habbe (Hg.): Als Feuer vom Himmel fiel. Der Bombenkrieg in Deutschland. München, S. 61 ff.

Deutschkron, Ingeborg (1978): Ich trug den gelben Stern. Köln

Dirks, Christian (2000): Greifer. Der Fahndungsdienst der Berliner Gestapo. In: Meyer, Beate/Hermann Simon (Hg.): Juden in Berlin 1938–1945. Begleitband zur gleichnamigen Ausstellung in der Stiftung »Neue Synagoge Berlin–Centrum Judaicum«, Mai bis August 2000, Berlin, S. 233–257.

Doerry, Martin (2002): »Mein verwundetes Herz«. Das Leben der Lilli Jahn 1900–1944. München

Drossel, Heinz (2001): Die Zeit der Füchse. Lebenserinnerungen aus dunkler Zeit. Waldkirch, 2. Aufl.

Dwork, Debórah (1994): Kinder mit dem gelben Stern. Europa 1933–1945. München

Frei, Norbert (1996): Vergangenheitspolitik. Die Anfänge der Bundesrepublik und die NS-Vergangenheit. München

Frei, Norbert (2001): Karrieren im Zwielicht. Hitlers Eliten nach 1945. Frankfurt am Main/New York

Friedländer, Henry (2008): Von der »Euthanasie« zur »Endlösung«. In: Klaus-Dietmar Henke (Hg.): Tödliche Medizin im Nationalsozialismus. Von der Rassenhygiene zum Massenmord. Köln, S. 185–202 Friedrich,

Heinz (Hg.) (1988): Mein Kopfgeld. Die Währungsreform–Rückblicke nach vier Jahrzehnten. München

Glaser, Hermann (2007): Kleine deutsche Kulturgeschichte von 1945 bis heute. Frankfurt am Main

Glatzer, Ruth (Hg.) (2000): Berlin zur Weimarer Zeit. Panorama einer Metropole 1919–1933. Berlin

Götz, Aly/Wolf Gruner/Susanne Heim u. a. (2009): Die Verfolgung der europäischen Juden durch das nationalsozialistische Deutschland 1933–1945. Band 2: Deutsches Reich 1938–August 1939, bearb. von Susanne Heim. München

Gruchmann, Lothar (2002): Justiz im Dritten Reich 1933–1940. Anpassung und Unterwerfung in der Ära Gürtner. 3., verb. Aufl. München

Gruner, Wolf (2009): Judenverfolgung in Berlin 1933–1945. Eine Chronologie der Behördenmaßnahmen in der Reichshauptstadt. 2., vollständig bearb. und wesentlich erw. Aufl. Berlin

Haffner, Sebastian (2003): Geschichte eines Deutschen. Die Erinnerungen 1914–1933. München

Hecht, Ingeborg (1984): Als unsichtbare Mauern wuchsen. Eine deutsche Familie unter den Nürnberger Rassengesetzen. Mit einem Vorwort von Ralph Giordano. Hamburg

Helwig, Gisela/Hildegard Maria Nickel (Hg.) (1993): Frauen in Deutschland 1945–1992. Berlin

Kaplan, Marion (2000): Der Mut zum Überleben. Jüdische Frauen und ihre Familien in Nazideutschland. Aus dem Amerikanischen von Christian Wiese. Berlin

Kershaw, Ian (2000): Hitler 1936–1945. Aus dem Englischen v. Klaus Kochmann. München

Kirschen auf der Elbe (2010): Erinnerung an das jüdische Kinderheim Blankenese 1946–1948. Hg. v. Verein zur Erforschung der Geschichte der Juden in Blankenese. Aus dem Hebräischen v. Alice Krück. Hamburg

Klattenhoff, Klaus/Friedrich Wißmann (2001): Jüdische Kindheit im Nationalsozialismus. In: Jüdisches Kinderleben im Spiegel jüdischer Kinderbücher. Eine Ausstellung der Universitätsbibliothek Oldenburg mit dem Kindheitsmuseum Marburg. Hg. von Helge-Ulrike Hyams/ Klaus Klattenhoff/Klaus Ritter u.a. Bd. 1 u. 2. 2., korr. und verm. Aufl. Oldenburg; Bd. 1, S. 137–160 (Katalog zur 17. Ausstellung der Universitätsbibliothek im Rahmen der Oldenburger Kinderund

Jugendbuchmesse 1998 im Stadtmuseum Oldenburg aus den Beständen der Universitätsbibliothek Oldenburg, dem Kindheitsmuseum Marburg und anderer Bibliotheken)

Klemperer, Victor (1995): Ich will Zeugnis ablegen bis zum letzten. Tagebücher 1933–1945. Bd. 1 u. 2. Berlin

Kuby, Erich (3. Aufl. 2010): Mein Krieg. Aufzeichnungen aus 2129 Tagen. Berlin

Lampert, Tom (2003): Ein einziges Leben. Geschichten aus der NS-Zeit. München

Lembeck, Elisabeth (1993): Exkurs: Eine vergessene Pionierin–Die Ministerialrätin Dorothea Hirschfeld. In: Dies.: Frauenarbeit bei Vater Staat. Weibliche Behördenangestellte in der Weimarer Republik. Freiburg, S. 137–146.

Lewyn, Bert & Saltzman Lewyn, Bev (2001): On the Run in Nazi Berlin. Holocaust Memoirs, printed in the USA. Xlibris Corporation

Lorenz, Ina S. (2002): Gehen oder Bleiben? Neuanfang der jüdischen Gemeinde in Hamburg nach 1945. Hamburg, Landeszentrale für politische Bildung

Meyer, Beate (1999): »Jüdische Mischlinge«. Rassenpolitik und Verfolgungserfahrung 1933–1945. Hamburg

Mitscherlich, Alexander und Margarete (1967): Die Unfähigkeit zu trauern. Grundlagen kollektiven Verhaltens. München

Möller, Horst (1995): Die Weimarer Republik. Eine unvollendete Demokratie. München

Müller, Ingo (1987): Furchtbare Juristen. Die unbewältigte Vergangenheit unserer Justiz. München

Perels, Joachim/Wolfram Wette (Hg.) (2011): »Mit reinem Gewissen«. Wehrmachtrichter in der Bundesrepublik und ihre Opfer. Berlin Pinl, Claudia (2003): Uralt, aber immer noch rüstig: der deutsche Ernährer. In: Erwerbstätigkeit von Frauen und Kinderbetreuungskultur in Europa. Aus Politik und Zeitgeschichte–Bundeszentrale für politische Bildung–(B44/2003): S. 6–8

Roth, Harald (Hg.) (2002): Mit falschem Pass und fremdem Namen. Junge Menschen im Holocaust. Gerlingen

Schildt, Axel/Siegfried, Detlef (2009): Deutsche Kulturgeschichte. Die Bundesrepublik von 1945 bis zur Gegenwart. München

Starke, Käthe (1975): Der Führer schenkt den Juden eine Stadt. Bilder, Impressionen, Reportagen, Dokumente. Berlin

Stein, André (1995): Versteckt und vergessen. Kinder des Holocaust. Wien/München

Steinkamp, Peter (2011): »Meine Richter müssen lernen, Unrecht zu tun.« Generalfeldmarschall Ferdinand Schörner–ein ehemaliger »Gerichtsherr« auf der Anklagebank. In: Perels/Wette, S. 48–63

Stoltzfus, Nathan (2002): Widerstand des Herzens. Der Aufstand der Berliner Frauen in der Rosenstraße 1943. Aus dem Amerikanischen v. Michael Müller. München

Totgeschwiegen 1933–1945 (1989): Zur Geschichte der Wittenauer Heilstätten, seit 1957 Karl-Bonhoeffer-Nervenklinik. Arbeitsgruppe zur Erforschung der Geschichte der Karl-Bonhoeffer-Nervenklinik, Wissenschaftl. Beratung Götz Aly. 2., erw. Aufl. Berlin (Stätten der Geschichte Berlins, Bd. 17)

Wette, Wolfram (Hg.) (1995): Deserteure der Wehrmacht. Feiglinge–Opfer– Hoffnungsträger? Dokumentation eines Meinungswandels. Essen

Wette, Wolfram (Hg.) (2003): Retter in Uniform. Handlungsspielräume im Vernichtungskrieg der Wehrmacht. 3. Aufl. Frankfurt am Main

Wette, Wolfram (Hg.) (2006): Filbinger–eine deutsche Karriere. Springe

Selected Literature in English

Deutschkron, Ingeborg (1990): Outcast: A Jewish Girl in Wartime Berlin

Doerry, Martin (2005): My Wounded Heart: The Life of Lili Jahn, 1900–1944

Frei, Norbert (2002): Adenauer's Germany and the Nazi Past

Haffner, Sebastian (2000): Defying Hitler: A Memoir

Kaplan, Marion (1999): Between Dignity and Despair: Jewish Life in Nazi Germany

Kershaw, Ian (2001): Hitler: 1936–1945 Nemesis

Klemperer, Victor and Chalmers, Martin (2001): I Will Bear Witness 1942- 1945: A Diary of the Nazi Years

Mitscherlich, Alexander and Mitscherlich, Margarete (1975): The Inability to Mourn: Principles of Collective Behavior

Stein, Andre (2014): Hidden Children: Forgotten Survivors of the Holocaust

Stoltzfus, Nathan (2001): Resistance of the Heart: Intermarriage and the Rosenstrasse Protest in Nazi Germany

Newspapers/Magazines

Die Zeit, 3. Juni 1948 (www.zeit.de/1948/23/volksbegehren-volkserpressung)

Die Zeit, 12. Mai 1978 (www.zeit.de/1978/20/erschiessen-sargen-abtransportieren)

Die Zeit, 16. Juni 1978 (www.zeit.de/1978/25/klarstellung)

»Deutschland: ›Er hat die Manneszucht zersetzt«. In: Der Spiegel, Nr. 16/1972 vom 10. April 1972, S. 49

»Affäre Filbinger: ›Was Rechtens war, . . .‹«. In: Der Spiegel, Nr. 20/1978 vom 15. Mai 1978, S. 23–27

Am Anfang war die Frau von der Jungfernbrücke. In: Frankfurter Allgemeine Sonntagszeitung, 20. April 2003, S. 5

Die 50er Jahre–Vom Trümmerland zum Wirtschaftswunder. SPIEGEL special, Nr. 1/2006

Online Sources/Documents

www.documentarchiv.de (Dokumentarchiv)

www.ns-archiv.de (NS-Archiv online)

www.dhm.de (Deutsches Historisches Museum Online)

www.luise-berlin.de

www.pcf.city.hiroshima.jp (Friedensgedächtnismuseum Hiroshima)

www.religionen-in-hannover.de (zur Website der Jüdischen Gemeinde Hannover)

www.ddr-wissen.de

Endnotes

1. Drossel, p. 16.
2. Möller, p. 324.
3. Nazi Archive, www.ns-archiv.de/krieg/1933/04-01-1933.php
4. Drossel, p. 35 f.
5. Emergency Regulation for the Protection of the People and the State, www.documentarchiv.de/ns/rtbrand.html
6. Haffner, p. 138.
7. Meyer, p. 192 f.
8. Drossel, p. 44.
9. Ibid., p. 76.
10. Ibid., p. 97.
11. Götz, p. 160 f.; Document 39.
12. German Historical Museum online, link "Aktion Arbeitscheu."
13. These estimates are based on Gruner (p. 168), Beata Meyer (an email from November 22, 2010), and Beata Kosmala (an email from August 1, 2012).
14. Drossel, p. 89.
15. Kuby, p. 18.
16. Klemperer, Vol. 1, p. 482, 485.
17. In 1940, the NSKK had over 500,000 members. Since 1934, it was affiliated with the SA Motor Corps. During the war, the NSKK was primarily involved in the deportation of Jews from the eastern areas.
18. Drossel, p. 113.
19. Ibid., p. 113 f.
20. Ibid., p. 121.
21. Kuby, p. 129.
22. Drossel, p. 123.
23. Quote taken from the NS-Archiv online portal.
24. Drossel, p. 126. And the following quote.
25. Kuby, p. 132 f.
26. Drossel, p. 148. And the following quote.
27. Drossel, p. 150.
28. From Hecht, p. 115. (Special Law, p. 361)
29. From her application for post-war restitution.
30. Totgeschwiegen, p. 77. One of the victims of this policy was the Jewish doctor Charlotte Alterthum. The lung specialist had sought in vain to leave Germany. Completely impoverished, the 50-year-old woman was deported to Minsk on November 16, 1941. There she was murdered. Ibid.
31. Friedländer, p. 188.
32. In April 1940, the department in charge of the euthanasia program moved to a confiscated mansion at Berlin's Tiergartenstrasse 4, hence the name *Aktion T4*.
33. All of the statistics were taken from: Totgeschwiegen, p. 185 ff.
34. Friedländer, p. 188.

35. Ibid., p. 199. "The murder of the handicapped preceded the killing of the Jews and Gypsies. This leads to the conclusion that the T4 murder program served as a model for the 'Final Solution.' The success of the euthanasia measures convinced the Nazi leaders that mass murder was technically possible, that completely normal men and women were prepared to kill countless innocent people, and that the civil service authorities tied to such unprecedented endeavors would willingly collaborate."
36. Beddies & Dörries (Ed.), p. 588.
37. Totgeschwiegen, p. 138.
38. Friedländer, p. 195.
39. Totgeschwiegen, p. 139.
40. Klemperer, Vol. 2, p. 104.
41. Hecht, p. 69.
42. Quoted in Kaplan, p. 81.
43. Klemperer, Vol. 2, p. 15.
44. All information about Dorothea Hirschfeld was taken from Lembeck.
45. See Sode-Madsen in Leo Baeck Yearbook 1993, XXXVIII, p. 275.
46. Adler, p. 22 f.
47. See Sode-Madsen in Leo Baeck Yearbook 1993, XXXVIII, p. 280 ff.
48. Kaplan, p. 117.
49. See Kaplan, p. 125.
50. Meyer, p. 403, Footnote 379.
51. For more information about Dobberke and the Gestapo arrests, see Dirks. Additional information about Dobberke can be learned through the Topography of Terror Foundation.
52. Stoltzfus, p. 295.
53. Ibid., p. 211.
54. Dirks, p. 233. Based on new research findings, historians often cite a total of 1,700 individuals who survived by living illegally.
55. Starting on July 4, 1940, groceries could only be purchased between 5:00 and 6:00 pm. (www.luise-berlin.de)
56. Notarized statement from December 6, 1951.
57. Klemperer, Vol. 2, p. 163.
58. Notarized statement from December 6, 1951.
59. Drossel, p. 153.
60. According to www.luise-berlin.de, 1940.
61. Starting in 1943, the nighttime carpet bombings by the British alternated with daytime precision attacks by the Americans.
62. Drossel, p. 153.
63. Ibid., p. 154.
64. Ibid., p. 158.
65. Ibid., p. 160.
66. Ibid., p. 163.
67. Ibid.
68. Klemperer, Vol. 2, p. 317 f.
69. Ibid., p. 164.
70. Ibid., p. 165.
71. Ibid., p. 169.
72. Ibid., p. 170.
73. Ibid., p. 178.
74. Ibid., p. 179.
75. Ibid., p. 183.
76. Ibid., p. 184.

77. Ibid., p. 186.
78. Ibid., p. 188 and 189.
79. Ibid., p. 189.
80. Ibid., p. 190.
81. Ibid., p. 192.
82. Ibid., p. 195.
83. Ibid., p. 197.
84. Ibid., p. 201.
85. Ibid., p. 203.
86. Born in 1892 in Munich, Ferdinand Schörner was the last supreme commander of the German Wehrmacht. In 1944, he took over the indoctrination of the troops into the Nazi worldview. He was infamous for his Draconian punishments and was considered sadistic by his contemporaries. He was kept in a Russian prison camp until 1954, after being caught trying to escape in civilian clothes. In 1957, "Bloody Ferdinand" was tried in West Germany for "desertion" and war crimes. He was sent to prison for a four-year term, but due to "health reasons," he gained an early release. In 1963, Federal President Lübke paid out to him part of the military pension that had been denied him. On July 2, 1973, Ferdinand Schörner died in Munich. See Steinkamp.
87. Drossel, p. 204.
88. Ibid., p. 208.
89. Ibid., p. 216.
90. Wette, 2003, p. 225.
91. Quoted in Ibid., p. 224.
92. Drossel, p. 216 f. In the first edition of his autobiography, Drossel described the situation differently. He told of how he went to the post office in order to find the telephone numbers. In September 2007, Drossel received a letter. The sender, who introduced herself as "the daughter of the maligned, 'dutiful Nazi' at the Senzig post office described in your book *Zeit der Füchse*," was upset: "My mother was not a member of the Nazi Party! You could have spared your uniform doo-dads on her. As I knew her, she was not impressed by such things!" In the second edition of his memoirs, Drossel's depiction of the events was also not precise: "In the second edition of the book . . . the events played out in the house of the Gladineck family who lived on his street. I was able to confirm five decades later that the telephone connection to this address was only first laid in 1968. No phone calls could have been made from her prior to that year!" Günter Fontheim confirmed, in its entirety, the version that appears in the second edition. He had wondered why Drossel first wrote a different version, but he never asked about it. Fontheim always assumed there were "legal reasons" for this, and this rationale sufficed for him.
93. Drossel, p. 221.
94. Ibid., p. 224. The following quote is from p. 224 f.
95. Ibid., p. 227.
96. Ibid., p. 229. The following quotes as well.
97. Ibid., p. 230.
98. Ibid., p. 232 f.
99. Ibid., p. 234.
100. Ibid., p. 235.
101. Ibid. After returning home, many German soldiers mentioned hearing numerous Russian soldiers use the phrase "Wojna kaputt" ("The war is over") over and over again.
102. Drossel, p. 236.
103. Ibid., p. 238. Also the following quote.
104. Ibid., p. 240.
105. Ibid., p. 242.

106. Ibid., p. 241.
107. Ibid., p. 242.
108. According to the summary provided on the website for the Hiroshima Peace Memorial Museum.
109. Drossel, p. 247. And the following quote.
110. In West Germany's public discourse through ca. 1985, people spoke of the "collapse" that occurred at the end of the war. See Schildt/Siegfried, p. 22.
111. Klemperer, Vol. 2, p. 650 and 653; entries from February 2 and 5, 1945.
112. Letter from July 20, 1948. Personal papers of Ernest Günter Fontheim.
113. Ibid.
114. Letter from February 23, 1948. Personal papers of Ernest Günter Fontheim.
115. Glaser, p. 166.
116. Schildt & Siegfried, p. 24.
117. Letter from July 15, 1948. Personal papers of Ernest Günter Fontheim.
118. Letter from July 20, 1948. Personal papers of Ernest Günter Fontheim.
119. See Friedrich, Appendix, p. 162.
120. Website for the Jewish Congregation Hannover: www.religionen-inhannover.de/ajudg.htm#hannover.
121. Lorenz, p. 9.
122. Ibid., p. 8.
123. Ibid., p. 10.
124. I received most of this information about the children's home on Kösterberg Hill from Prof. Ina S. Lorenz at the Institute for the History of the Jews in Hamburg.
125. Kirsche auf der Elbe, p. 35.
126. Stein, p. 262.
127. Ibid., p. 48 f. Also, the following quote.
128. Ibid., p. 64.
129. Personal papers of Ernest Günter Fontheim.
130. Letter from August 15, 1948. Personal papers of Ernest Günter Fontheim.
131. Letter from July 20, 1948. Personal papers of Ernest Günter Fontheim.
132. Ibid.
133. Letter from August 15, 1948. Personal papers of Ernest Günter Fontheim. And also the following quotes.
134. Letter from August 24, 1948. Personal papers of Ernest Günter Fontheim.
135. Letter from May 25, 1949. Personal papers of Ernest Günter Fontheim.
136. Letter from July 31, 1949. Personal papers of Ernest Günter Fontheim.
137. Letter from October 20, 1949. Personal papers of Ernest Günter Fontheim.
138. Letter from January 16, 1950. Personal papers of Ernest Günter Fontheim.
139. Quoted in Schildt & Siegfried, p. 133 f.
140. Quoted in Frei 1996, p. 31.
141. Quoted in Ibid., p. 39.
142. Ibid., p. 37.
143. Ibid., p. 50.
144. Frei 1996, p. 51. The following quotations are from p. 52 and p. 53.
145. Martin Bormann was convicted *in absentia*. Hermann Göring escaped his death sentence through suicide.
146. *Spiegel* Special, Nr. 1/2006, p. 118.
147. Ibid., p. 116.
148. Mitscherlich, p. 30.
149. Schildt & Siegfried, p. 140.
150. Ibid., p. 136.
151. Ibid.

152. Mitscherlich, p. 15.
153. Schildt & Siegfried, p. 127.
154. Mitscherlich, p. 23.
155. Gruchmann, p. 318.
156. The letter is printed in the Documents appendix of this book, p. 191.
157. Letter from June 13, 1962, to the Senator for Labor. See the Documents appendix of this book, p. 191.
158. See Merlind Theile, "Aufbruch ins Gestern." *Spiegel* special, No. 1/2006, p. 162.
159. Schildt & Siegfried, p. 103.
160. Ibid., p. 99.
161. Pinl, p. 6.
162. *Spiegel* special, Nr. 1/2006, p. 161.
163. Schildt & Siegfried, p. 142.
164. Ibid., p. 122 f.
165. See Frei, "Das Straffreiheitsgesetz von 1954." Ders. 1996, p. 100-131, especially p. 123-125.
166. Schildt & Siegfried, p. 142.
167. Ibid., p. 141.
168. At this time, the jurisdiction of the social courts was administered by the Ministry. Today it falls under the supervision of the Ministry of Justice.
169. Hochhuth based his claims on an account of a war tribunal ruling that had been published in *Spiegel* (Nr. 16/1972). In its editorial comments, *Spiegel* quoted the defendant Petzold, who recalled that in May 1945, Filbinger praised "our beloved Führer," who "had raised up the Fatherland." Filbinger sued *Spiegel*. The opinions expressed in the article remained undisputed, but the news magazine was forbidden from further dissemination of the former defendant's quote.
170. *Die Zeit*, May 12, 1978.
171. *Der Spiegel*, Nr. 16/1972, p. 49.
172. *Der Spiegel*, Nr. 20/1978, p. 25.
173. Wette, 2006, p. 9.
174. *Der Spiegel*, Nr. 20/1978, p. 26.
175. Wette, 2006, p. 22.
176. Ibid., p. 20.
177. Mitscherlich, p. 31.
178. See Wette, 2006, p. 20.
179. Drossel, Foreword to the 2nd edition.
180. Wette, 2006, p. 11.
181. *Frankfurter Allgemeine Sonntagszeitung*, April 20, 2003, p. 5.
182. Paul Drossel uttered this sentence to his son Heinz on the occasion of his first communion. See page 12 of this book.
183. Excerpt from a letter to the author from July 30, 2011. See the Documents appendix of this book, p. 191.

Photographic Sources

Acknowledgments

I pursued research in the following archives and institutions: Centrum Judaicum (New Synagogue Foundation); International Search Service, Bad Arolsen; Medical History Institute, Berlin; Military History Museum, Dresden; World Zionist Organization (Sharon Visser from the Family Research Department), Jerusalem; Topography of Terror, Berlin; Yad Vashem, Jerusalem. I would like to thank all of the employees here who made both materials and their knowledge available to me.

I would also like to thank Dr. Susanne Urban, who was in Jerusalem at that time; Gisela Kuck, the staff member at the German Embassy who was involved in the honoring of Heinz Drossel as "Righteous among the Nations"; Dr. Claudia Steuer of the Topography of Terror Foundation, who shared important information with me, especially concerning the detention camp in the Schulstrasse and SS man Walter Dobberke; Sabine Boehlich, MA, from the Society of Jews in Blankenese, and Prof. Ina Lorenz, from the Institute for the History of the German Jews, who told me about the Warburg children's home; Dr. Beate Meyer, also from the Institute for the History of the German Jews, who even answered my questions about the Nazi "mixed race" policies all the way from America; and Dr. Elisabeth Lembeck, who gave me valuable insights into Pauline Hirschfeld's life. I would also like to warmly thank my colleagues from *Der Spiegel*, including Dr. Heiko Buschke, Dr. Martin Doerry, Johannes Eltzschig, Heiko Paulsen, Ursula Wamser, and Karin Weinberg, for their valuable advice and support.

I owe a special thanks to Ruth Drossel. She was a valuable source of information, telling many stories from her family's past and bringing her mother, Marianne Drossel, nee Hirschfeld, closer for me.

I would also like to thank Judis, who put her trust in me, and her sons Andreas and Stefan for their openness.

Without Ernest Günter Fontheim, this book would never have been possible. He made valuable sources available to me from his personal papers, and he provided support and advice to me through his time and his friendship. His family warmly accepted me.

The University of Michigan made it possible for me to take part in the award of the Raoul Wallenberg Medal to Heinz Drossel in 2004. Reinhard Egge accomplishes so many incredible things through his contribution to enlightening young people. His engagement inspired me. I had important conversations with Heinz Drossel's good friends Renate Silabetschki and Uli Weißberger, who convinced him to be involved with the youth work at the Waldkirch High School.

Prof. Wolfram Wette is responsible for making sure that Heinz Drossel was not to be forgotten. He shared his knowledge with me and provided a connection to my editor Maria Matschuk with Aufbau Verlag. Her insightful recommendations were exciting and helpful.

My parents Karl and Ursel Uelsmann, my siblings Ute and Jörg with Simone and my nephew Felix, my friends Reiner Ahlschwedt, Dr. Claudia Benthien, Katie and Sven Böttcher (with heart's blood), Doja Hacker, Beate Lakotta, Maik Pippig and Angele Stresemann, Susanne Lando, Gacks Lütje, Rainer and Marita Schmitt, Traudel Sperber, Peter Theophil (with enthusiasm), and Konnie Vogler have all motivated and supported me tirelessly.

Without my friend and mentor Michael Schmidt-Klingenberg, I would never have started this project. He passed away in 2004. I am grateful to have known him, and I still miss him.

The biggest thank-you goes to my husband Henning. His patience, his tenacity, and his forbearance were inexhaustible. His praise, as well as his criticism, was always helpful. His love has inspired me.